UNIVERSITY OF NORTH CAROLINA AT CHAPEL HILL
DEPARTMENT OF ROMANCE LANGUAGES

NORTH CAROLINA STUDIES
IN THE ROMANCE LANGUAGES AND LITERATURES

ESSAYS; TEXTS, TEXTUAL STUDIES AND TRANSLATIONS; SYMPOSIA

Founder: URBAN TIGNER HOLMES

Distributed by:

UNIVERSITY OF NORTH CAROLINA PRESS
CHAPEL HILL
North Carolina 27514
U.S.A.

NORTH CAROLINA STUDIES IN THE
ROMANCE LANGUAGES AND LITERATURES
Texts, Textual Studies and Translations

Number 5

LUIS VÉLEZ DE GUEVARA:
A CRITICAL BIBLIOGRAPHY

LUIS VÉLEZ DE GUEVARA:
A CRITICAL BIBLIOGRAPHY

BY

MARY G. HAUER

CHAPEL HILL

NORTH CAROLINA STUDIES IN THE ROMANCE
LANGUAGES AND LITERATURES
U.N.C. DEPARTMENT OF ROMANCE LANGUAGES

1975

Library of Congress Cataloging in Publication Data

Hauer, Mary G.
　　Luis Vélez de Guevara.

　　(North Carolina Studies in the Romance Languages and Literatures: Texts, textual studies, and translations; no. 5)

　　"Sources": p. 168.
　　Includes index.

　　1. Vélez de Guevara y Dueñas, Luis, 1579-1644 — Bibliography. I. Series.

Z8931.15.H38　　　　　　016.868'3'09　　　　　　74-28216

ISBN: 978-0-807-89162-9

DEPÓSITO LEGAL: V. 3.757 - 1975

ARTES GRÁFICAS SOLER, S. A. - JÁVEA, 28 - VALENCIA (8) - 1975

TABLE OF CONTENTS

	Page
Preface	9
Introduction	11
Chapter	
I. LUIS VÉLEZ DE GUEVARA — THE MAN	13
II. LUIS VÉLEZ DE GUEVARA — POET, DRAMATIST AND PROSE WRITER	19
III. CONCLUSIONS	31
The Critical Bibliography	37
Sources	168
Index	172

PREFACE

Luis Vélez de Guevara's fortunes through the centuries have been varied, and his true position among the literary figures of his day has yet to be determined. This bibliography of criticism of Vélez is offered as a basis for further study of this talented author, whose writings should be evaluated with impartiality.

Expressions of criticism cited in the bibliography include those by Vélez' contemporaries: Cervantes, Lope de Vega, Quevedo, Montalbán, Claramonte, and others; and by writers of the eighteenth, nineteenth, and twentieth centuries, up through the year 1971.

It is with much gratitude that I take the opportunity to thank Professor Frederick A. de Armas, of Louisiana State University, Department of Foreign Languages, for his interest and patience in directing the original.

INTRODUCTION

Luis Vélez de Guevara (1579-1644) was a playwright, poet, and prose writer who was well-known in seventeenth century Spain and was regarded as one of the popular idols of the theater-going public along with Lope de Vega, Tirso de Molina, and others. He was accorded a position of esteem among the literary men of his time if the words of praise by Lope, Cervantes, Montalbán, and Claramonte are to be taken at face value. During the eighteenth century, Luis Vélez was almost forgotten but was remembered for *El diablo cojuelo,* partly due to Lesage's imitation, *Le diable boiteux.* A few of Vélez' dramatic works, notably *Reinar después de morir,* continued to be represented in the theaters of Madrid. The playwright was brought into view in the nineteenth century but the criticism was rather severe on the part of some and he was assigned a place as a good second-rate dramatist. The twentieth century has seen a reappraisal of the works of Luis Vélez de Guevara but a true appreciation of his literary production has not been fixed with satisfactory exactness.

Baena, Pellicer, and Vélez himself indicate that four hundred *comedias* were composed by the author but the greater portion of them seem to have been lost. In the publication, *The Dramatic Works of Luis Vélez de Guevara: Their Plots, Sources, and Bibliography,* Spencer and Schevill give the titles of ninety-four dramatic compositions, including works written in collaboration with other playwrights. Vélez' literary production was not collected and published during his lifetime nor have his *obras* been assembled to this day. Some of his *comedias* were printed as *sueltas* and in collections of theatrical works by different authors, but in order to make a complete study of Vélez' compositions, it is necessary to seek out materials located in various libraries.

It is hoped that this bibliography, which contains many critical expressions of Luis Vélez' literary ability, will encourage further study of this playwright whose works deserve to be better known.

The compilation of items presented does not pretend to be definitive. Every effort has been made to examine all materials of a critical nature which pertain to Luis Vélez de Guevara, and in addition, the items which give biographical facts of importance to a sketch of what the man was really like. The works included in the bibliography are listed in alphabetical order under the name of the critic, complete bibliographic information is given, followed by a paragraph stating insofar as possible the opinion expressed by the author. Each entry in the listing has a number to facilitate location. The commentaries are designed to present a picture of Luis Vélez de Guevara and his works as seen through the eyes of his critics, during the time in which he lived and in the centuries following the Golden Age.

Preceding the bibliography, "Luis Vélez de Guevara — the Man," is treated in Chapter I, followed by "Luis Vélez de Guevara — Poet, Dramatist and Prose Writer," in Chapter II, which includes a summary of criticism from the seventeenth century to the present, and "Conclusions" in Chapter III. A list of resources used in locating materials and an index are provided.

Chapter I

LUIS VÉLEZ DE GUEVARA — THE MAN

Luis Vélez was born in Écija at the end of July 1579, the son of the "licenciado" Diego Vélez de Dueñas and Francisca Negrete de Santander. The father, though poor, was a poet of note as was also Luis' brother, Diego. Luis received his education at the University of Osuna where he was granted permission to study *gratis* since he was labeled as "pobre," graduating "de bachiller en Artes" July 1596. Vélez entered the service of the Archbishop of Seville, Rodrigo de Castro, whom he accompanied to Madrid and Valencia in connection with the wedding of Philip III and Margarite of Austria. For the festivities Vélez wrote a poem entitled *Las bodas de los Católicos Reyes de España don Felipe y doña Margarita de Austria celebrados en la insigne ciudad de Valencia,* which was published in 1599. Rodrigo de Castro died in 1600 and Vélez became a soldier, spending a short time abroad. By 1603 he was back in Spain, in Valladolid, and in 1604 in Seville. In 1608 when Vélez published *Elogio del Ivramento del serenissimo Príncipe don Felipe Domingo, Quarto deste nombre,* he had changed his name from Santander to Guevara and was in the service of the Conde de Saldaña.

Luis Vélez was married four times, though the first marriage is not mentioned by Juan, his son. According to Rodríguez Marín in the *Prólogo* of his edition of *El diablo cojuelo* (p. xvi, note 1) there can no doubt since Salcedo Coronel refers to the first marriage in the *Canción* dedicated to Vélez when he died. The poem is found in *Cristales de Helicona* (Madrid, Diego Díaz de la Carrera, 1649-1650) and reads as follows:

> Coronado de aplausos y victorias
> volviste a España, que fiel previno
> en agradables lazos de Himeneo
> refrenar la inquietud de tu destino.
> Ingrato el esplendor a tus memorias
> ardió en las teas que encendió el deseo,
> y entre infaustos gemidos sin aseo,
> al tálamo condujo temerosa
> pronuba Juno a tu querida esposa,
> que en dulce nudo apenas
> se vió a tu firme voluntad unida,
> cuando, de acerbo golpe interrumpida,
> sulcó estigias arenas:
> Eurídice feliz fuera, si el llanto
> no impidiera la fuerza de tu canto. [1]

The second wife, Úrsula Ramisi Bravo de Laguna, was the mother of Juan, and her death occurred in 1618; the third was Ana María del Valle who died after two years of marriage. Vélez then left the house of the Conde de Saldaña and entered the service of the Marqués de Peñafiel. Luis Vélez was in dire financial straits, for it seems the noblemen were not always forthcoming with promised payments for service, and during the years 1622 and following, his circumstances were described in the *Memoriales* which he wrote asking for money. Finally, he became a member of the household of the king as "ujier de Cámara de Su Majestad," a position which actually was more of an honor than a compensatory one.

Vélez married for the fourth time in 1626. His last wife was a young widow, María López de Palacios, who possessed some means but the property was sold and the funds vanished in raising a family and Luis Vélez lived in need until his death November 9, 1644. In his will he lists a large number of small debts: "Item, declaro que por el presente estoy muy alcançado y necesitado de hacienda, para poder disponer y dejar las misas que yo quisiera por mi alma." [2]

A look at the facts concerning the life of Luis Vélez de Guevara brings to mind a number of questions. Why did the play-

---

[1] Francisco Rodríguez Marín, *El diablo cojuelo* (Madrid: Espasa-Calpe, S. A., 1969), p. xvi, note 1.

[2] Cristóbal Pérez Pastor, *Bibliografía madrileña* (Madrid: Tipografía de la "Revista de Archivos, Bibliotecas y Museos," 1906-1907), p. 513.

wright change his name? Why was Luis Vélez constantly in financial difficulties when other playwrights of his time did not suffer such deprivation? What was the man really like?

The first question may be explained by the fact that there is a possibility that Luis Vélez was of Jewish descent. Américo Castro[3] and Rodríguez Cepeda[4] say that he was. Cotarelo[5] indicates that a Luis de Santander of Écija was apprehended by the Inquisition and burned to death. At that period in Spain, the last thing anyone wanted to admit was that a member of his family had been punished by the Inquisition and least of all Vélez. To be named Santander and from Écija was not a recommendation for membership in one of the "Órdenes caballerescas." Several facts along the lines mentioned above are evident in the following *Memorial* directed to the King in 1629:

> Luis Vélez, señor, en fin,
> que no pudo merecer
> entre tanta cruz, siquiera
> ser caballero montés
> o por lo luengo, pendón
> de Calatrava o con el
> lagarto de Santiago
> perrochia de San Ginés
> o con el perejil mojarse
> de Alcántara para que
> los que de él están ahitos
> le arrostrasen a comer:
> pues soy de varón Guevara
> y desde Ávila del Rey
> de los trescientos hidalgos
> que ganaron a Jerez.[6]

It seems very reasonable that the above facts could offer an explanation for his change of name. Another possibility is that the vanity of Vélez, which included a strong desire to be of noble

---

[3] Américo Castro, *Los españoles: cómo llegaron a serlo* (Madrid: Taurus, 1965), pp. 33-34, note 1.
[4] Enrique Rodríguez Cepeda, Review of "Note critiche sull'opera di Vélez de Guevara," by Maria Grazia Profeti, *Segismundo*, II (1966), 215.
[5] Emilio Cotarelo y Mori, "Luis Vélez de Guevara y sus obras dramáticas," *Boletín de la Real Academia Española*, III (Diciembre de 1916), 638.
[6] *Ibid.*, III, 637.

birth, caused him to assume the name "Guevara," certainly an important one in Spain. A personal wish of Luis Vélez was to become a member of one of the military orders — a prerequisite for entrance was "sangre limpia." Vélez never succeeded in attaining the prized honor and thus in *El diablo cojuelo* appears what is considered to be satire of the nobility.

The second question concerning Vélez' financial problems may be explained by his being a vain man and something of a "Beau Brummell." A bit of evidence to indicate his lack of care in handling funds can be offered in the inventory made of his possessions before his marriage to María López de Palacios. After a list is given of Vélez' household effects, in which the following statement appears: "Para su despacho sólo tenía una escribanía de ébano de Portugal con sus cantoneras negras, y su biblioteca se reducía a un libro de *Refranes* de Malara y otros 24 libros 'chicos y grandes,'" Vélez' wardrobe is itemized:

> Un vestido de hombre de jerga noguerada, forrado en tafetán noguerado, acuchillado el dicho vestido con mangas de tela de lama con flores de oro, medias y ligas nogueradas y un jubón de ámbar, con un pasamano de oro al canto, y un tahalí bordado de seda, que valía 1.700 reales.
>
> Un capotillo de campaña de este mismo vestido (100 reales).
>
> Un calzón y ropilla de terciopelo labrado con mangas de raso nuevo, sin estrenar, con un ferreruelo de bayeta, con sus medias de seda negra y ligas (900 reales).
>
> Otro vestido de hombre, de bayeta (200 reales).
>
> Un jubón de cordobán, de ámbar, traído (50 reales).
>
> Un vestido de damasco acuchillado, con mangas de tafetán acuchillado y ferreruelo de bayeta y medias de seda y ligas negras (200 reales).
>
> Otro vestido de tafetán acuchillado, calzón, ropilla y jubón (150 reales).
>
> Un ferreruelo de tela de cebolla (40 reales).
>
> Seis camisas de Holanda con puntas. Otras tres camisas traídas.

Una espada, que la hoja es de Pedro de Archega, de Como, que tiene más de ochenta años, con su guarnición, daga y talabarte (400 reales).

Un troquel de palo de higuera, grande, verde en su cerco y chapa de hierro (100 reales).

Un coxín y un portamanteo de terciopelo verde en 20 ducados (220 reales). [7]

As can be seen, Vélez' wardrobe was certainly not that of a poor man. There have been references to the fact that he was "excesivamente apasionado al bello sexo," [8] which would cause him to "dress up."

The third question, "What was the man really like?" is answered in the very revealing discussion of the dual roles played by Luis Vélez, written by Entrambasaguas, "El Haz y el envés." [9] According to the critic, the playwright wanted to be noble so he created a name for himself as well as for his second wife; he wanted to be an important warrior, in reality he was an undistinguished soldier for several years. Vélez apparently longed to be something that he was not, thus he created a world suitable to his desire but he was never able to have sufficient funds to manage to live as he would have liked and constantly wrote *Memoriales* begging for money.

In spite of the apparent two-sided personality of Luis Vélez, he was a very talented poet, dramatist, prose writer and wit. At times, Vélez could be very caustic in his writings as can be seen in the following *décima* written to a wealthy Portuguese Jew who sent thirty *reales* instead of the fifty *escudos* requested:

> Por un papel en que os pido
> dineros, necesitado,
> con treinta volvió el criado...

---

[7] Pérez Pastor, *op. cit.*, p. 510.

[8] Ramón de Mesonero Romanos, *Dramáticos contemporáneos a Lope de Vega* (Madrid: Librería de los Sucesores de Hernando, 1924), p. x.

[9] Joaquín de Entrambasaguas, "Un tricentenario — Haz y envés de Luis Vélez de Guevara," *Atenea*, XCVI (Marzo de 1950), 188-203.

¡Notable número ha sido!
Pero, dime, ¡fementido
tesorero de Israel!:
mi mal escrito papel
¿qué talle o fisonomía
de Jesucristo tenía,
que diste treinta por él? [10]

---

[10] Cotarelo y Mori, *op. cit.*, IV (Abril de 1917), 170.

CHAPTER II

LUIS VÉLEZ DE GUEVARA — POET, DRAMATIST AND PROSE WRITER

Manuel Muñoz Cortés says in the *Prólogo* to his edition of *Reinar después de morir y El diablo está en Cantillana:* "La obra dramática de Luis Vélez de Guevara ha experimentado últimamente una valoración crítica superior en apreciación positiva y más rica en matices que la que tuvo, tanto en su época como en los tiempos posteriores."[1] It will be noted in the summary of criticism which follows that Muñoz Cortés' statement appears to be a just one. Criticism of the works of Luis Vélez is treated by century, beginning with the seventeenth and coming up through 1971.

Seventeenth Century

Luis Vélez de Guevara was esteemed by his contemporaries for his poetic eloquence and his incomparable wit. Claramonte speaks of the "floridissimo ingenio de Ezija," of whom great works were expected and who had already written many excellent *comedias*. Cervantes calls Vélez a "quita pesares," or trouble soother, and refers to the "pomp, tumult, pageantry, and grandeur" of his plays. Lope de Vega thought of Vélez as "a new Apollo" and says that the *ecijano* "tenía / en éxtasis las musas, que a sus labios / Iban por dulce néctar y ambrosía." Fernando de Vera praises Vélez as "el Rey de Romanos," and Pérez de Montalbán in *Para*

---

[1] Manuel Muñoz Cortés, *Reinar después de morir y El diablo está en Cantillana* (Madrid: Espasa-Calpe, S. A., 1959), p. vii.

todos writes: "Luis Vélez de Guevara, ingenio el más claro, fértil, agudo, y floridíssimo destos tiempos...." Nicolás Antonio considers Vélez to possess great talent for spreading joy with his witty sayings and eloquence in speaking and indicates that the author's poetic ability places him on a level with Lope de Vega and any other playwright. Quevedo in *Perinola* tells Montalbán to leave the writing of *comedias* to Lope, to Luis Vélez, to Pedro Calderón and others, which seems to assign to Vélez a place by the side of Lope and Calderón. J. P. Wickersham Crawford, in his study of Suárez de Figueroa, states that even though there was criticism of the national theater in *El Pasajero,* the public paid no attention to it for Lope de Vega, Tirso, and Luis Vélez de Guevara were the popular idols and at two o'clock in the afternoon the theaters of La Cruz and El Príncipe were filled, from the *mosqueteros* in the pit to the *Señores* in their boxes, all equally eager for the "follies" of their beloved *comedia*. Here Vélez is ranked with Lope and Tirso.

Another indication of the position enjoyed by Vélez is found in José de Pellicer's *Avisos históricos,* in which he notes that the playwright's body was buried in the "Monasterio de doña María de Aragón," in the chapel of the dukes of Veraguas, an honor bestowed upon him because of his merit.

Two letters written by Gerónimo Dalmao y Casanate, commissioned to have a "comedia a lo divino" composed to commemorate in 1616 the beatification of Isabel, Queen of Portugal who became Santa Isabel, show the reputation Luis Vélez de Guevara enjoyed as author of "comedias de santos." In the first letter, Gerónimo Dalmao writes that Lope de Vega, the one he was supposed to have compose the play, was in Valencia, but that some of the people with whom he talked told him that Luis Vélez, "poeta moderno" would write a good one, for concerning dramas "a lo divino" he does them almost better than Lope. In the second letter, Gerónimo Dalmao writes again on the same matter, asking if the poet about whom he had talked would please his Majesty, that all the authors assure him that he will do it very well; his name is Luis Vélez and in matters "a lo divino" is the one who does them best at this time.

Cotarelo points out that Vélez must have been a famous poet to be called "poeta" in a baptismal record, that of his son Juan

Crisóstomo, 1611, since such documents usually employ "el desesperante laconismo."

Further evidence of Vélez' importance is the fact that he presided during the Academia del Buen Retiro in 1637, at which time he delivered *una oración* and Francisco Rojas read a *vejamen*. There were many *Academias literarias* in Spain and burlesques were put on frequently by the writers for Philip IV. José Sánchez considers the "academias" and the important part they played in the development and evolution of the Golden Age literature in the book that he wrote on the subject, *Academias literarias del siglo de oro español*.

All expressions concerning Vélez were not complimentary. Francisco Santos in his *Arca de Noé y Campana de Belilla* (1697) speaks of *El diablo cojuelo* as "digno de que le consumiera vn Polvorista: está sin enseñança buena, ni moralidad y esto sobre acabar como la nieve...."

From the foregoing opinions written by Golden Age writers, it appears that Luis Vélez de Guevara was esteemed and respected, with one notable exception, by his contemporaries as an important poet, dramatist and superb wit. He was very much in the midst of what was going on in both the theater proper and in the "Academias" with their burlesques. Luis Vélez was regarded by some, as indicated by Nicolás Antonio, Quevedo, and the authors referred to in the letters written by Gerónimo Dalmao, as being on a level with Lope de Vega, at least in certain areas of the drama.

Eighteenth Century

Luis Vélez de Guevara seems to have been pretty much forgotten during most of the eighteenth century with the exception of interest in *El diablo cojuelo* and several of his dramas, notably *Reinar después de morir*.

In 1707, Lesage wrote his *Le diable boiteux*, taking the title and idea from Vélez' story and granting to Luis Vélez the honor of invention. The French author acknowledges his debt to Vélez in the prologue to his *Diable boiteux* but claims that he did not translate the Spanish work. A second edition was published in 1717, also dedicated to Vélez, in which quite a few changes were made. There were many French versions on the "diablo" theme, which was tremendously popular in France. Lesage's *Diable boiteux* was translated into Spanish and also enjoyed a wide audience, so great in fact that Bonilla was inspired to present his edition in 1902 of the *Diablo cojuelo* to remind readers of the original Spanish work created by Luis Vélez, for as he says, some Spanish enthusiasts attributed to the Spanish author the *Diable boiteux*.

There were Spanish editions of Vélez' story in the eighteenth century as noted by the title *El diablo cojuelo, verdades soñadas y novelas de la otra vida traducidas a estas, añadido al fin con ocho Enigmas curiosos y dos novelas,* published in Madrid (Imprenta de Ramón Ruiz) in 1798.

Laurenti[2] in his *Ensayo de una bibliografía de la novela picaresca española* cites translations of *El diablo cojuelo* in Denmark, England, Germany, Holland, Italy, France, Russia and Sweden in the eighteenth century.

Two versions of Vélez' *Reinar después de morir* appeared in Amsterdam: *De gekroonde na haar dood, treurspel* (Amsteldam: Erfgen van J. Lascailje, 1701), and *De gekroonde na haar dood, treurspel* (Amsteldam: J. Duim, 1735).

Cotarelo notes criticism which appeared in the *Memorial Literario,* a Spanish newspaper. Comments on several plays by Vélez which where performed in 1787 are as follows: *El alba y el Sol* is called truly "extravagante y desaforada," and *La Duquesa de Sajonia* is condemned for the "horrorosa crueldad del Duque de Sajonia de hacer dormir a la Duquesa con el cadáver del que creyó adúltero." In the same newspaper in 1784, a review of *Reinar después de morir* indicates that "Esta es una de las comedias más famosas de nuestros teatros,... causa una fuerte impresión en los espectadores...," and in 1786 *El vasallo perseguido y el lucero de Castilla,* which Cotarelo says may be a new variation or "refundición" of *El privado perseguido,* is praised as "bueno en los caracteres, trama y desenlace..."[3]

The eighteenth century may be considered as a period when there was a temporary lapse of interest in Luis Vélez de Guevara.

---

[2] Joseph L. Laurenti, *Ensayo de una bibliografía de la novela picaresca española, años 1554-1964* (Madrid: C. S. I. C., 1968), pp. 120-126.

[3] Emilio Cotarelo y Mori, "Luis Vélez de Guevara y sus obras dramáticas," *Boletín de la Real Academia Española,* IV (October 1917), 432.

The influence of *El diablo cojuelo* was felt early in the century as indicated by Lesage's imitation, *Le diable boiteux,* and as noted, there was a Spanish edition of the *Diablo cojuelo* in 1798, as well as translations into many different languages. Also, a few of Vélez' plays were represented as is evident from Cotarelo's citations from the *Memorial Literario.*

Nineteenth Century

In the eighteen hundreds, Luis Vélez de Guevara began to emerge from the apparent eclipse of the previous century, though some of his critics were not very kind to him. Alberto Lista was very severe in his judgment, indicating that Vélez was inferior to Tirso in the description of characters and comic element, to Mira de Amescua in versification, and to Montalbán, in the art of directing the action though he was his equal in high-flown style and exaggeration. He further states that Vélez disfigures the heroes of Spanish history depicted in his plays by having them use the language of ruffians and bullies, and that there are few traces in Luis Vélez' works of the improvements in dramatic art advanced by Lope. Lista grants that Vélez was not lacking in talent but says that his taste was abominable.

Eugenio de Ochoa includes *Reinar después de morir* in the fourth volume of *Tesoro del teatro español* published in 1838. In his opinion, *Reinar después de morir* is one of the "dramas más bellos de nuestro teatro" and since he believes it is very superior to the other works of Luis Vélez de Guevara, it alone is enough to give readers an appreciation of the dramatic talent of the playwright.

The view of Mesonero Romanos is that if *Reinar después de morir* were the only work by Vélez which had been preserved, it would be enough to accord him a distinguished place among the best authors of Spain. Mesonero Romanos believes that Vélez knew how to invent an argument, develop it and put it skillfully onto the stage but was weak and lacked success in the denouement, thereby taking away all the interest created by the action. A great step forward was taken by the inclusion of six of Vélez' plays in Mesonero Romanos' *Dramáticos contemporáneos a Lope* de Vega (*Biblioteca de Autores Españoles*, Vol. XLV). The dramas are:

Más pesa el Rey que la sangre y blasón de los Guzmanes
Reinar después de morir
Los hijos de la Barbuda
El ollero de Ocaña
El diablo está en Cantillana
La luna de la sierra

In his *Manual de literatura*, published in 1844, Antonio Gil y Zárate contends that Vélez imitated Lope de Vega in every way and that the playwright did not enjoy the reputation that he had at the time in which he lived. Of Vélez' verse, he says that in general it is "flúida y sonora, aunque a veces con resabios de mal gusto." Gil y Zárate praises *El diablo cojuelo* for the novelty of the idea and the lightness and grace of the style.

Adolf Friedrich von Schack, in his *Historia de la literatura del arte dramático en España,* translated by Eduardo de Mier, wrote that Vélez was one of the most distinguished poets of his time; perhaps he could not be counted among the dramatists of the top level but should be one of the principal ones of the secondary group. Schack believes that Vélez' best dramas are those based on national history, such as *Si el caballo vos han muerto,* and *Más pesa el Rey que la sangre.* In his opinion, Vélez' *Reinar después de morir* is unquestionably the best dramatic work treating the Inés de Castro theme.

Another German critic, Adolf Schaeffer, analyzes in detail thirty-six of Vélez' dramas in his *Geschichte des spanischen Nationaldramas,* published in 1890. According to Schaeffer, Vélez was never guilty of literary piracy as were most later writers, and when he did borrow from Lope *(La desdichada Estefanía, El Hércules de Ocaña, El Rey Don Sebastián),* he adapted the material in his own independent manner. The critic adds that Luis Vélez, like Lope, was a source from which later dramatists drew without hesitation. In his *Ocho comedias desconocidas,* Schaeffer includes four plays which he says are by the pen of Vélez: *El capitán prodigioso, Príncipe de Transilvania, La devoción de la misa, El Rey Don Sebastián,* and *El Hércules de Ocaña.*

Menéndez y Pelayo, in *Obras de Lope de Vega,* classifies Vélez as an outstanding dramatist among those of the second category who at happy moments come to vie with those of the first order, and he adds that the playwright imitated Lope's style with such perfection that at times the works of the two authors are confused.

Louis de Viel-Castel writes in his *Essai sur le théâtre espagnol* that Luis Vélez is one of the playwrights who was admired by his contemporaries but who is today regarded with less indulgence by the few readers of his works which remain. Another French critic, Alfred Gassier in his *Le théâtre espagnol,* contends that Montalbán's praise of Vélez in *Para todos* is exaggerated. He indicates that Luis Vélez' dramas are full of spectacles, apparitions, battles, etc. Gassier recognizes as one of the models of the Spanish theater Vélez' *Reinar después de morir,* which he says is much more vigorous and more inspired than the works treating the Inés de Castro theme that preceded it.

In the United States, George Ticknor in his *History of Spanish Literature* comments on a number of Vélez' plays. He indicates that a good deal of skill is shown in putting the subject of the *comedia, Más pesa el Rey que la sangre,* into a dramatic form, and adds that in Vélez' religious dramas there is the disturbing element of love adventures mingled with what ought to be very spiritual and above human passion.

The English writer Thomas Roscoe in his *Spanish Novelists: A Series of Tales from the Earliest Period to the Close of the Seventeenth Century* gives a biographical sketch of Luis Vélez, stating that the author possessed a brilliant wit which infused life and spirit into the court of Philip IV of Spain, and that Vélez' fame as a lively writer in both prose and verse was little inferior to that of Lope de Vega.

Cayetano Alberto de la Barrera y Leirado's opinion is that Vélez' *Reinar después de morir* is his best drama and that it alone would assure Luis Vélez a distinguished place in Spain's dramatic Parnassus.

In his *Narraciones extremeñas,* Vicente Barrantes y Moreno compares *La serrana de la Vera* by Luis Vélez with Lope's play bearing the same title and states that Vélez' *comedia* is less rich in poetic details than that of Lope but follows more closely the "tradición."

At the end of the century, in 1899, the German critic, L. Hohmann, wrote *Studien zu Luis Vélez de Guevara,* in which he gives a biographical sketch of the playwright and an overview of his literary production. Four plays are analyzed: *Reinar después de morir, El diablo está en Cantillana, La luna de la sierra,* and *Más pesa el Rey que la sangre.* Outstanding features of each *comedia* are discussed as are also the characters in the different dramas which he considers to be well-drawn. Hohmann avers that *Reinar después de morir* is the best dramatic work dealing with the Inés de Castro theme.

In the nineteenth century, Luis Vélez de Guevara gradually progresses from the state of almost complete oblivion to that of being considered by many as a good second rate dramatist. The consensus by the critics of the period is that *Reinar después de morir* is the most outstanding play about Inés de Castro and that it alone should accord to Vélez a distinguished place among the best authors of Spain. The playwright suffers at the hands of the critics for his bad taste, weakness in the denouement of his plays, slavish imitation of Lope de Vega, *comedias* full of spectacles, apparitions, battles, etc., mixing love adventures in Biblical dramas, and high-flown style and exaggeration. Generally, he is given credit for creating poetry that is "flúida y sonora" and for imitating Lope's style with such perfection that at times the works of the two authors are confused.

Twentieth Century

With the turn of the century Luis Vélez de Guevara began to come into his own as more and more attention was devoted to the study of his works. In 1902, Bonilla y San Martín published *El diablo cojuelo* from the "edición príncipe de Madrid, 1641" with many notes and commentaries to aid the reader in understanding Vélez' allusions, metaphors, etc. Felipe Pérez y González, in 1903, produced his work on *El diablo cojuelo,* with notes and commentaries and new information for the biography of Luis Vélez. Many documents which had never been reproduced appear in the edition. In 1904, Antonio Paz y Melia published Vélez' autograph *comedia, El águila del agua,* in the *Revista de Archivos, Bibliotecas y Museos,* X and XI (1904) and stated that he was adding one more work to the "preciada" collection of plays by Vélez. Two dissertations on the Inés de Castro theme are of importance to the study of Vélez. The first, by Ángel Apraiz y Buesa, *Doña Inés de Castro en el teatro castellano* (Universidad Central, Vitoria, Spain), 1911, treats *Reinar después de morir* which Apraiz says is not only Vélez' masterpiece but is "uno de los timbres de gloria con que cuenta el teatro español." The second, by Heinrich Theodor Heinermann, *Ignez de Castro* (Münster, Germany, 1914), contains a discussion of the *romance* element in *Reinar después de morir.* The author notes that the drama enjoyed great favor with Vélez' contemporaries and in addition was effective on the stage for a long time to come.

In 1916, the first major comprehensive study of the life and works of Luis Vélez de Guevara was made by Emilio Cotarelo y Mori (*Boletín de la Real Academia Española,* III [1916] and IV [1917]). Not only does he give much biographical information which had never been published but lists the plays, tries to establish authorship, gives origins, models and imitations, and includes the characters in each. He indicates where and when the first publications were made, lists other printings and in the case of manuscripts tells the library in which they can be found. Cotarelo also gives a summary of criticism of Vélez and to this adds his own. He states that because of his lack of originality Vélez cannot be considered on a level with Guillén de Castro, Mira de Amescua, Montalbán nor Jiménez de Enciso, but outside of these playwrights, he does not yield in merit to any other of his contemporaries, among those of the second order.

Also in the year 1916, the great Spanish scholar Ramón Menéndez Pidal, together with his wife María Goyri, published *La serrana de la Vera* as the first in the series *Teatro antiguo español,* in which the critics indicate that Vélez' play is superior to that of Lope de Vega in "vigor dramático." The second drama by Luis Vélez to appear in the *Teatro antiguo español* series was *El rey en su imaginación,* the edition of J. Gómez Ocerín, published in 1920 as Volume III. In 1931, Ángel Lacalle brought out an edition containing three *autos* by Luis Vélez, including the *Auto de la mesa redonda,* a rare combination of the eucharistic allegory together with chivalric adventures.

The monumental work of Spencer and Schevill (started in 1921 by Spencer and completed by Schevill in 1937 due to the untimely death of Spencer) includes the titles of ninety-four dramas by or attributed to Vélez, with the first and last two or more lines, date of the first printed text together with the library in which it may be found, the number of the play on Cotarelo's list, cast of characters, a well-condensed resumé of each *comedia* and in some instances a brief critical comment. According to Spencer and Schevill, Vélez deserves a prominent place among the chief dramatists of the seventeenth century — he derives from Lope and points unmistakably to Calderón.

Richard H. Olmsted prepared a critical edition of Vélez' autograph *comedia, El conde don Pero Vélez y don Sancho el Deseado,* which was to have been published as Volume X of the *Teatro antiguo español* series but copy and proofs were completely destroyed in the civil war during 1936. Olmsted contends that "Luis Vélez de Guevara es, a no dudarlo, uno de los grandes escritores del Siglo de Oro, y tanto por su teatro como por su novela merece uno de los primeros puestos en la historia de la literatura castellana."

Several critics who see little merit in *La serrana de la Vera* are: Milton A. Buchanan, who, in his review of the *comedia* says that it is of scant merit and that the folklore and ballad interest must have appealed to the authors to persuade them to make the play accessible in print; Ernest Mérimée indicates that the exploits of the ferocious virago in the *sierra* would be intolerable today in the theater, even the Spanish.

John M. Hill, in reviewing the Spencer and Schevill work, says that earlier critics have been disposed to dismiss Vélez as a servile imitator of Lope but it now appears clear that the indebtedness was far less than has generally been supposed. In his review of Muñoz Cortés' edition of *Reinar después de morir y El diablo está en Cantillana,* Samuel Gili Gaya indicates that the attention devoted to *El diablo cojuelo* probably contributed to relegating to a secondary role the copious dramatic production of Luis Vélez. Gili Gaya states that present century scholars are correcting the error and Luis Vélez de Guevara is beginning to acquire the esteem which in the opinion of Valbuena Prat "habrá de situarle al lado de los seis grandes poetas de nuestra escena clásica."

In 1941, Joaquín de Entrambasaguas reproduced "Un olvidado poema de Vélez de Guevara, *Elogio del juramento del serenissimo Príncipe don Felipe Domingo, Qvarto deste nombre.*" He contends that if Vélez is admired as the excellent dramatic author of *Reinar después de morir* and as the reflective satirical novelist who wrote *El diablo cojuelo,* he well deserves to have added to his literary merits the composition of the fine poem, forgotten but a brilliant facet of his work.

Since the 1950's, with more and more attention being centered on the study of Luis Vélez de Guevara and with greater value being placed on his artistic production, there have appeared a considerable number of theses and dissertations on some phase of the playwright's work or critical editions of his plays, in addition to studies on Luis Vélez published in scholarly journals.

Editions of works previously published have been made available with new ideas and information concerning the author, such as Luisa Revuelta's *La luna de la sierra,* Enrique Rodríguez Cepeda's *La serrana de la Vera,* Giuseppe Rossi's *Reinar después de morir,* Enrique Rodríguez Cepeda and Enrique Rull's *El diablo cojuelo,* and others.

In 1970, Diego Catalán in his book *Por campos del Romancero* devotes a section to "Dos romances inspiradores de Vélez de Guevara." According to Catalán, the *romance de Grifos Lombardo (o Conde preso)* provided the argument for *La romera de Santiago,* now considered a play by Vélez, and *El conde don Pero Vélez* gave the story for Luis Vélez' *El conde don Pero Vélez y don Sancho el Deseado.* Catalán says that the presence of the *romance, El conde don Pero Vélez,* in modern tradition is undoubtedly linked to the success that the *romance* attained in the theater, thanks to the interest of Luis Vélez de Guevara in the "hazaña" of his "antepasado."

Raymond R. MacCurdy published in 1971 *Spanish Drama in the Golden Age: Twelve Plays,* in which he states that the most important playwrights of Lope's generation include: Tirso de Molina, Guillén de Castro, Mira de Amescua, Juan Ruiz de Alarcón, and Luis Vélez de Guevara. One of the twelve plays in the anthology is Vélez' *Reinar después de morir.*

The twentieth century has been a time in which renewed interest in the literary production of Luis Vélez de Guevara is evident. Beginning in 1902 with Bonilla's *príncipe* edition of *El diablo cojuelo,* followed in 1916 by Cotarelo's study of Vélez and his dramatic works and the publication of *La serrana de la Vera* by the Señores Menéndez Pidal, the number of studies treating Luis Vélez has increased steadily and includes critical editions of *comedias* which were not easily accessible. Critics have attempted to determine the place of Luis Vélez de Guevara among Spanish authors of the seventeenth century. Some of them believe that he should be ranked with the six great dramatists of the *Siglo de Oro:* Lope, Tirso, Alarcón, Calderón, Rojas and Moreto.

CHAPTER III

CONCLUSIONS

Opinions of Luis Vélez de Guevara through the centuries show different points of view, from high praise in the seventeenth century, a temporary lapse of interest in the eighteenth, an increase in the study of Vélez with some severe criticism in the nineteenth, to a re-evaluation in the twentieth. Just what should Vélez' place be in Spanish literature? Mesonero Romanos believed that the theater of the dramatist displayed appreciable gifts of talent that should not be passed over and that Vélez had not been studied sufficiently nor judged impartially. According to Mesonero Romanos, Lista condemned Luis Vélez without being completely familiar with his *comedias,* a confession made by Lista himself.

It seems that the main difficulty in an unbiased appraisal of Vélez has been the inaccessibility of his works. If Vélez' writings were assembled, it would afford scholars an opportunity to make an over-all study of the author's literary production. Until the Señores Menéndez Pidal published *La serrana de la Vera* in 1916, the only works which could be obtained with any ease were *Reinar después de morir,* which appeared in print in 1838, the six *comedias* included by Mesonero Romanos in *Dramáticos contemporáneos a Lope de Vega,* and *El águila del agua,* reproduced by Paz y Melia in the *Revista de Archivos, Bibliotecas y Museos* in 1904. Four of Vélez' plays appear in Schaeffer's *Ocho comedias desconocidas,* a volume not easily available. In 1920, Gómez Ocerín published *El rey en su imaginación* and in 1931, Lacalle put into print three *autos* by Vélez. Up until 1936 when Olmsted prepared his critical edition of *El conde don Pero Vélez y don Sancho el*

Deseado, the aforementioned were the only plays which could be obtained except in manuscripts, *sueltas* and collections of plays by different authors in various libraries. An effort has been made since the late 1930's in the United States to prepare critical editions of Vélez' works; also several notable recent publications of his plays have appeared not only in Spain but in Italy and other countries. Still, the works are not together in *Obras completas* which would make possible a complete study of the ninety-four *comedias* that remain of the four hundred written by Vélez.

From the criticism of scholars, it is noted that pretty generally *Reinar después de morir* is regarded as Vélez' masterpiece and also as one of the best plays in the Spanish theater. The fact that it is still in the repertory of the modern theater affords proof of the lasting interest in Vélez' work. Some critics, notably Astrana Marín, consider *La serrana de la Vera* the most outstanding. Most scholars list as the best dramas by Vélez *Reinar después de morir, La serrana de la Vera,* and *La luna de la sierra.* Editions of these three plays have appeared within the last ten or fifteen years and publications of *El diablo cojuelo* have also been prepared with new ideas as to meanings of allusions, metaphors, etc. In 1964, *El diablo cojuelo* was translated into the Russian language and in 1968 into Romanian.

Little by little modern critics are bringing out of obscurity the dramatic works of Luis Vélez de Guevara, and some of them, as Ynduráin and Valbuena Prat, are claiming for him a place at the side of the great dramatists of the *Siglo de Oro:* Lope, Tirso, Alarcón, Calderón, Rojas, and Moreto. Whether modern scholars will accord to Vélez a place among the top dramatists of the Golden Age of Spain depends on further study, and as Claude E. Anibal points out in his review of the Spencer and Schevill work, there is a need for an analysis of Vélez' whole literary personality (technique, versification, ideology, style, imagery, word patterns, etc.), a complete reappraisal of his relative virtues and defects and thus his exact position and significance among his contemporaries.

Luis Vélez de Guevara was a talented poet, dramatist, prose writer and superb wit. He created characters that are not soon forgotten, especially Gila in *La serrana de la Vera* — a bit wild and woolly perhaps but certainly unforgettable. Inés de Castro is another memorable personage, as is also Blanca, the Infanta of

Navarre. In a theater where it was difficult to attain individuality, as pointed out by Reichenberger in his article "The Uniqueness of the *comedia*," Vélez succeeded in gaining a certain identity for himself by his creation of strong characters — both men and women. Other features of Vélez' works, though not unique to him, include the particular use he makes of the old *romances,* and the wit which is sprinkled throughout much of his literary production.

THE CRITICAL BIBLIOGRAPHY

1. Ackerman, Stephen H. "A Tentative Edition, with Introduction and Notes, of Luis Vélez de Guevara's *La corte del demonio*." Unpublished Master's thesis, The Ohio State University, 1951.

> Ackerman's edition of *La corte del demonio* was prepared from a photostat copy made from the volume entitled *Comedias nuevas de los mejores ingenios desta Corte* (Madrid, 1667), located in the Ticknor Collection, Boston, Massachusetts. The critic indicates that the above book contains the only known version of the *comedia*. Ackerman says that Vélez has adapted effectively a Biblical story for presentation on the stage but that the *ecijano* has assigned the role of protagonist to the devil instead of Jonah. The critic states that the playwright, working with Lucero in the leading role, provides the city of Nineveh with a character of its own and one sees this historical place as a single person following the lead of the devil but finding ultimate salvation in penitence and humility. Ackerman compares Lucero in Vélez' *La corte del demonio* with Angelio in Amescua's *El esclavo del demonio* and points out that the devils differ in that Angelio has the specific purpose of winning the individual soul of don Gil whereas Lucero desires to gain the entire city of Nineveh.

2. Adams, Nicholson B. "*Siglo de Oro* Plays in Madrid, 1820-1850," *Hispanic Review*, IV (1936), 342-357.

> An interesting note for the study of Luis Vélez de Guevara is that in Madrid, 1820-1850, Vélez ranked thirteenth in the list of authors whose plays were performed during that period: Vélez de Guevara. 35 performances: 1. *El alba y el sol*, 22. 2. *Los encantos de Merlín*, 9. 3. *Reinar después de morir*, 4. Comparative figures for other playwrights are given by Adams; several of these are as follows: Ruiz de Alarcón, 57 performances; Belmonte, 106; Rojas Zorrilla, 182; Moreto, 273; Calderón, 275; Lope de Vega, 458; Tirso, 541.

3. Ahrens, Theodor G. *Zur Charakteristik des spanischen Dramas im Anfang des XVII. Jahrhunderts (Luis Vélez de Guevara und Mira de Mescua.)* Halle: Waisenhaus, 1911.

    Ahrens analyzes ten dramas by Luis Vélez de Guevara and discusses their sources. The author treats in detail the *romance* element in *Más pesa el Rey que la sangre* and *Reinar después de morir,* and compares Vélez' *El Hércules de Ocaña* and Lope de Vega's *El valiente Céspedes.* Ahrens says that Lope's play follows much more closely the biography of Céspedes than that of Vélez, the latter having changed the episodes to achieve new dramatic effects.

4. Alborg, Juan Luis. *Historia de la literatura española,* Tomo II: *Época barroca.* 2nd ed. Madrid: Gredos, 1970.

    Alborg says that among the followers of Lope de Vega, with the exception of Tirso de Molina, perhaps Luis Vélez de Guevara may be the dramatist "de mayor riqueza teatral." The critic discusses Vélez as a playwright, indicating that in his opinion, the most noteworthy compositions are *La serrana de la Vera, La luna de la sierra,* and *Reinar después de morir.* The critic points out that the greater part of Vélez' plays are replete with romantic happenings, violence, crime, virtue taken to impossible perfection or passions of abnormal or rude primitivism, noting that the playwright knew what would excite the interest of the spectators and he gave them what they wanted. Alborg states that when Vélez' themes are not concerned with the *romance* or popular element he lapses into *gongorismo,* and as a prose writer *(El diablo cojuelo),* he turns to *conceptismo,* taking as his model Quevedo.

5. Alonso Cortés, Narciso. *Historia de la literatura española.* 6th ed. Valladolid: Librería Santaren, 1943.

    In the opinion of Alonso Cortés, Luis Vélez de Guevara is one of the best dramatists of the Golden Age, and though he frequently used the subjects of other authors, especially Lope de Vega, he always knew how to add his own innovations. Continuing, the critic states that Vélez inserts into his *comedias* very skillfully and at opportune moments *romances* and *cantarcillos populares.* Alonso Cortés remarks that the tone of *El diablo cojuelo* is humorous, tending toward social satire and that the *novela* "peca de exceso de ingeniosidad, por el abuso de conceptos alambicados y juegos de palabras que llegan en ocasiones hasta lo ininteligible."

6. Álvarez y Baena, Joseph Antonio. *Hijos de Madrid, ilustres en santidad, dignidades, armas, ciencias y artes. Diccionario histórico por el orden alfabético de sus nombres que consagra al Illmo. y Nobilísimo Ayuntamiento de la Imperial y Coronada Villa de Madrid.* 4 vols. Madrid: Benito Cano, 1789-91.

Álvarez y Baena includes in his *Hijos de Madrid* Juan Vélez de Guevara, son of Luis Vélez, and says that the latter wrote various works in verse and prose and more than four hundred *comedias*. Álvarez y Baena states that Juan possessed a talent for poetry, having learned how to write it from his father whom he imitated in "la gallardía del verso." According to the compiler of *Hijos de Madrid*, the son, Juan, surpassed the father in "lo festivo y gracioso." (Vol. III, p. 236)

7. Amorós, Andrés. "Aubrun y el teatro español," *Cuadernos Hispanoamericanos,* CXCVIII (1966), 615-620.

In considering Aubrun's statements on the Spanish theater, Amorós says that he is not in agreement with the little esteem that the French critic holds for Luis Vélez de Guevara. "... un parásito ... sus obras carecen de toda conciencia histórica o social." Amorós points out that Vélez is the author of a work, *La serrana de la Vera,* which "queda al margen de todos los convencionalismos de nuestra comedia clásica y plantea problemas absolutamente apasionantes para el hombre de nuestros días."

8. Anderson, Carleton Q. "The Evolution of the Inés de Castro Story in Drama." Unpublished Ph. D. dissertation, Brigham Young University, 1970.

Anderson studies the Inés de Castro theme, tracing the development from the *Chrónica de El Rei, Dom Pedro I* by Fernão Lopes in the early part of the fifteenth century up to Gondin da Fonseca's *Inés de Castro* written in 1957. The critic states that *Reinar después de morir* by Luis Vélez de Guevara, great dramatist of the Spanish Golden Age, is one of the best known versions of the story. Anderson contends that Vélez raised the dramatic tone of the play to a lofty height by the use of old ballads, good poetic lines, intrigue and appeal to the passions of love and jealousy. According to the critic, Vélez created characters who display their interior feelings dramatically and convincingly: the passionate appeal made by Inés for her life; the profound, frustrating feeling of defeat sensed by King Alfonso; the haughty pride and subsequent sadness felt by the Infanta; and the torment which engulfed Pedro are all evidence of the author's skill. Anderson further states that by portraying Pedro and Inés as persons possessing deep sentiments of love for each other despite all opposing forces and by adding the posthumous coronation scene with the thought that Inés could reign after death, Vélez also gives the interpretation that love exceeds the bounds of death.

9. Anibal, Claude E. "Observations on *La Estrella de Sevilla*," *Hispanic Review*, II (1934), 1-38.

In his study concerning the authorship of *La Estrella de Sevilla*, Anibal suggests that an intensive study of Luis Vélez de Guevara might lead to illuminating material of great importance in determining the identity of the author. Anibal believes that there is striking analogy between *La Estrella de Sevilla* and the Vélez formula as it occurs in *Más pesa el Rey que la sangre*, etc. Anibal adds that whoever the author of this play may be, his moments of satire and his *conceptismo* indicate the influence of Quevedo; his allusion to golden apples at Colchis cannot justly be interpreted as due merely to a mistake in mythology.

10. ———. Review of *El conde don Pero Vélez y don Sancho el Deseado*, by Luis Vélez de Guevara, ed. of Richard Hubbell Olmsted, *Hispanic Review*, XII (1945), 258-262.

In reviewing Olmsted's work, Anibal mentions the fact that the present edition of the "autógrafo" was sent to press in 1936 in Madrid where it was to have been published as Volume X of the Centro de Estudios Históricos' series, *Teatro Antiguo Español*, but copy and proofs were completely destroyed in the civil war. According to Anibal, there are omissions in Olmsted's commentaries but the presentation of the text itself is a precious service. In considering the historical characters in *El conde don Pero Vélez y don Sancho el Deseado*, Anibal says that Vélez, whose historical sense is generally underestimated, has invested Sancho with a well-defined character that faithfully conforms to that recorded by the more reliable chronicles. He also states that don Manrique de Lara's potential villainy is revealed with fine understatement and the personage constitutes a first-rate creation. The critic indicates that those familiar with the civil dissension instigated by Manrique during the minority of Alfonso VIII will recognize in his characterization a portrait so keenly prophetic as to compel some reappraisal of Vélez' competence in historical drama.

11. ———. ———. *The Dramatic Works of Luis Vélez de Guevara: Their Plots, Sources, and Bibliography*, by Forrest Eugene Spencer and Rudolph Schevill, *Hispanic Review*, VIII (1940), 170-177.

Anibal says that the place of Luis Vélez de Guevara in the literary history of Spain's Golden Age has not been fixed with satisfactory exactness and there is a need for an analysis of Vélez' whole literary personality (technique, versification, ideology, style, imagery, word patterns, etc.), a complete reappraisal of his relative virtues and defects and thus his exact position and significance among his contemporaries. According to Anibal, a project of this nature is not easy to accomplish due to the general inaccessibility of the majority of Vélez' plays. Anibal indicates that toward the achievement of a complete study of Vélez, the work of Spencer and Schevill is a contribution of such readily appreciable and fundamental value as to make it a point of departure for all subsequent investigation of Vélez as a dramatist. Anibal concludes that nothing would be more helpful than publication of the sixty-one *comedias* which remain generally unobtainable.

12. ———. ———. *The Estrella de Sevilla and Claramonte*, by Sturgis E. Leavitt, *Hispanic Review*, I (1933), 343-352.

In his review of Leavitt's book on *La Estrella de Sevilla*, Anibal comments on the author's assertions and questions whether along the lines of plot-analogy followed by him, a stronger case — even with the perplexing *Cardenio* — might, for instance, be established for the unquestionably superior Luis Vélez de Guevara, or perhaps even for Mira de Amescua, than has been possible for the generally mediocre Claramonte. Anibal suggests that since Vélez displays a predilection for just the dramatic recipe and its variations found in *Estrella* and his *Más pesa el Rey que la sangre*, and since *Estrella* is already regarded as probably influenced by the works of Tirso and Lope if not Claramonte, would it not be well to test this resultant of various dramatic components also for Vélez' influence? Anibal points out that in both *Estrella* and *Más pesa el Rey que la sangre*, there is not only an extraordinarily energetic expression of monarchical sentiment, but a loyalty to king which involves both the protagonist's honor and his sacrifice of a life as dear to him as that of the lady with whom, at first sight, the king has in each play become passionately enamored.

13. Anonymous. Review of *El rey en su imaginación* by Vélez de Guevara, ed. of J. Gómez Ocerín, *Boletín de la Real Academia Española*, VIII (1921), 451-453.

    The reviewer states that there are many manuscripts in the Biblioteca Nacional of true interest for the study of the history of Spanish dramatic art of which critical editions should be published. With the appearance of *El rey en su imaginación*, the critic says, the turn has come to the famous and fertile author of *Reinar después de morir*, a playwright who merited the praise of Lope de Vega, Montalbán, and others, a man of "carácter franco y festivo" of whom Cervantes wrote in *El viaje del Parnaso* "Este que es acogido entre millares, / de Guevara Luis Vélez es el bravo, / que se puede llamar quitapesares."

14. Antonio, Nicolás. *Bibliotheca Hispana Nova: sive Hispanorum scriptorum qui ab anno MD. ad MDCLXXIV, floruere notitia*... nunc primum prodit, recognita emendata aucta ab ipso auctore. Tomus 1 - 2. Matriti: J. de Ibarra, 1783-88.

    Nicolás Antonio praises Ludovicus Vélez de Guevara (vol. 1, pp. 68-69) for his incomparable talent for spreading joy with his witty sayings and eloquence in speaking, and says that Vélez' poetic ability places him on a level with Lope de Vega and any other playwright. Following Ludovicus Vélez de Guevara, Nicolás Antonio lists the name Ludovicus de Santander, whom he apparently considers a different person.

15. Apraiz y Buesa, Ángel. *Doña Inés de Castro en el teatro castellano*. Tesis presentada el año 1905 al Claustro de Doctores de la Facultad de Filosofía y Letras de la Universidad Central, para la obtención de dicho grado en la misma Facultad. Vitoria: Establecimiento Tipográfico de Domingo Sar, 1911.

    Apraiz examines literary works which are concerned with the Inés de Castro theme, beginning with Portuguese literature — the *Trovas* of García de Resende and the *Os Lusíadas* of Camoens — continuing with Spanish compositions which have as their subject the famous legend. According to the critic, the most interesting part of his study is that which has to do with Vélez de Guevara's *Reinar después de morir,* published in 1652, and he says that works about Inés de Castro written previous to Vélez' are "regueros que conducen agua cristalina al caudal de inspiración reunido en *Reinar después de morir.*" Apraiz compares Vélez' play with *Tragedia famosa de doña Inés de Castro* by Mexía de la Cerda pointing out similarities especially the element of jealousy and the ire of the rejected sweetheart, introduced by Mexía. According to the critic all of the characters in Vélez' work are well delineated, especially doña Inés "... celosa primero de los encantos de su rival..., temerosa luego de su poder, pero fuerte y valiente cuando tiene que defender ante ella el amor de su esposo e hijos; blanda y acariciadora con el Rey y siempre triste e inquieta...." Apraiz states that *Reinar después de morir* is not only Vélez' masterpiece but is "uno de los timbres de gloria con que cuenta el teatro español."

16. Arrom, José Juan. "Representaciones teatrales en Cuba a fines del siglo XVIII," *Hispanic Review,* XI (1943), 64-71.

   Arrom discusses the theater in Cuba at the end of the eighteenth century and lists the plays represented there during the year 1791 according to the announcements published in the *Papel Periódico de la Havana.* Noted in the groups of *comedias* are several works by Luis Vélez de Guevara and by the *ecijano* in collaboration with other playwrights.

   Feb. 8. *El catalán Serrallonga* (Coello, Vélez de Guevara y Rojas Zorrilla).

   Feb. 26. *Reinar después de morir, Doña Inés de Castro* (Vélez de Guevara).

   March 6. *También la afrenta es veneno* (Rojas Zorrilla, Coello y Vélez de Guevara).

   Aug. 4. *El catalán Serrallonga* (Coello, Vélez de Guevara y Rojas Zorrilla).

   Aug. 28. *El cerco de Roma por el Rey Desiderio* (Vélez de Guevara).

   Oct. 27. *Doña Inés de Castro* (Vélez de Guevara).

   Dec. 1. *Doña Inés de Castro* (Vélez de Guevara).

17. Ashcom, Benjamin B. "Concerning 'La mujer en hábito de hombre' in the *comedia,*" *Hispanic Review,* XXVIII (1960), 43-62.

Ashcom discusses Carmen Bravo-Villasante's book, *La mujer vestida de hombre en el teatro español — Siglos XVI-XVII* (Madrid: Revista de Occidente, 1955), and points out that throughout the book one dramatist, Luis Vélez de Guevara, "brilla por su ausencia." The critic notes that Vélez is mentioned three or four times but that his plays are not discussed nor are they included in the list of "Principales obras teatrales en que aparecen mujeres vestidas de hombre" — a list that includes five plays by Matos, seven by Diamante, four by Zárate and on through Bances Candamo, Lanini and Cañizares, all third and fourth rate dramatists. Ashcom contends that Vélez, a playwright of major stature, presents women in male attire in at least fifteen plays and that more important is the fact that Vélez is much the greatest exponent of "la mujer varonil."

18. ―――. "Luis Vélez de Guevara's *El gran Iorge Castrioto y Príncipe Escanderbey,* a Critical Edition, with Introduction and Notes." Unpublished Ph. D. dissertation, University of Michigan, 1938.

Ashcom's dissertation presents a critical, annotated edition of one of a group of three Spanish plays inspired by the life of the Albanian hero, George Castriot, called Scanderbey. The dramas in question are: *El Príncipe Escanderbey,* 1634; *El gran Iorge Castrioto y Príncipe Escanderbey,* 1679, and *El Príncipe esclavo,* 1720?, all associated with the name of Luis Vélez de Guevara. A thorough study is made of the historical Scanderbey and of the three *comedias* which Ashcom believes were written by Vélez and he offers evidence to bolster his argument. One proof is that Montalbán, in the preface to his *Auto* on the subject, states that the *ecijano* had written two plays on the Scanderbey theme and since his work follows the outline of Vélez' drama as he sketches it in the preface he probably was not familiar with the third play which is a continuation of the first two. Ashcom contends that Belmonte did not write the first play, as has been proposed, for there are many characteristics of Vélez in the first Scanderbey *comedia;* for example, the superhuman heroes and heroines; Vélez' penchant for having characters throw or threaten to throw around both persons and things; the use of violent language by secondary characters; the lion scene, etc. Ashcom avers that Vélez wrote both the first and second plays as well as the third and that the *ecijano* reworked the first to make the *comedia* more suitable for presentation at the court of Philip IV.

19. ———. "Notes on the *comedia:* A New Edition of a Vélez de Guevara Play," *Hispanic Review,* XXX (1962), 231-239.

>The reviewer states that Professor Ramón Rozzell has earned the gratitude of Hispanists by making available the text of one of Vélez de Guevara's better plays (*La niña de Gómez Arias* por Luis Vélez de Guevara. Edición, Introducción y Notas de Ramón Rozzell. Granada, 1959, 291 pp. Colección Filológica de la Universidad de Granada XVI.) Ashcom remarks that "Professor Rozzell's notes are at times enlightening and erudite, at times no more than adequate and at times irritating ... too often skimpy and undocumented ... Vélez is an important dramatist and his theater has not been edited so frequently as to make ample annotation either unnecessary or undesirable."

20. ———. Review of *El embuste acreditado,* by Luis Vélez de Guevara, ed. by Arnold G. Reichenberger, *Symposium,* XIII (1959), 343-350.

>According to Ashcom, *El embuste acreditado* is no masterpiece but it is better than many critics have thought even if less important than the length and seriousness of Reichenberger's discussion would lead one to believe. The critic adds that Vélez wrote well when his interest was aroused as it was by the comic, the heroic, and the folkloric, but when he was not interested he might not even write competently — his attention wandered; his ideas, vague and dispersed, became hopelessly involved. Ashcom says the action picks up speed in *El embuste* when Merlín arrives — he is the center of the action and is one of Vélez' best *graciosos* and Vélez' *graciosos* can be very good indeed. The critic indicates that *El embuste acreditado* is run-of-the-mine Vélez, but the *comicidad* of the play is far better than its vehicle.

21. Astrana Marín, Luis. "El rumbo y tropel de Vélez de Guevara," in *Cervantinas y otros ensayos,* Madrid: Afrodisio Aguado, S. A., 1944, pp. 173-176.

>Astrana Marín contends that Vélez' *comedias* have not grown old and have continued to be of interest because Vélez was concerned primarily with national and popular themes, heroic and dramatic types, popular songs and "romances." According to the critic, Vélez' *Reinar después de morir* and *La luna de la sierra,* two incomparable jewels of Spanish dramatic art, still seem "frescas y jugosas en nuestras tablas." Astrana Marín

considers Vélez' masterpiece, without doubt, to be *La serrana de la Vera,* inspired by the famous *romance* "Allá en Garganta la Olla, / en la Vera de Plasencia..." and avers that it is very superior to the play written by Lope de Vega with the same title. The critic believes that the moment in which Gila throws her seducer over the precipice shows intensity truly Shakespearean.

22. Atkinson, William C. Review of *The Dramatic Works of Luis Vélez de Guevara: Their Plots, Sources and Bibliography,* by Forrest E. Spencer and Rudolph Schevill, *Modern Language Review,* XXXIII (1938), 611-613.

    The reviewer states that in Spencer and Schevill's work no conclusions are reached — the book ends when the last summary has been dealt with — but that some aspects of Vélez the dramatist do emerge even from the re-telling of the plots. Atkinson cites as characteristics of Vélez' compositions: love of the spectacular and the fantastic; static, one-sided conception of character; lessening concern for national values; rhetorical tirades and *culteranismo.* The critic indicates that these elements serve to determine the passage from Lope de Vega to Calderón. Atkinson notes that a critical evaluation of Vélez' art and achievement has not been made.

23. Aubrun, Charles V. "*El Diablo cojuelo* et *Le Diable boiteux:* Deux définitions du roman," in *Mélanges à la mémoire de Jean Sarrailh,* Paris: Centre de Recherches de l'Institut d'Etudes Hispaniques, 1966, Vol. I, pp. 57-73.

    An enlightening comparison is made between Vélez' *Diablo cojuelo* and Lesage's *Diable boiteux,* with emphasis on the differences between the two works. Aubrun examines in the syntax and style of the *Diablo cojuelo* the reflection of its aim of producing *engaño.* The French critic sees the *Diablo cojuelo* as an attack on the mercantilist challenge to the *ancien régime* and points out that in the eyes of the *ecijano,* there is no spectacle as comic as that of the merchant, the miser, or the usurer made victims of the sharper, thief or brigand. Aubrun states that Vélez uses the *roman* to describe the relations between man and the universe, giving it a structure flexible enough to permit in the same work three ways of considering the relations: objectively, ideally, and allegorically. The French critic indicates that Lesage's *Diable boiteux* extols and rewards middle-class virtue, as opposed to Vélez' scorn of man and hatred of the bourgeois.

24. ———. *La comedia española (1600-1680)*, tr. by Julio Lago Alonso. Madrid: Taurus, 1968.

>Aubrun contends that Vélez lacked imagination and "se limitó a trasponer al plano de la tragedia heroica las obras de otros, cuya técnica imitaba muy bien." The critic continues saying that Vélez liked heroic and historic *comedias* in which he could distribute with absolute freedom not justice as other dramatists but rather censure and praise in a very original manner. Aubrun indicates that *Los novios de Hornachuelos* probably is Vélez'; *García del Castañar* is attributed to him; and *La luna de la sierra* is his with more certainty. The critic states that Vélez begged during his whole life for a pittance, always insufficient to take care of his excessive desires and that few dramatists of that period really were needy since they all had patrons. Aubrun adds that if Vélez and Cáncer frequently lacked funds it was due to their carelessness. The following words by the critic are not very complimentary to the *ecijano:* "este maníaco de nobleza usurpaba el alto nombre de los Guevara; halagó el snobismo de la alta burguesía, lo cual no dejaba de halagar y de irritar a la vez a la verdadera aristocracia; sus obras dramáticas testimonian una idea de la generosidad tan alta que sus nobles protectores no consiguen elevarse hasta ella; él se lo reprocha abiertamente y echa en cara al siglo que vaya perdiendo la sublime grandeza de antaño."

25. ———. "*Régner après la mort* de Vélez de Guevara et *La reine morte* de Montherlant," in *Le Théâtre tragique*, ed. by Jean Jacquot. 2nd ed. Paris: Editions du Centre National de la Recherche Scientifique, 1965, pp. 191-197.

>The author compares Vélez de Guevara's *Reinar después de morir* and Montherlant's *La reine morte* and indicates that the time in which each play was written influenced the composition of the work. When Vélez wrote his drama there existed conflicts between personal freedom and the good of the State, thus he brought to the stage two of the major preoccupations of his day: the conflict of two generations, each attempting to suppress the other, and the conflict between "raison d'état" and personal freedom. Aubrun points out that the Spanish conception of tragedy is tragicomedy and not real tragedy because whatever has to happen or whoever has to die to permit others to live or to restore the situation to normal, this must be done. French tragedy derives from the Greek in which the personages do not choose their destiny as the King in *Reinar después de morir* had to choose, none is free. Aubrun believes that tragedy is

linked with history and tragedy in the theater becomes possible in periods when society is changing. The function of tragedy is to bring about a crisis which will help people to surmount the purging of the past and to face the future. In Vélez' play, the death of Inés is necessary to re-establish order in the kingdom.

26. ———. Review of *Reinar después de morir y El diablo está en Cantillana* by Luis Vélez de Guevara, ed. of Manuel Muñoz Cortés, *Bulletin Hispanique,* LI (1949), 81-82.

Aubrun says that the merit of Muñoz Cortés in his laborious study of the literary history of the legend of the "Reine morte" consists in having posed the problem of the source of the story used by Vélez de Guevara. The question is that of the relationship between the *romance* of don Fadrique, "Yo me estaba en Coimbra," the "trovas" about Inés de Castro of García de Resende, "polos campos de Mondeguo / cavaleiras vi somar" and the *romance* doña Isabel, "Yo me estando en Giromena / ... por los campos de Monvela / caballeros vi asomar." The critic concludes that in Vélez' *Reinar después de morir,* the legend of the "Reine morte" is nothing more than a mere detail.

27. Avalle-Arce, Juan Bautista. "El cantar de *La niña de Gómez Arias,*" *Bulletin of Hispanic Studies,* XLIV (1967), 43-48.

Avalle-Arce states that during the sixteenth and seventeenth centuries "el cantar de *La niña de Gómez Arias*" was so popular that it came to be, in the words coined by Margit Frenk Alatorre, "cantar proverbializado." The same "cantar" provides the subject of two plays with the title, *La niña de Gómez Arias,* one by Luis Vélez de Guevara and the other by Pedro Calderón de la Barca. Avalle-Arce indicates that Ramón Rozzell has studied exhaustively the "cantar" in his edition of Vélez' *La niña de Gómez Arias,* and that on the basis of his observations, it may be concluded that the original "cantar" has been lost. Avalle-Arce believes it is possible to attempt an approximation of what the lost "cantar" was like by comparing three texts: "una glosa" by Sebastián de Horozco, the play by Vélez, and the one by Calderón. In the three texts, Gómez Arias seduces a woman and sells her to the Moors. In the two *comedias,* he sells her to a certain person, the "alcaide moro de Benamejí." In Horozco's "glosa" Benamejí is not mentioned but Córdoba is. The geographical area is the same.

According to Avalle-Arce, there is an historical basis for the Gómez Arias story, and he quotes a passage from the *Crónica de Alfonso XI* to support his statement. Gómez Arias was the "alcaide" in 1333 of the fortress of Benamejí, which through his negligence fell into the hands of the Moors and opened the way for their army to reach Córdoba. Benamejí remained in the hands of the Moors from 1333 to 1341. As a monument to the infamy of Gómez Arias, the castle even today is called "el castillo de Gómez Arias." Avalle-Arce believes that the "cantar de *La niña de Gómez Arias*" came into being between the years 1333 and 1341.

28. Barrantes y Moreno, Vicente. "*La serrana de la Vera*," *América*, XV, no. 23 (1871), 8-9, no. 24, 5-8; XVI, no. 1 (1872), 11-12, no. 2, 9-10, no. 3, 7-8. (Reprinted in his *Narraciones extremeñas*.).

29. ———. *Narraciones extremeñas*. Pt. I, II, Madrid: Impr. de J. Peña, 1872-73.

Barrantes gives background information on the legend of *La serrana de la Vera* and reproduces a *romance* bearing the same title which appears in a very rare book, *Amenidades, florestas y recreos de la provincia de la Vera alta y baja en la Extremadura, con un tratado* ... by Gabriel Azedo de la Berrueza, Madrid, Andrés García de la Iglesia, 1667. Barrantes adds that the *romance* must have been very popular in the seventeenth century since Lope de Vega and Vélez de Guevara copied to the letter some of the lines. The critic compares Lope's drama, *La serrana de la Vera*, with Vélez' play of the same title, giving a summary of each and quoting numerous passages from both works. Barrantes concludes by saying:

> Tal es la obra inédita y casi desconocida de Vélez de Guevara, menos rica que la de Lope de Vega en detalles poéticos; pero más ajustada a la tradición y a la verdad en cuanto a los hechos y a los personajes que intervinieron en las aventuras de la *Serrana de la Vera* (pp. 97-98).

30. Barrera, Isaac J. *Estudios de literatura castellana: El siglo de oro*. Quito: Editorial Ecuatoriana, 1935.

Barrera begins his discussion of Luis Vélez by saying that if there is a life which is the epitome of the picaresque it is that of the *ecijano:* he never had any money and was always writing "epístolas" and "memoriales" asking for aid. Yet, the critic continues, Vélez was esteemed by his contemporaries for his delightful conversation as noted by Cervantes "Topé a Luys Vélez..." In pointing out certain facts about *El diablo cojuelo*, Barrera says that among the humorous and picaresque details can be found literary curiosities which offer a basis for comparison with discussions today. The critic continues by stating that Cleofás found in the "Premáticas y Ordenanzas" that not only "culta" words were censured but also symbols. In speaking of the "fénix" in the "Premática," it is said that however much the "fénix" was celebrated in the Academy previously "...mandamos que se ponga perpetuo silencio en su memoria..." Barrera asks "¿Este pregón burlesco no recuerda al 'tuércele el cuello al cisne' con que se ha expresado el fastidio de nuestra época por el uso de otro símbolo, del cual abusaron los buesos y los malos poetas?"

31. Barrera y Leirado, Cayetano A. de la. *Catálogo bibliográfico y biográfico del teatro antiguo español desde sus orígenes hasta mediados del siglo XVIII*. Madrid: Rivadeneyra, 1860.

> Before listing the works by Luis Vélez de Guevara, Barrera gives a biographical sketch of the poet and says that he occupies a prominent place among the "más felices ingenios" of whom Spain can be proud. Barrera indicates that Vélez devoted himself almost exclusively to dramatic works and that of the four hundred plays written by him there are scarcely eighty which are known to be his. According to the critic, most of Vélez' *comedias* are "dramas de grande espectáculo teatral, comedias de ruido," the characters are well drawn, and the poetry is elegant and harmonious. Barrera states that Vélez' tragedy, *Reinar después de morir* o *Doña Inés de Castro* is without doubt the best that he composed and it alone would assure the *ecijano* a distinguished place in Spain's dramatic Parnassus.

32. Bell, Aubrey F. G. *Castilian Literature*. Oxford: Clarendon Press, 1938.

> Bell says that the witty Vélez de Guevara brought life and animation to subjects of ancient and contemporary history, the battle of Lepanto or the story of Guzmán el Bueno, but that Mira de Amescua, a greater dramatist than Vélez, derived his subjects from the Bible and from lives of the saints, writing also some delightful comedies of manners. The critic indicates that humor during the Golden Age was broad and it depends on the reader's taste as to whether he finds Vélez de Guevara's *El diablo cojuelo* rude and primitive when compared with

Lesage's *Le diable boiteux,* or Lesage's novel insipid by the side of Vélez' *Diablo.*

33. Berndt, Robert J. "A Qualitative Analysis of the Versification of Selected *Comedias* of Luis Vélez de Guevara." Unpublished Ph. D. dissertation, Western Reserve University, 1956.

> Berndt is concerned in the dissertation with qualitative versification and analyzes seven plays by Luis Vélez de Guevara to determine whether he followed the formula established by Lope de Vega in *El arte nuevo de hacer comedias en este tiempo* for the use of specific meters. Tables are included for each of the seven plays showing "Distribution of Verse Forms," "Summary for Each Act," and "Summary of Qualitative Versification." Berndt's findings show that Vélez attempted to suit the verse form to the subject matter but he expanded on the rules by adding innovations of his own, thus underscoring different elements and giving his plays greater flexibility than otherwise would have been possible. Berndt states that Vélez stands between Lope de Vega and Ruiz de Alarcón. Lope emphasized *comedias de capa y espada,* or those in which action and plot development were prime factors, and Juan Ruiz de Alarcón placed emphasis on character rather than on plot. Vélez at times creates a play in which plot is the more important element and other times, the character far outshines the plot itself. According to Berndt, Vélez as a lyric poet achieves the heights of the master and on certain occasions surpasses him. Berndt concludes his study with the following statement:
>
>> With the increased interest in Luis Vélez de Guevara and the presentation of new studies of his literary abilities, his relative position among his contemporaries will be raised, for while he does follow established formulas he is quite capable of demonstrating originality accompanied by native ability. (p. 300)

34. ———. "A Tentative Edition, with Introduction and Notes, of Luis Vélez de Guevara's *El príncipe viñador.*" Unpublished Master's thesis, The Ohio State University, 1951.

> Berndt explains that the thesis is a "tentative" edition only because the Introduction and the Notes are not as complete as the subject demands, but in spite of this, it is hoped that the work will help in furthering a better understanding of Luis Vélez de Guevara and evaluating his relative position among his contemporaries. A synopsis of the play is given, together with an

analysis of versification and sources discussed. Berndt points out that Vélez, like many of his seventeenth century contemporaries, drew source material for his dramatic works from the *romances* and this is true in the case of *El príncipe viñador*. A comparison is made between Vélez' *comedia* and Lope's *El vaquero de Moraña*, in which the same plot is used with a few variations. Berndt believes that Lope's play influenced Vélez' work, for in addition to using the same theme, the *graciosos* are similar, even to having the same name. Another play which deals with the same *romance* is *Mientras yo podo las viñas* by Agustín de Castellanos.

35. Bininger, Robert J. "A Critical Edition, with Introduction and Notes, of Vélez de Guevara's *El conde don Sancho niño*." Unpublished Ph. D. dissertation, The Ohio State University, 1955.

    Bininger considers *El conde don Sancho niño* to be a mediocre play and says that a curious aspect in this connection is that the drama is well constructed, simple, direct and cohesive, rare virtues in the theatrical works of the period. According to the critic, the reason why *El conde don Sancho niño* is not a good *comedia* is that in spite of its technical qualites, it is not inspired with any real conviction: the total effect is one of detached, mathematical coldness and precision. Beninger says that he has edited the play because these mediocre works are of extreme importance to the history of the Spanish drama for they are the raw material of which the *chef-d'œuvres* are made.

36. ———. Review of *El embuste acreditado*, by Luis Vélez de Guevara, ed. of Arnold G. Reichenberger, *Nueva Revista de Filología Hispánica*, XII (1958), 422-424.

    According to the reviewer, it is regrettable that in drawing parallels between *El embuste acreditado* and three other *comedias* by Vélez, Reichenberger did not include *El conde don Sancho niño*, which not only was written at about the same time but has many characteristics in common with the three plays (*El caballero del Sol, La niña de Gómez Arias, El conde don Pero Vélez*) and in less measure with the *Embuste*. Bininger indicates that as a literary creation *El embuste acreditado* cannot be placed above the level of mediocre: to Cotarelo the argument seems absurd and ridiculous and Grillparzer seems to have the same opinion. Anibal, for whom few *comedias* were completely bad, limited himself to say that it was worthy of an edition. Only Spencer and Schevill dare to consider it one of the best *comedias novelescas* of Vélez, along with *La serrana de la Vera* and *La luna de la sierra*. Bininger remarks that Reichenberger fails to mention *La corte del demonio,* another *comedia* by Vélez in which there are important elements of magic: a miraculous flight through the air which is "justamente el plato fuerte del *Embuste*." The reviewer adds that the artistic deficiences of the play do not lessen the value of this edition as a contribution to the study of the theater of the *Siglo de Oro* in general and that of Vélez de Guevara in particular.

37. Blanco, Noemí Campos. "El tema de Inés de Castro en el siglo XX." Unpublished Master's thesis, Louisiana State University, 1968.

   The historical background of the Inés de Castro legend is given and the literary development is traced. Noemí Blanco says that probably Luis Vélez de Guevara's *Reinar después de morir* has influenced contemporary dramatists more than any other work treating the Inés de Castro theme. She mentions the fact that Vélez introduced into the story the jealous Infanta, moved by strong passions — that of love and pride — and indicates that the other characters become pale in comparison with her. The critic points out that Inés is a victim of destiny, the king of his weakness, and the Infante of his blindness before danger.

38. Blecua, José M. *Academia burlesca en Buen Retiro a la Magestad de Philippo Quarto el Grande.* (Ms. Madrid, 1637.) Valencia: Tip. Moderna, 1952.

   José M. Blecua has reproduced from the Manuscript of 1637 the *Academia burlesca en Buen Retiro,* presided over by Luis Vélez de Guevara, and attended by Antonio de Solís, Francisco de Rojas, Luis de Belmonte Bermúdez, and many other literary figures of the day. Luis Vélez delivered an oration, Francisco de Rojas "un vejamen" and many *memoriales, cédulas, poemas,* etc., were written for the occasion, all of which are included in Blecua's reproduction of the manuscript.

39. Bonilla y San Martín, Adolfo. "Algunas poesías inéditas de Luis Vélez de Guevara sacadas de varios manuscritos," *Revista de Aragón,* III (1902), 573-583.

According to Bonilla y San Martín, most of the nine poems composed by Luis Vélez de Guevara which he reproduces had not been published before 1902. Four of the poems contain information of interest for the biography of the author. They are the following:

1) Luis Vélez de Guevara al conde de Olivares.
2) Memorial de Luis Vélez de Guevara.
3) Memorial de Luis Vélez de Guevara pidiendo al rey merced de ayuda de guardarropa en Madrid.
4) Luis Vélez pretendiendo la cámara del infante cardenal.

Bonilla y San Martín says in the brief introductory remarks:

...Hubiéramos querido precisar en algunas, especialmente en la III, los datos nuevos e importantes que contienen para la biografía de Vélez, pero hemos temido dar demasiada extensión a este artículo, cuyo único objeto es la publicación de los mencionados textos.

40. ———. "Carta abierta al Sr. D. Manuel Serrano y Sanz (observaciones acerca de *El diablo cojuelo*)," *Revista de Archivos, Bibliotecas y Museos*, VI (1902), 382.

Bonilla y San Martín is concerned with giving an interpretation of several phrases in *El diablo cojuelo:* "Mula de Liñán," "puerta de Guadalajara," and "velicomen." Bonilla does not believe that the reference to "mula de Liñán" can be interpreted as the "mula" of Pedro Liñán de Riaza, and even if it could this would not explain Vélez' use of the phrase in *El diablo cojuelo*. The "puerta de Guadalajara" the critic says is a place of business for merchants and is referred to by Quevedo in Chapter XV of the *Buscón*. Bonilla contends that "velicomen" means "vaso" as used by Quevedo in *La hora de todos*. The critic indicates that the word comes from German "Wilkommenbecher" as stated by Ramón Menéndez Pidal in *Etimologías españolas*.

41. ———. *El diablo cojuelo* por Luis Vélez de Guevara, reproducción de la edición príncipe de Madrid, 1641. Vigo: Librería de Eugenio Krapf, 1902.

The critic indicates that the similarity between the *Sueños* of Quevedo and Vélez' *Diablo cojuelo* is apparent not only in the satirical intent but in the likeness of the style. According to Bonilla y San Martín, Vélez, resembling Quevedo, is "un escolástico del idioma" and his *Diablo* must not be read hurriedly but carefully in order to savor the daring metaphors, the extravagant narrative, the stupendous puns and the arbitrary license in which he delighted. In commenting on Lesage's *Diable boiteux,* published in 1707, Bonilla calls it a "refundición" of the *Diablo cojuelo* in which there is scarcely a vague resemblance to the original. A new edition of Lesage's work, that of 1726-27, attracted the attention of the Spaniards more than the story by Vélez, and in the nineteenth century the Spanish editions of the translation of the *Diable boiteux* were so numerous that there were even some who attributed to Vélez the text of the French author. Bonilla states that it was time for a faithful reproduction of the original text, the edition of 1641, of the *Diablo cojuelo* to be published, which he has done. Following the *novela,* the critic adds detailed notes in the section, "Comentario de algunos vocablos y modismos usados en *El diablo cojuelo.*"

42. ———. "Más 'diabluras.' (Comentario y Notas a unas 'Notas' y a unos 'Comentarios' sobre un Comentario y unas Notas," in *Anales de la literatura española (Años 1900-1904),* Madrid: Est. Tip. de la Viuda e Hijos de Tello, 1904, pp. 193-200.

Bonilla y San Martín writes this article in answer to the ones composed by Felipe Pérez y González for *La Ilustración Española y Americana* and later published in book form, in which he amplified or corrected some of Bonilla's comments. Concerning the "deslices" which Bonilla says Pérez y González seemed to enjoy pointing out, the author of this article remarks that the corrector made some slips himself. In defending his explanations, Bonilla asks why Pérez y González did not explain passages like the following: "ayuntamiento de las ranas del molino quemado," "golfo lanzado," "mula de Liñán" and "río navarrisco," which are really difficult and new information would be of great value.

43. ———. Review of *La serrana de la Vera,* by Luis Vélez de Guevara, ed. of Ramón Menéndez Pidal y María Goyri de Menéndez Pidal, *Revista Crítica Hispanoamericana,* III (1917), 176-182.

The reviewer discusses Luis Vélez de Guevara's *La serrana de la Vera* and the play by Lope de Vega with the same title, making mention also of the *serranillas* of the Arcipreste de

Hita and the Marqués de Santillana. Lope's play was published for the first time in *Parte séptima* of his *Teatro* (Madrid, 1617) but the title appears in the first list of *El peregrino en su patria,* which would mean that it was written before 1603. Vélez' *comedia* was published in 1916. Menéndez y Pelayo and Menéndez Pidal say that Vélez' play could not have been composed before 1613 (not 1603 as indicated on the manuscript). Bonilla is not convinced that the date 1613 is correct, an opinion expressed also by Milton A. Buchanan. One fact to support belief in the 1603 date is that Jusepa Vaca, for whom Vélez' *comedia* was written, was in Valladolid in 1603 and not in 1613. Bonilla indicates that if neither date, 1603 nor 1613, seems to be correct, all things considered, why pick 1613 instead of 1603? The critic adds that if Vélez' *Serrana de la Vera* is not a play of extraordinary merit, it is certainly one of the best dramatic works of the famous but forgotten Vélez de Guevara and is superior to Lope's play on the same subject. According to Bonilla, the Sres. Menéndez Pidal made a good choice in selecting Vélez' *La serrana de la Vera* for the first of the *comedias* in the *Teatro antiguo español* series.

44. ———. "Sobre un tomo perdido de Lope de Vega," in *Miscelânea de estudos em honra de D. Carolina Michaëlis de Vasconcellos,* Coimbra: Imprensa da Universidade, 1933, pp. 101-110.

   Bonilla mentions three volumes of the works of Lope de Vega, Numbers 131, 132, and 133, which were in the Biblioteca de Osuna, as indicated by Schack in *Nachträge,* 1854. The critic says that by 1904 when H. A. Rennert published his *Life of Lope de Vega,* the three volumes had disappeared. Bonilla had the good fortune to find one of the volumes, Number 132, which he describes in detail. A note of interest for the study of Luis Vélez de Guevara is that included in this volume is the following: "*Comedia famosa del Conde don Pedro Vélez,* written by Lope de Vega Carpio." Bonilla says: "Esta interesante comedia, no es de Lope, sino de Luis Vélez de Guevara, puesto que precisamente se conserva en la Biblioteca Nacional el autógrafo de este último."

45. Brenan, Gerald. *The Literature of the Spanish People from Roman Times to the Present Day.* Cambridge: University Press, 1953.

   Brenan calls *El diablo cojuelo* a "satirical-fantastical work, written in a breathless style of elaborate conceits and endless clauses in apposition which makes it tedious to read," and says that Vélez' novel owes its fame chiefly to Lesage's *Diable boiteux,* derived from the Spanish story. Brenan speaks of religion and Spain in the seventeenth century and quotes the following lines by Luis Vélez de Guevara:

> Yo bien podré ser también
> mal cristiano pero buen
> católico ¡vive Dios!

46. Bruerton, Courtney. "Eight Plays of Vélez de Guevara," *Romance Philology,* VI (1952-1953), 248-253.

Verse statistics for eight plays by Luis Vélez de Guevara are presented as evidence in an attempt to determine probable dates of the plays. The versification of *La hermosura de Raquel I,* with *quintillas* heavier than *redondillas,* light *romance,* a single long passage of *tercetos,* varied act openings and closings, 21.4 percent of Italian lines, point to an early date. *La hermosura de Raquel I* was probably written after Vélez' return to Spain in 1602. By comparing the number of *quintillas, redondillas, romances, décimas,* etc., the author of this article proposes the following dates for the eight plays:

El prodigioso príncipe transilvano	1597?-1602
	(1599-1600?)
La hermosura de Raquel I	1602-1605
La hermosura de Raquel II	1602-1608
La devoción de la misa	1604-1610
El rey don Sebastián	1604-1608
La obligación de las mujeres	1606-1610
El espejo del mundo	1606-1610
Los hijos de la Barbuda	1608-1610

47. ———. "*La ninfa del cielo, La serrana de la Vera,* and Related Plays," *Estudios hispánicos,* in *Homenaje a Archer M. Huntington,* Wellesley, Mass.: Spanish Department, Wellesley College, 1952, pp. 61-97.

Courtney Bruerton compares the *comedias de bandoleras* by Lope de Vega *(La serrana de la Vera, Las dos bandoleras);* Mira de Amescua *(El esclavo del demonio);* Luis Vélez de Guevara *(La serrana de la Vera);* and *La ninfa del cielo* (known by two other titles, *La condesa bandolera* and *Obligaciones de honor),* attributed to Tirso de Molina in two MSS of the Biblioteca Nacional and ascribed to Luis Vélez in a MS of the Biblioteca Palatina in Parma. Bruerton says that there are indications that point to Vélez as the author: the attribution to him in what appears to be the manuscript copy of earliest date extant (that of the Biblioteca Palatina), and the versification disagrees in a number of respects with Tirso's verse habits about 1613 (the date of the play). Bruerton's final statement is that if Vélez did not write the whole play — and the *gracioso's* speeches suggest that to be the case — the most probable conclusion seems to be that the play was written in collaboration with Tirso de Molina.

48. ———. "*La quinta de Florencia*, fuente de *Peribáñez*," *Nueva Revista de Filología Hispánica*, IV (1950), 25-29.

   A point of interest for the study of Luis Vélez de Guevara in the above article is that Bruerton states that *El infanzón de Illescas* and *Los novios de Hornachuelos* are by Vélez de Guevara (p. 25).

49. ———. "The Date of Schaeffer's *Tomo antiguo*," *Hispanic Review*, XV (1947), 346-364.

   Bruerton indicates that in 1887 Adolph Schaeffer, having discovered a very old volume of Spanish plays which lacked the cover and preliminary pages, published the eight rarest texts of the twelve contained in the volume. He believed that the book was printed between 1612 and 1616. A number of the plays included in Schaeffer's work have not appeared in any other volume to date. By analyzing the versification as to number of *redondillas*, *quintillas*, *romances*, etc., Bruerton attempts to date the plays in Schaeffer's *Tomo antiguo*. He concludes that the volume was not published before 1626 and perhaps not until later. Bruerton says of Vélez' *Hércules de Ocaña*, printed only in Schaeffer, that Vélez may have been the imitated, not the imitator.

50. Buchanan, Milton A. Review of *La serrana de la Vera*, by Luis Vélez de Guevara, ed. by Ramón Menéndez Pidal and María Goyri de Menéndez Pidal, *Modern Language Notes*, XXXII (1917), 423-426.

   The reviewer believes that the *Serrana de la Vera* is of scant merit as a piece of literature: "A ranting female 'miles gloriosus' who, when her virtue suffers compromise, becomes one of the numerous brigands and murderers of the Spanish drama, and, after wreaking vengeance upon her betrayer, meets an inglorious death on the gallows almost within view of the spectators, is hardly a heroine to inspire a masterpiece. It was undoubtedly the folklore or ballad interest of the play which appealed to the editors and persuaded them to make the play accessible in print." Buchanan does not agree with the Sres. Menéndez Pidal that the date could not be 1603 and believes that the *comedia* could have been written for presentation before the Queen in Valladolid at that time since the play is not of the type intended for the stage of an ordinary theater but was probably acted in the court of a palace.

51. Capdet, Françoise. *El hijo del águila,* de Luis Vélez de Guevara, avec une introduction historique et des notes. Diplôme d'études Supérieures, Université de Montpellier, 1966.

(This item could not be located.)

52. ———— and Jean-Louis Flecniakoska. "Le Bâtard Don Juan d'Autriche, personnage de théâtre," in *Dramaturgie et Société,* ed. by Jean Jacquot, with the collaboration of Elie Konigson and Marcel Oddon, 2 vols., Paris: Centre National de la Recherche Scientifique, 1968, pp. 125-132.

Capdet and Flecniakoska consider three plays on the theme of don Juan of Austria: *El señor don Juan de Austria* by Pérez de Montalbán, *El hijo del águila* and *El águila del agua* by Luis Vélez de Guevara. The authors indicate that the first of the *comedias* by Vélez treates the early life of Jerónimo, surname of don Juan of Austria, his arrival at Villagarcía, up to the day of his recognition at court, and the second play the events immediately preceding the battle of Lepanto, the battle itself in the third act which is a veritable reconstitution of the fight at sea. The critics state that the oarsmen are seen, the cannon is heard, and the victory is symbolized by the spoils laid at the feet of don Juan by the Turks. The authors see don Juan as more than a theatrical personage in the plays of Montalbán and Vélez de Guevara: he is the public defender of the values of a past that one would wish to be an example and stimulant for Spain, already feeling the weight of a decline fully primed. Capdet and Flecniakoska believe that don Juan was given the main role in the above plays for the purpose of political propaganda.

53. Caro Baroja, Julio. "¿Es de origen mítico la 'leyenda' de la serrana de la Vera?" *Revista de Dialectología y Tradiciones Populares*, II (1946), 568-572.

>   Referring to the edition of *La serrana de la Vera* by Ramón Menéndez Pidal and María Goyri de Menéndez Pidal, Caro Baroja mentions that the Sres. Menéndez Pidal give no indication as to the origin of the story which served as a basis for the *romances* and the other literary works that they study but they do state that it has been said that the legend of the *serrana* does have historical foundation. Caro Baroja believes that the story of *La serrana de la Vera* is not an historical theme but is a mythical one which has remained in the folklore and that Spanish folkloric material shows that "la serrana de la Vera es el último avatar de una vieja divinidad de las montañas." Caro Baroja notes that in the Basque country there exists the myth of "Mari," a divinity who resided in mysterious caves in the mountains, which seems to him to have some relation with the myth of the *serrana*.

54. "Cartas de D. Gerónimo Dalmao y Casanate a los diputados del Reino de Aragón, participándoles noticias de la Corte de España," *Revista de Archivos, Bibliotecas y Museos*, VIII, Ser. 1 (1878), 76-77.

>   Excerpts from letters written by Gerónimo Dalmao y Casanate, commissioned to have a "comedia a lo divino" composed to commemorate in 1616 the beatification of Isabel, queen of Portugal who became Santa Isabel, show the reputation that Luis Vélez de Guevara enjoyed as author of "comedias de santos":

>   Carta 7.ª

>   Despues de hauerse partido el ordinario de ayer me dieron su carta de V. S., de 12 deste, y assi aunque escriui el sabado passado no pude responder á lo que V. S. me manda; pero harelo hagora, diziendo el contento grande que tuue con el auisso que V. S. me á dado de la concesion que Su Santidad a dado para que se venere y reze á la Sta. Reyna Isabel, de cuyo despacho me cabe mucha parte, assi por que lo deseaua como por hauer hecho yo diligencias en esta Corte para que se diesse, y fio en Nuestro Señor que se conseguirá tambien su canoniçacion, y es muy justo que V. S. solemnize la fiesta con hazer la comedia; pero no está aqui Lope de Vega, á quien me manda V. S. que se la haga componer de la santa vida de la Reyna, porque a muchos dias que se fué á Valencia;

pero anme asegurado algunas personas pláticas que Luis Velez, poeta moderno, la hará muy bien por que las que son á lo diuino haze cassi mejor que Lope de Vega. V. S. verá lo que en esto le parece, ó si gustará que se escriba á Valencia para que la haga Vega........ De Madrid a 22 de Julio, 1616.

Carta 9.ª

... ...
Ya escriui a V. S. desde el Escurial como hauia recibido la carta en que me manda V. S. trate con Lope de Vega de que haga una comedia de la vida de la Santa Reyna Isabel, y tanbien lo que en esto se hauia hecho; y como Lope de Vega está en Valencia, que es la persona á quien V. S. me ordena que la encomendasse, V. S. verá si el poeta que le escriui será de su gusto, que todos los autores me aseguran que la hará muy bien: llámase Luis Velez; es en cossas á lo diuino quien mejor haze agora.
... ...
De Madrid 6 de Agosto, 1616.

55. Castro, Américo. *Los españoles: cómo llegaron a serlo.* Madrid: Taurus, 1965.

A note of interest for the study of Luis Vélez de Guevara is the following quotation from Américo Castro's *Los españoles: cómo llegaron a serlo,* which indicates that Vélez was of Jewish descent:

... Luis Vélez de Guevara (también de ascendencia judía) habla en *El diablo cojuelo* (1641, tranco III) de "la ropería de los agüelos, donde cualquiera..., porque el suyo no le viene bien o está muy traído ('viejo, gastado, como la ley vieja de los judíos'), se viene aquí, y por su dinero, escoge el que le está más a propósito. Mira allí aquel caballero *torzuelo* ('de baja condición') cómo se está probando una agüela que ha menester, etc." Note 1, pp. 33-34.)

56. ———. "Noruega, símbolo de la oscuridad," *Revista de Filología Española,* VI (1919), 184-186.

In considering the allusions to remote countries used from time to time by Spanish authors during the Golden Age, Américo Castro says that the most curious ones are those in which Norway becomes a synonym for night and darkness. The critic indicates that Luis Vélez de Guevara speaks of "la más oscura Noruega" in *El diablo cojuelo,* and in *El rey en su imaginación,* Carlos speaks to Diana, queen of Sicily in the following terms:

> Muchas albas amanezca
> vuestra majestad, señora,
> en las noches de su ausencia,
> que estos horizontes son
> de vuestros rayos Noruega
> donde muere mi esperanza
> hasta amanecer en ella.
>
> (ll. 1674-1680, ed. J. G. Ocerín)

57. ———. Review of *El diablo cojuelo,* by Luis Vélez de Guevara, ed. of Francisco Rodríguez Marín, *Revista de Filología Española,* VII (1920), 77-78.

Commenting on Rodríguez Marín's edition of *El diablo cojuelo,* Américo Castro points out the curious investigation of the popular theme of the "crippled devil" based on proceedings of trials for witchcraft before the Inquisition in 1532, 1600, 1633, etc. The critic disagrees with Rodríguez Marín's interpretation of the meaning of "encrucijada de apellidos," indicating that Vélez alludes to the fact that the "apellidos eran robados." Américo Castro cites several works by J. Gómez Ocerín concerning Luis Vélez de Guevara which Rodríguez Marín failed to mention (Articles in *Revista de Filología Española* 1916 and 1917).

58. ——— and Hugo A. Rennert. *Vida de Lope de Vega, (1562-1635).* New York: Las Americas Publishing Company, 1968.

Américo Castro has brought up to date the 1919 edition of the *Vida de Lope de Vega* by Hugo A. Rennert and Américo Castro. A few statements concerning Luis Vélez de Guevara are noted. In a letter to Antonio Hurtado de Mendoza, "poeta de la corte," written by Lope in 1628, the following appears:

> ...Estos días se decretó en el Senado cómico que Luis Vélez, don Pedro Calderón y el doctor Mescua hiciesen una comedia, y otra en competencia suya el doctor Montalván, el doctor Godínez y el licenciado Lope de Vega, y que se pusiese un jarro de plata en premio. Respondí que era este año capellán mayor de la Congregación, y que para el que viene aceptaba el desafío. Grande invención, solemne disparate, desautorizada cosa, gran plato para el vulgo. (p. 290)

Concerning *Los novios de Hornachuelos,* which has been attributed to both Luis Vélez and to Lope, Américo Castro says on page 480: "Este es un caso típico, en que no podemos saber con exactitud de quién sea la comedia." On page 546, the author says: "Es dudoso que *Los novios de Hornachuelos* sea obra de Lope; más parece de Vélez de Guevara." On page 487, Américo Castro says that "El verdadero autor" of *El Príncipe Escanderberg* is Luis Vélez.

59. Catalán Menéndez Pidal, Diego. *Por campos del Romancero, estudios sobre la tradición oral moderna.* Madrid: Gredos, 1970.

In the section of his book "Dos romances inspiradores de Vélez de Guevara" (pp. 122-185), Catalán discusses the *Romance de El conde preso* in the *comedia La romera de Santiago,* formerly attributed to Tirso but now to Luis Vélez de Guevara. Catalán says that the historical basis of Vélez' play is fantastic: the action occurs in the time of King Ordoño de León and the Spanish count Garci Fernández, but the feminine protagonist is the daughter of don Manrique de Lara and the "conde preso" is don Lisuardo, a name unknown in any of the chronicles, historical or novelistic. Catalán agrees with S. Griswold Morley (*Bulletin Hispanique,* XVI [1914], 186, 191-192 and 203-205), that "puede decirse que la comedia toda no es otra cosa que un edificio construido sobre el tema del poemita épico." The *romance viejo* which provided the argument for the *comedia* is introduced in scene XII of the third act: don Lisuardo is in jail for having "forzado a doña Sol de Lara" when she was returning from a pilgrimage to Santiago, and he hears voices singing his story. Catalán indicates that the *Romance de Grifos Lombardo (o El conde preso)* is on the way toward extinction or if the story is retained there is a tendency to adopt a new structure.

El conde don Pero Vélez y don Sancho el Deseado, the autograph manuscript of which is in the Biblioteca Nacional in Madrid, is based on a *romance.* Catalán notes that apparently Vélez was attracted to the story because the name of the protagonist, Pero Vélez, was considered to be that of one of his ancestors. The critic points out that since in "la tradición moderna" the two *romances, El conde don Pero Vélez* and *El conde preso,* seem to be intermingled, one is led to believe that Vélez knew a version of *El conde don Pero* which had been influenced by *El conde preso,* but Vélez himself could have changed the scene of the sentence of *El conde don Pero Vélez.* Catalán is of the opinion that the presence of *El conde pero Vélez* in "la tradición moderna" is undoubtedly linked to the success the *romance* reached in the theater thanks to the interest Vélez had for the "hazaña" of his "antepasado."

60. Cejador y Frauca, Julio. *Historia de la lengua y literatura castellana,* Vol. IV: *Época de Felipe III.* Madrid: Tip. de la "Revista de Arch., Bibl. y Museos," 1916.

    Cejador y Frauca notes that Vélez de Guevara wrote *comedias* which are spectacular in nature and in which the delineation of the characters and the dramatic qualities reveal the talent and inspiration of the poet. Concerning *El diablo cojuelo,* the critic states that the first five *trancos* are the best, each of the succeeding ones losing the verve of the first. Cejador y Frauca points out that the incidents in the *Diablo* are of less importance than the ingeniousness of the thought, the elegant subtlety, the perfection and suitability of the language, very similar to that of Quevedo, from whom Vélez took not a few phrases, playing with the language in a marvelous manner.

61. Cervantes Saavedra, Miguel de. *Obras completas,* Vol. I: *Comedias y entremeses,* ed. of Rudolph Schevill and Adolfo Bonilla. Madrid: Imprenta de Bernardo Rodríguez, 1915.

    In the "prólogo al lector" to his *Comedias y entremeses,* Cervantes makes note of "el rumbo, el tropel, el boato, la grandeza" of Vélez' compositions. Cervantes' selection of words — "pomp, tumult, pageantry, and grandeur" — seems to typify perfectly some of the plays written by Vélez.

62. ———. *Obras completas,* Vol. XVII: *Viage del Parnaso,* ed. of Rudolph Schevill and Adolfo Bonilla. Madrid: Gráficas Reunidas, S. A., 1922.

    Cervantes, the *ecijano's* greatest contemporary, mentions Luis Vélez de Guevara twice in *El Viaje del Parnaso.* In the following lines, he refers to Vélez as a "quitapesares" presumably because of his ready wit and humor:

> Este, que es escogido entre millares
> de Gueuara Luiz Velez es el brauo,
> que se puede llamar quitapesares:
>   es poeta gigante, en quien alauo
> el verso numeroso, el peregrino
> ingenio, si vn Gnaton nos pinta, o vn Dauo.
>   (p. 29)

In the second reference to Luis Vélez, Cervantes speaks affectionately of him as a personal friend:

Topé a Luys Velez, lustre y alegria
y discrecion del trato cortesano,
y abraçele, en la calle, a medio dia.
(p. 117)

63. Chabás, Juan. *Nueva y manual historia de la literatura española*. La Habana: Cultural, S. A., 1960.

Chabás notes that Luis Vélez de Guevara is very adept in inserting popular *romances* and legends into his dramas at the most intense moment and that in delineating feminine characters, he even surpasses Tirso: Gila of *La serrana de la Vera*, harsh, masculine and energetic; Blanca of *El conde don Pero Vélez*, sweet, jealous and sad; Inés de Castro of *Reinar después de morir*, valiant, worthy and passionate, all speak a poetic language adorned with images. Chabás believes that Luis Vélez de Guevara "merece ser recordado en el primer lugar de nuestros dramaturgos" and considers *La luna de la sierra* to be one of the *ecijano's* most beautiful *comedias*.

64. Chandler, Frank W. *Romances of Roguery, an Episode in the History of the Novel*. Two parts. (Part I: *The Picaresque Novel in Spain*). New York: Macmillan, 1899. (Tr. by P. A. Martín Robles, *La novela picaresca en España*. Madrid: La España Moderna, 1935).

The *Diablo cojuelo* by Vélez de Guevara is included by Chandler in the last chapter "The Decadence of the Picaresque Novel." He says that the fundamental conception of a rascal serving, defrauding and satirizing masters, traversing all society to describe its faults and foibles was bound to lose its popularity in time. According to Chandler, new methods were sought to portray adventure in the picaresque mould and this Vélez does by a trip through the air conducted by the *diablo cojuelo*. The reader is given a satirical view of Madrid society, with the deceits being unveiled in the ten *trancos* or strides through space and as Chandler says, the human comedy is laid bare.

65. Chandler, Richard R., and Kessel Schwartz. *A New History of Spanish Literature*. Baton Rouge: Louisiana State University Press, 1961.

Chandler and Schwartz very briefly mention Luis Vélez de Guevara under "Lesser Dramatists of the Golden Age." The authors indicate that two of Vélez' best known plays are *Más pesa el Rey que la sangre* and *Reinar después de morir*. Vélez is also included among "Minor picaresque writers."

66. Cilley, Melissa A. *El teatro español, las épocas en el desarrollo del drama*. Madrid: Blass, S. A., 1934.

Under "Dramáticos de segundo orden" Cilley lists Luis Vélez de Guevara, stating that the playwright's style is similar to that of Lope de Vega and even the subjects of his plays are drawn from the great master. According to the critic, Vélez excels in character delineation. Cilley lists a total of twenty-one works by the *ecijano*, which are divided into the following groups: *Comedias históricas, Comedias de espectáculo, Comedias bíblicas*, and *Entremeses*.

67. Cioranescu, Alejandro. "El autor del *Príncipe transilvano*," in *Estudios de literatura española y comparada*. Canary Islands: Universidad de la Laguna, 1954, pp. 91-113.

Cioranescu devotes a section to the study of the authorship of *El Príncipe transilvano*, attributed variously to Lope de Vega, Luis Vélez de Guevara, Juan de Matos in collaboration with Agustín Moreto, and Montalbán, and the critic concludes that all indications seem to point to Luis Vélez de Guevara as the true author of the *comedia*. In order to arrive at his decision, Cioranescu presents detailed information on the history of Segismundo Báthory, available at the time the play was written only in manuscript form or by oral communication, and points out the possibility that Vélez might have had access to the facts while in the service of the Archbishop of Seville, Rodrigo de Castro. The Archbishop was slated, before the death of Felipe II, to be in charge of the wedding festivities of Felipe III and Margarita de Austria, sister of Segismundo's wife. According to Cioranescu, *El Príncipe transilvano*, spectacular enough to indicate certain dramatic merit but amateurish enough to betray the unskilled hand of a beginner, could have been composed by Vélez for the celebration at the request of Rodrigo de Castro.

68. Cirot, Georges. "A propos du *Diablo cojuelo* aperçus de stylistique comparée," *Bulletin Hispanique*, XLVI (1944), 240-251.

In making a stylistic comparison between Vélez de Guevara and prose writers of the *Siglo de Oro* with whom there appears to be a marked kinship, Cirot cites passages from works by the authors he mentions, including: Cervantes *(Don Quijote),* Zavaleta *(El día de fiesta por la tarde,* 1660), Antonio Liñán y Verdugo *(Aviso y guía de forasteros que vienen a la corte,* 1620), Vicente Espinel *(Marcos de Obregón,* 1618), Gracián *(El criticón,* 1651), Quevedo *(Los sueños,* 1627), Antonio de Guevara *(Menosprecio de corte,* 1539), and the anonymous *Lazarillo de Tormes,* 1554). The French critic states that a characteristic of Spanish prose seems to be a tendency toward a piling up of details and Vélez reaches the maximum in that respect. According to Cirot, one is attracted to the *ecijano* by the use that he makes of words that are surprising and bold, expressions which are full of zest, not aimed at eloquence but realism attained in part by the truth of his statements and by the application of the spoken language. The critic adds that in spite of the effort necessary to read Vélez' work, it is worth the trouble to do so.

69. ———. "Le procédé dans *El diablo cojuelo,*" *Bulletin Hispanique,* XLV (1943), 69-72.

Cirot indicates that the action in *El diablo cojuelo* moves rapidly and a great deal takes place in a few pages but that sometimes the sentences are loaded with details — "un pêlemêle" not always easy to understand. As to vocabulary, the French critic points out that Vélez would not permit the intrusion of neologisms and that his attitude with regard to borrowed words directly or indirectly from Latin, is in opposition to "culteranismo." Cirot adds as an explanation for Vélez' point of view that he desired to use popular language and that he was reacting against the "invasion savante" favored by the clerics from the time of Berceo in the thirteenth century. Other characteristics of Vélez' style noted by Cirot are that the language is expressive and alive — that used in everyday life; and that the author is not afraid to use vulgar, bold and even repugnant scenes. The French critic concludes by saying that in every way the *Diablo cojuelo* keeps close to the route of the *Zahurdas de Plutón* of Quevedo.

70. ———. "Le style de Vélez de Guevara," *Bulletin Hispanique,* XLIV (1942), 175-180.

Cirot believes that there are elements of the baroque in Vélez' *Diablo cojuelo.* He states that the work generally is complicated by incidental items but that the structure, even though synthetical and massive, is at the same time attractive; that the language is that spoken by Vélez and not a special way of speaking created for a character in a book. The French critic compares *Le diable boiteux* of Lesage with Vélez' *Diablo cojuelo,* pointing out differences and says that Lesage found the idea for his work in the story of the Spanish author but did not translate it. Cirot indicates that similarities can be noted between the devil in Quevedo's *El alguacil alguacilado* and the one in *El diablo cojuelo.*

71. ———. Review of *El rey en su imaginación,* by Luiz Vélez de Guevara, ed. of J. Gómez Ocerín, *Bulletin Hispanique,* XXVII (1925), 170-172.

    The reviewer's opinion is that the principal theme of *El rey en su imaginación* is treated by Vélez de Guevara with spirit and ingenuity but that is about the only feature which makes the play worthwhile since it borders too frequently on buffoonery. The French critic adds that it takes the genius of a Shakespeare or a Cervantes to create scenes of folly which are of interest, and that the main argument of the *comedia* — the protagonist being of royal birth unbeknown to him feels instinctively a king — does not hold deep attraction for the piece. Cirot says that the "gongorisme" is heavy, citing the first scene as being nothing more than a long working of a play on the words "dar celos" and "pedir celos." The critic further states that the editing should have been more extensive, for the *comedia* is not lacking in obscurities. Cirot declares that truly he does not admire the dramatic work.

72. Cirre, José F. "Luis Vélez de Guevara y su tiempo," *Revista de las Indias,* XXII (1944), 337-348.

    Cirre says that Luis Vélez de Guevara accepted a secondary role as an author by using as models Lope in drama and Quevedo in prose, and that probably the economic difficulties in which the playwright found himself would not permit the luxury of original work. Cirre is of the opinion that if Vélez had lived during another period in history his image would have been greatly enlarged for he had undeniable talent and great ability. The author of this article concludes that Vélez was a man of his time — Spain was tired and lacked the force of creating new goals and from the absence of stimulus and the recognition of decadence comes the deep skepticism of Vélez.

73. Claramonte y Corroy, Andrés de. *Letanía moral,* followed by *El Inquiridion de los ingenios invocados.* Sevilla: 1613. (Cited in Felipe Pérez González, *El diablo cojuelo,* p. 181.)

In his *Letanía moral,* Claramonte writes the following lines dedicated to San Luis, in which he praises "dos sabios Luises," Luis Vélez and Luis Góngora:

> Sancte Ludovice
> ¿Por qué mi pluma pedis
> Viendo que dos sabios Luises
> Os haran, sagrado Luis
> Entre vuestras blancas lises
> Con sus plumas otra lis?
> Parto son de la sutil
> Cándida espuma de Tetis,
> Y, en lo dulce y lo gentil.
> Uno, oráculo del Betis:
> Otro, Anfriso del Genil.
> Ellos inmortales sumas
> Os deben conforme a ley
> Que como rizas espumas.
> En la gorra de tal Rey
> Bien parecerán sus plumas.
> Piedras dara, pues le toca
> Vélez para entretejerlas
> En ella, con fe no poca
> Y Góngora os dará perlas
> Pues las vierte de su boca...

In the *Inquiridion* which follows the *Letanía moral,* Claramonte says: Vélez. Luys Vélez de Guevara, floridissimo ingenio de Ezija de quien esperamos grandes escritos y trabajos, y a hecho hasta oy muchas famosas comedias."

74. Clark, Fred M. *Objective Methods for Testing Authenticity and the Study of Ten Doubtful comedias Attributed to Lope de Vega.* Chapel Hill: The University of North Carolina Press, 1971. *(Studies in the Romance Languages and Literatures,* Number 106.)

Fred M. Clark includes *El prodigioso príncipe transilvano* in his study of ten doubtful plays attributed to Lope de Vega. Some critics believe Luis Vélez de Guevara to be the author of this dramatic work. Clark states that *El prodigioso príncipe transilvano* differs from both playwrights' autographed *comedias* in the orthoepy. He indicates that there is little in the way of unusual hiatus which would exclude Lope or Vélez as the author, but he adds that in the treatment of the individual word there is sufficient evidence for rejecting the play as an authentic work of either dramatist. The majority of the non-Lopean elements in the *comedia* are found in the treatment of the individual word and in the rhyme schemes. The treatment of the individual word also offers variations from Vélez' usual orthoepic preferences. Clark believes that the twenty-six strophes in which both consonance and assonance are employed, the eighty-six autorhymes, the presence of false Andalusian rhymes, and the number of times that consonance is employed for assonance in *romance* passages offer additional evidence for rejecting the play as being by Lope. The strophic patterns, as Morley and Bruerton indicate, differ from Lope's authentic works also.

75. Cornil, Suzanne. *Inès de Castro, Contribution à l'étude du développement littéraire du thème dans les littératures romanes de l'histoire à la légende et de la légende à la littérature.* Bruxelles: Palais des Académies, 1952.

   A comprehensive study, tracing the literary development of the Inés de Castro theme, is presented by Suzanne Cornil, who avers that the best dramatic interpretation of the story in Spanish literature is *Reinar después de morir* by Luis Vélez de Guevara. The critic states: "Il (Vélez) a les défauts de son siècle, mais aussi son imagination débordante et sa grande richesse d'expression" (p. 78). Cornil indicates that the fact that *Reinar después de morir* is still in the repertory of the modern theater affords proof of the lasting interest in Vélez' *comedia*. The critic gives a summary of the play, mentions works by the playwright's predecessors, and points out that Vélez introduced the *romance* "¿Dónde vas el caballero?" which announces the death of Inés, and also was the first to use the comparison of the flight of the heron with the life of a woman in danger. Cornil finds that the characters are not well developed: Inés is a very beautiful and deserving woman who only wants to live in peace; Alfonso IV is superficial and lacking in force; the prince is so overwhelmed by the events bursting upon him that he scarcely has time to study them; Blanca is the best drawn — agitated by the sentiments of love, jealousy and pride — and she is entirely original. Cornil states that in five centuries about three hundred texts have treated the Inés de Castro theme.

76. Coster, Adolphe. Review of *La serrana de la Vera,* by Luis Vélez de Guevara, ed. of Ramón Menéndez Pidal and María Goyri de Menéndez Pidal, *Revue Critique d'Histoire et de Littérature,* ns. LXXXII (1916), 162-163.

   Coster praises the excellent edition of *La serrana de la Vera* by the Sres. Menéndez Pidal and hopes to see it followed by many others. The critic points out that the editors scrupulously respect the original orthography except the old equivalence of the *u* and the *v* which in the texts of the Centro de Estudios Históricos preserves in the first the character of the vowel and in the second that of the consonant. Coster believes that texts should not be modernized for this makes serious study of the old language impossible.

77. Cotarelo y Mori, Emilio. *Colección de entremeses, loas, bailes, jácaras y mojigangas desde fines del siglo XVI a mediados del XVIII.* 2 vols. Madrid: Casa Editorial Bailly/ Baillière, 1911. (*Nueva Biblioteca de Autores Españoles,* vol. XVIII.)

  Cotarelo says that among the words of praise for Luis Quiñones de Benavente's *Jocosería,* the most curious and important are those written by Luis Vélez de Guevara in his *Aprobación,* dated August 26, 1644, which probably were the last to come from his pen since he died November 10 of the same year. Luis Vélez says:

> Enseña ingeniosamente y ayuda a ellas (las buenas costumbres) con lo moral, lo peregrino, lo raro, conceptuoso, nuevo y nunca de otro talento comunicado a la alabanza general con tantos aplausos, nunca a otro tan dignamente debidos; que nadie en el mundo, no solamente no le ha imitado, sino que solos lejos y sombras de su pluma no se ha atrevido a rastrear, siendo el más singular ingenio en esta provincia de cuantos ha tenido España. (p. lxxvii)

Cotarelo discusses four *entremeses* by Luis Vélez: *La burla más sazonada, La sarna de los banquetes, Los atarantados,* and *Antonia y Perales.* He gives a brief summary of each but does not reproduce any of them. Cotarelo also mentions another *entremés, Los sordos,* and two *bailes, La colmeneruela* and *Los moriscos.* The critic says that Vélez was an excellent "entremesista" especially in "lo satírico como era de esperar de su ingenio agudo y mordicante."

78. ———. "Luis Vélez de Guevara y sus obras dramáticas," *Boletín de la Real Academia Española,* III (1916), 621-652, IV (1917), 137-171, 269-308, 414-444.

  Cotarelo makes a comprehensive study of Luis Vélez de Guevara, giving detailed biographical information, a list of the playwright's dramatic works with origins, models, imitations, first publication, etc., followed by opinions of critics from the time in which Vélez lived up to 1917. One of the criticisms of Luis Vélez' work is that he lacked originality and imitated Lope de Vega in many of his *comedias*. Cotarelo says that the imitations and reworkings by Vélez of the *comedias* of Lope are so numerous that he cannot omit the titles which he lists on pages 442-443. The critic adds that of those plays for which we do not know a model, there are some excellent dramas, such as *El diablo está en Cantillana, La luna de la sierra, Más pesa el Rey que la sangre*, etc. Cotarelo concludes by stating:

> ...por su falta de originalidad no creemos que pueda Vélez igualarse con Guillén de Castro, con Mira de Amescua, con Montalbán ni con Jiménez de Enciso; pero, fuera de éstos, no cede en mérito a ningún otro de sus contemporáneos, entre los de segundo orden.

79. Crawford, J. P. Wickersham. *The Life and Works of Cristóbal Suárez de Figueroa*. Philadelphia: University of Pennsylvania Press, 1907.

According to Crawford, Suárez de Figueroa's *El Pasajero* (1617) contains the most severe criticism of the national theater at the beginning of the seventeenth century. Crawford states that the public paid no attention to the critics for Lope de Vega, Tirso, and Luiz Vélez de Guevara were the popular idols and at two o'clock in the afternoon the Teatro de la Cruz and the Teatro del Príncipe were filled, from the place of the *mosqueteros* in the pit to the *Señores* in their boxes, all anxiously awaiting the "follies" of their beloved *comedia*.

80. Delano, Lucile K. "The *gracioso* Continues to Ridicule the Sonnet," *Hispania*, XVIII (1935), 383-400.

Lucile Delano points out that the merit of the *culteranistas* was judged by the obscurity of their metrical compositions, if we are to believe Laín, *gracioso* in Vélez de Guevara's *El príncipe de Escanderbey:*

> Yo soy poeta, Señor,
> y en España los poetas
> tienen sus ocultas setas,
> para escribir con primor;
> porque advierto en su favor
> que claramente se ha visto
> ser cualquiera dellos listo
> por lo culto, y lo discreto
> para hurtar cualquier conceto

> aún del mismo altar de Cristo.
> ....
> y soy poeta, que ignoro
> aquello mismo que he escrito;
> con un soneto acredito
> mis poéticos cuidados,
> puestos de los afamados
> poetas, y no entendidos,
> que son pocos escogidos,
> aunque muchos los llamados.
>
> (*Biblioteca de Autores Españoles* LXIX, 500)

81. Dellepiane de Martino, Ángela Blanco. Review of *Reinar después de morir y El diablo está en Cantillana*, ed. of Manuel Muñoz Cortés, *Filología* (Universidad de Buenos Aires), III (1951), 240-241.

    Ángela Blanco Dellepiane indicates that the collection of the *Clásicos castellanos* has always been sparse in publications of the classical theater and perhaps the desire to increase the number of dramatists of that period induced them to include an edition of Vélez de Guevara, an author always given an inferior place in his role of "comediógrafo." The reviewer states that Muñoz Cortés has made possible the "actualización" of the theater of Vélez and has chosen for this purpose two *comedias*: *Reinar después de morir*, based on the well-known legend of doña Inés de Castro, and *El diablo está en Cantillana*, a pleasing work in which veiled irony is discernible. Dellepiane does not consider the edition to be well annotated and adds explanations for a number of terms and phrases used in the two plays which might be of value to the reader.

82. Devoto, Daniel. "Para la historia de *Los novios de Hornachuelos*," *Bulletin Hispanique*, LXXI (1969), 579-584.

    According to Devoto the text of *Los novios de Hornachuelos*, attributed to Lope de Vega and in recent times restored to Luis Vélez de Guevara, has not been studied scrupulously by modern Spanish editors. The critic discusses the attribution of the *comedia* to Lope de Vega by Menéndez y Pelayo and the contention of John M. Hill that Luis Vélez is the author. Devoto calls attention to the manuscripts and *suelta* which were known to exist and indicates that he found two additional *sueltas* in the Bibliothèque Nationale de Paris. One of the *sueltas* agrees with the copy in the British Museum which was used by Hill for his study; the other *suelta* seems more recent than the first though apparently of the seventeenth century. Devoto believes that the second *suelta* is the one mentioned by Salvá in his *Catálogo*, the location of which heretofore has not been determined.

83. Díaz de Escovar, Narciso, and Francisco de P. Lasso de la Vega. *Historia del teatro español*, Vol. I: *Desde el origen del teatro hasta el siglo XVII*. Barcelona: Montaner y Simón, Editores, 1924.

> Díaz de Escovar and Francisco de P. Lasso de la Vega remark that Vélez attained more renown for his novel than for his dramatic work, even though he wrote more than four hundred *comedias* and was the one who not only corrected the plays written by Felipe IV but also collaborated with him in writing them. In citing Vélez' plays, the authors contend that, without doubt, all of his works reveal defects — disarranged arguments, foolish happenings, incredible situations, monstrous inventions, extravagances and nonsense — but these things are not enough to authorize the severe criticism suffered by Vélez. The critics point out that there are to be found in Vélez' work many beautiful aspects both in form and substance — well-delineated characters, flexible and harmonious versification, and varied style.

84. Díaz-Plaja, Guillermo. *Historia general de las literaturas hispánicas*, Vol. III: *Renacimiento y barroco*, introd. by Ramón Menéndez Pidal. Barcelona: Editorial Barna, S. A., 1953.

> Díaz-Plaja says that Luis Vélez de Guevara is one of the most outstanding figures in the theater of the *Siglo de Oro*, and that for many critics is considerably more than a very brilliant second-rate writer, ranking on a level with Moreto, Rojas, Alarcón and even Tirso in the area of the heroic and dramatic *comedia*. According to Díaz-Plaja, Vélez resembles Quevedo in his caricatures and numerous elements of style but lacks the bitterness of the great Spanish satirist. Commenting on *El diablo cojuelo*, Díaz-Plaja states that Vélez does not moralize but rather limits himself to seeing and painting — the visual aspect of society grotesquely stylized is all that matters to him.

85. Dugdale, B. E. C. "Inés de Castro and Pedro of Portugal," *The Quarterly Review*, CCXXIV (1915), 356-378.

> In the opinion of Dugdale, Vélez de Guevara is undoubtedly the writer who has made the most of Pedro and Inés. The critic

points out that *Reinar después de morir* has been acted in quite modern days and is a very fine tragedy. Dugdale contends that although as a whole *Reinar después de morir* is by far the most beautiful work of imagination which has been written on the subject, the ending of it is perhaps the weakest of all the dramatic expedients that have ever been tried. The critic thinks that La Motte and the queen's poison, Ferreira and death duly announced by messenger are better than Vélez' horrible picture of Pedro bending over the murdered corpse and demanding a crown, which is promptly brought from behind the scene and placed by him upon the lady's head.

86. Endres, Valerie F. "The Aesthetic Treatment of *Romancero* Material in the *comedias* of Luis Vélez de Guevara." Unpublished Ph. D. dissertation, University of Arizona, 1966.

Romancero material used by Luis Vélez de Guevara in twelve of his *comedias* is discussed and an attempt is made to arrange the plays in chronological order. Endres says that she does not presume to have carried out this endeavor without error, adding that the majority of Vélez' plays have not been dated with certainty. The critic believes that the adjective "great" could rarely be applied to Vélez' dramatic works, but an examination of his treatment of the *romances* shows that the playwright was a conscious craftsman who merits attention because of the care with which he incorporated ballads and other traditional material into the fabric of his works and because of his ability to evoke the beauty and charm of his *Romancero* material.

87. Entrambasaguas, Joaquín de. *Estudios sobre Lope de Vega*. 3 vols. Madrid: Consejo Superior de Investigaciones Científicas, 1946.

In volume II, Entrambasaguas mentions the friendship of Lope de Vega and Luis Vélez de Guevara which may have begun in 1599, as has been proposed, since Vélez composed a sonnet for Lope's edition of his *Rimas*, published in 1604. The critic indicates that Vélez and Lope remained friends for many years as is apparent in the praises of Vélez which appear in a number of Lope's works, such as *El Jardín de Lope de Vega, Laurel de Apolo*, etc. Concerning Vélez' change of name from Santander to Guevara, Entrambasaguas says that there were other writers of the time who assumed appellations of famous people, notable among them Lope de Vega, who exchanged Fernández for Carpio to give the idea that he was a descendant of the great Bernardo del Carpio.

88. ———. Review of *Estudios de literatura española y comparada*, by Alejandro Cioranescu, *Revista de Literatura*, VI (1954), 408-410.

    Entrambasaguas does not agree with Cioranescu that the authorship of *El Príncipe transilvano* can be settled definitely in favor of Luis Vélez de Guevara, for there are many circumstances which seem to point to Lope de Vega as the possible composer of the *comedia*. The critic contends that until there are more convincing reasons than those presented by Cioranescu, he believes the matter will remain unsolved as it has been in the past.

89. ———. "Un olvidado poema de Vélez de Guevara," *Revista de Bibliografía Nacional*, II (1941), 91-176.

    The *portada* of the poem published by Entrambasaguas reads as follows: ELOGIO DEL IURAMENTO DEL SERENISSIMO PRÍNCIPE DON FELIPE DOMINGO, QVARTO DESTE NOMBRE DE LUYS VÉLEZ DE GUEVARA, CRIADO DEL CONDE DE SALDAÑA DIRIGIDO A LA SEÑORA DOÑA CATALINA DE LA CERDA, DAMA DE LA MAGESTAD CATÓLICA DOÑA MARGARITA DE AUSTRIA, REYNA DE ESPAÑA, MADRID, MIGUEL SERRANO DE VARGAS, 1608. The critic indicates that the poem is written in *octavas reales* (133 of them), in which the poet describes with surprising exactitude courtly dress of the seventeenth century, as well as aspects of official life and customs of the time. Entrambasaguas adds that if Vélez de Guevara is admired as the excellent dramatic author of *Reinar después de morir* and as the reflective satirical novelist who wrote *El diablo cojuelo*, he well deserves to have added to his literary merits the composition of the fine poem, forgotten, but a brilliant facet of Vélez' work.

90. ———. "Un tricentenario — Haz y envés de Luis Vélez de Guevara," *Atenea*, XCVI (1950), 188-203.

    To commemorate the *tricentenario* of the death of Luis Vélez de Guevara (1644), Entrambasaguas gives a biographical sketch of the poet, indicating the dual role that he played throughout his life — the real and the imaginary characterizations. The critic points out that Vélez considered himself to be an *hidalgo* assuming the aristocratic name Guevara, with a wife whose family was no less important than his, and an illustrious warrior, but in reality he was not of noble birth nor was his wife and neither was he a great soldier. Entrambasaguas adds that the unquestionable truth of his life is his literary brilliance, and says that if Vélez had not left us his theater — excellent, full of popular flavor and even almost *juglaresco* — another work of his would be enough for his *tricentenario* to be remembered, *El diablo cojuelo,* with its sharp and sparkling satire.

91. ———. "Una nueva comedia de Lope de Vega sobre Santa Teresa de Jesús, estudio bibliográfico," *Revista de Literatura,* XXV (1964), 5-47. (Facsimiles of manuscripts reproduced.)

    Entrambasaguas unravels the mystery of the lost text of a Lope de Vega play, *Vida y muerte de Santa Teresa de Jesús,* confused with the one by Luis Vélez de Guevara, *La bienaventurada Madre Santa Teresa de Jesús, monja descalza de Nuestra Señora del Carmen.* It seems that since the titles of the *comedias* were so similar, part of Lope's play was put with Vélez' and vice versa, so that the Manuscript in the Biblioteca Nacional in Madrid has the first and third acts of the Vélez play and the second of Lope's with *línea autógrafa,* while the Manuscript in the Parma Library has the first and third acts of Lope's *comedia* and the second of Vélez'. How did this mix-up come about? Entrambasaguas says it is difficult to tell. He believes that the mutilation was not intentional but probably due to the similarity of the two titles.

92. Entwistle, William J. Review of *El conde don Pero Vélez y don Sancho el Deseado,* by Luis Vélez de Guevara, ed. by Richard H. Olmsted, *The Modern Language Review,* XL (1945), 145-147.

    The reviewer states that *El conde don Pero Vélez y don Sancho el Deseado* is not of great intrinsic importance and its author is decidedly one of the second rank but that the play possesses certain peculiarities of interest and serves to classify Luis Vélez de Guevara with more precision than heretofore has been achieved. Entwistle indicates that Vélez found the hero for *El conde don Pero Vélez* in Timoneda's fake ballad, *El conde Vélez y el rey Sancho el Deseado,* and availed himself of the ballad, *Conde de Saldaña* for further details. Entwistle points out that there is no history in Vélez' *comedia* nor any notable degree of plausibility: "the characters are of papier-mâché and the kings and princesses are only too obviously strutting players." The reviewer concludes by saying that verve and gusto make the play exciting while the performance lasts but when looked at in clear cold light, it fails to stand the test.

93. Fernández de Navarrete, Eustaquio. *Novelistas posteriores a Cervantes con un bosquejo histórico sobre la novela española.* Vol. XXXIII of *Biblioteca de Autores Españoles.* Madrid: M. Rivadeneyra, 1854.

Fernández de Navarrete calls Luis Vélez de Guevara an author of first note and says that the information left to us by his contemporaries does not equal his reputation. According to the critic, *El diablo cojuelo o novela de la otra vida,* published in 1641, is an ingenious satire in which Vélez, by means of a new invention, portrays the customs of the court during his time and by so doing fixed his reputation and made it eternal. The influence of *El diablo cojuelo* is discussed and Fernández de Navarrete notes the popularity of Lesage's *Le diable boiteux* and mentions many other offspring of Vélez' "devil." The critic states that the story of *Estebanillo González* is believed by many to be a work by Luis Vélez but that don Nicolás Antonio indicated that the author was Esteban González, "bufón" who had belonged to Octavio Picolonini de Aragón. The fact that the work was first published in Brussels makes plausible to Navarrete the opinion of Nicolás Antonio.

94. Fitzmaurice-Kelly, James. *Historia de la literatura española desde los orígenes hasta el año 1900,* tr. del inglés y anotada por Adolfo Bonilla y San Martín, con un estudio preliminar por Marcelino Menéndez y Pelayo. Madrid: La España Moderna, 1901.

Fitzmaurice-Kelly considers Luis Vélez de Guevara as a dramatist and states that even the most severe critics have praised *Más pesa el Rey que la sangre.* According to the English author, there have been few instances in the ancient Castilian tradition of loyalty to King which have been expressed with "tal energía y colorido." Fitzmaurice-Kelly indicates that Luis Vélez is best known for his satire, *El diablo cojuelo,* which contains verbal pictures of life among all classes of Madrid society of the time. The critic believes that Lesage improved notably the work of Vélez but that the original "es de un humorismo extremado y su estilo es tan castizo como puede serlo el de la mejor obra castellana." An interesting note made by Fitzmaurice-Kelly is that he attributes to Vélez de Guevara the *novela, Los tres hermanos* with the date given as 1641.

95. Flores García, Francisco. *La corte del rey-poeta (recuerdos del Siglo de Oro)*. Madrid: Ruiz Hermanos, 1916.

Flores García dedicates a chapter in his book to Luis Vélez de Guevara and states that his desire is to give an idea of what this famous author was as a man and as a writer. The critic remarks that Vélez, a very talented person on whom fortune did not smile, wasted a great deal of his keen-edged wit on composing autobiographical poetry which was nothing more than a group of *memoriales* asking for money, work, or favors of some kind. Flores García points out that Vélez was highly respected by his associates as is evidenced by the fact that he presided over the literary *certamen* at El Buen Retiro, with such important people as El Príncipe de Esquilache, Antonio Hurtado de Mendoza, and others acting as judges. The critic concludes by saying that Luis Vélez had everything except the necessary means to live as he deserved in proportion to his great merit.

96. Foulché-Delbosc, R. "Un fragment de traduction française du *Diablo cojuelo*," *Revue Hispanique*, VI (1899), 200-203.

Foulché-Delbosc reproduces a fragment of a French translation of the *Diablo cojuelo* by Vélez de Guevara. The passage appears at the beginning of the story, *Les Avantures de Dom Leandre*, fifth adventure in the book entitled *Diverses Avantures de France et d'Espagne, Nouvelles Galantes et Historiques*. A Paris, chez Pierre Ribou... M.DCCVII, by "le chevalier de Mailly." According to Foulché-Delbosc, the first paragraphs are almost a literal translation of Vélez' *Diablo*, but the rest of the story bears no resemblance to Vélez' work.

97. García Blanco, Manuel. "Cervantes y el *Persiles:* un aspecto de la difusión de esta novela," in *Homenaje a Cervantes*, ed. by Francisco Sánchez-Castañer, II. *Estudios cervantinos*, Mediterráneo, 1959, pp. 102-106.

In discussing Cervantes' use of Norway as a symbol of darkness in *El Persiles*, García Blanco mentions Vélez de Guevara's reference to the far away place in several of his works, notably *El diablo cojuelo*, in *Tranco* VI where Vélez mentions "...los neblíes de la más oscura Noruega puntas a diferentes partes." Other compositions by Vélez in which Norway is designated as a place of darkness are: *El rey en su imaginación* (ed. of J. G. Ocerín, ll. 1674-1680), *La romera de Santiago* (Act III, scene 8), and in *El marqués del Vasto* an analogous passage with the same lines appearing as those in *La romera de Santiago.*

98. Gassier, Alfred. *Le théâtre espagnol.* 2nd ed. Paris: Paul Ollendorff, Editeur, 1898.

> According to Gassier, Luis Vélez de Guevara was one of the most prolific writers of a superabundant epoch, having written four hundred *comedias.* The French critic contends that Montalván's praise of Vélez in *Para todos* is exaggerated, for in the Spaniard's opinion all of Vélez' works are masterpieces. Gassier discusses briefly the plays by Vélez which he says are the most important of those that have been saved and indicates that the playwright's dramas are full of spectacles, apparitions, battles, etc. Gassier recognizes as one of the models of the Spanish theater Vélez' *Reinar después de morir,* which he says is much more vigorous and more inspired than the works treating the Inés de Castro theme that preceded it.

99. Gil y Zárate, Antonio. *Manual de literatura, principios generales de poética y retórica y resumen histórico de la literatura española.* 10th ed. Paris: Librería de Garnier Hermanos, 1889.

> Gil y Zárate contends that Luis Vélez de Guevara imitated Lope de Vega in every way and that he did not enjoy in the nineteenth century the position that as a dramatic poet he had during the time in which he lived. The critic adds that "en medio de su desarreglo, tiene, sin embargo, rasgos muy felices; sus caballeros son siempre nobles, valientes y generosos, y las damas brillan por su honestidad y recato, siendo su versificación por lo general flúida y sonora, aunque a veces con resabios de mal gusto." Of the *Diablo cojuelo,* Gil y Zárate says that the idea is an ingenious one: that of flying over Madrid, with the rooftops raised permitting the author to criticize various social classes and many customs of the time. The novelty of the story, together with the lightness and grace of the style, delight the reader. The critic indicates that Vélez' work deserves to be more known and not subordinated to Lesage's imitation, which in Spanish translation is the most familiar. A long passage from *El diablo cojuelo* is quoted, in which Vélez describes various types of Madrid society of the time.

100. Gili Gaya, Samuel. Review of *Reinar después de morir y El diablo está en Cantillana,* by Luis Vélez de Guevara, ed. of

Manuel Muñoz Cortés, *Nueva Revista de Filología Hispánica,* III (1949), 196-197.

Gili Gaya indicates that the attention given to *El diablo cojuelo* probably has contributed to relegating to a secondary role the copious dramatic work of Luis Vélez de Guevara. The critic says that in the present century scholars are correcting the error and the playwright is beginning to acquire the esteem which, in the opinion of Valbuena Prat "habrá de situarle al lado de los seis grandes poetas de nuestra escena clásica." Gili Gaya states that Muñoz Cortés gives an analysis by act of *Reinar después de morir* and *El diablo está en Cantillana* and relates characters, themes and situations with various works by Vélez and by other authors. According to the critic, Muñoz Cortés causes us to see how the legend of doña Inés de Castro replaces the historical to leave a lyrical sediment without regard to time or place and the aesthetic quality overpowers the historical and determines the legendary development of the theme.

101. Gillet, Joseph E. "El flamenco en algunos textos españoles antiguos," *Revista de Filología Española,* XV (1928), 384-388.

The derivation of various phrases used in several early Spanish texts is discussed by Gillet with examples from the works of Torres Naharro, Lope de Vega and Vélez de Guevara. The words *el nitesgut español,* used by Vélez in *El diablo cojuelo* (ed. of Bonilla, p. 50), according to Gillet must be derived from the Flemish *niets goed (malo de toda manera)* rather than the German *nichts gut,* which would have preserved some of the *ch* sound. Gillet believes that the hypothesis of Bonilla (English "naughty guest") cannot be accepted.

102. Givanel Mas, J. "Observaciones sugeridas por la lectura del drama de Coello, Rojas y Vélez: *El Catalán Serrallonga y Vandos de Barcelona,*" *Boletín de la Real Academia de Buenas Letras de Barcelona,* XVIII (1945), 159-192.

The critic gives an analysis of the play, stating that the last act was written by Luis Vélez de Guevara, who lends a picaresque note in keeping with his joyful muse without losing the character given to the personages in the *comedia.* Givanel Mas cites the delightful jail scene in which pass in review types worthy of figuring in a gallery of caricatures. According to the critic, Vélez expresses sharpness of wit in the comic scenes but at the side of this note, there is tenderness shown in the character of the father of the protagonist and a feeling of tragedy revealed in the words of the captain addressed to his sweetheart before entering the chapel.

103. Glaser, Edward. "El patriarca Jacob, amante ejemplar del teatro del siglo de oro español," *Bulletin Hispanique*, LVIII (1956), 5-22.

In his study of Jacob as an exemplary lover in the theater of the Spanish Golden Age, Glaser discusses at length Luis Vélez de Guevara's *La hermosura de Raquel*. The critic indicates that the work is based on three fundamental episodes of the Biblical story: the blessing of Jacob by his father, his enslavement, and his return to Israel. Glaser points out that Vélez pictures Jacob as a handsome young man whose virtues equal his physical appearance, and even more worthy of praise is his religious zeal. According to the critic, the principal part of Vélez' work is consecrated to the triumphs and tribulations of Jacob *enamorado*, and that the many metaphors, similes and pastoral parables suggest a certain analogy with bucolic literature. Glaser believes that Vélez' vision of the Biblical episode was influenced by Camões' *Sete annos*, in fact the sonnet, which is a *bucolización* of the love of the patriarch, exercised such a fascination for the author that he repeated it twice in his play. Glaser contends that the piece loses its enchantment by the playwright having the patriarch play the role of a *filósofo de amor*, when Jacob reaches the conclusion that love and jealousy are incompatible. The critic says that in developing the story of the love of Jacob and Rachel, Vélez has dwelled on minute details while on the other hand the psychological characterization lacks depth and subtlety.

104. Gómez Ocerín, J. *El rey en su imaginación*, by Luis Vélez de Guevara. (*Teatro antiguo español*, Tomo III). Madrid: Imprenta de los Sucesores de Hernando Quintana, 1920.

El rey en su imaginación, insofar as Gómez Ocerín was able to determine, had not been published before the edition of 1920 which he prepared. The autograph manuscript of the play, located in the Biblioteca Nacional in Madrid, is described in detail and an attempt is made to date the *comedia*. Gómez Ocerín establishes the fact that the work could not have been written before 1615 nor later than August 1625. An analysis of *El rey en su imaginación* follows and included in this study is a discussion of *comedias* by other authors based on a theme similar to Vélez'. The critic indicates that the lack of chronological data precludes a comparative study of imitations, sources and influences, but one cannot assume that Lope de Vega is always the initiator and the imitated. Gómez Ocerín believes that the central theme of the *comedias* treating *El rey en su imaginación* comes from *libros de caballerías*. The young people in these stories grow up not knowing their true origin and although they live as rustics their nature forces them not to be content with that life but to aspire to great things. Thus the image of the *príncipe villano* is commonplace in the chivalric story. *Observaciones y notas* and *observaciones métricas* are included after the reproduction of the play.

105. ———. Review of *La serrana de la Vera*, by Luis Vélez de Guevara, ed. of Ramón Menéndez Pidal y María Goyri de Menéndez Pidal. (*Teatro antiguo español*, I), *Revista de Filología Española*, IV (1917), 411-414.

The reviewer is concerned with observations made by Milton A. Buchanan in his comments in *Modern Language Notes*, XXXII (1917), 423-426, and George T. Northup in *Modern Philology*, XV (1917), 447-448. Gómez Ocerín does not agree with Northup that the method of using old Spanish spelling with modern accents is disagreeable nor with Buchanan that the play is a spectacular one which would have had to be performed in the patio of a palace. The critic agrees with Northup that the publication of *La serrana de la Vera* is of great value and concludes by saying that only by remembering the popular sources of themes in Spanish drama can one understand the theater of Spain not as an historical curiosity but as a marvelous art.

106. ———. "Un nuevo dato para la biografía de Vélez de Guevara," *Revista de Filología Española*, IV (1917), 206-207.

Gómez Ocerín publishes the document in which Felipe IV granted to Luis Vélez de Guevara, because of his past and future services, the meat stall in the *carnicería* which had become vacant due to the death of Juan Ladrón de Guevara, making available to Luis Vélez all the privileges enjoyed by his predecessor, dated Madrid, April 7, 1636. Reprinted from Archivo Histórico Nacional. Consejo de Castilla. Decretos de gracia. Leg. 13197 a. 1636, núm. 13.

107. ———. "Un soneto inédito de Luis Vélez," *Revista de Filología Española*, III (1916), 69-72.

    The following poem is quoted:

      De Luis Vélez al conde de Olivares
       Cavalleriça tiene Vuecelencia,
       cámara tiene Vuecelencia y todo;
       y soy del mismo quebradiço lodo
       que hizieron a Quincoces y a Canençia.
      Bálgame por servicios la paçiençia
       con que a uger destos fieros me acomodo:
       rey tengo natural, español, godo,
       y en bos está su humana omnipotençia.
      Yo nasí en el rinión de Andaluçía,
       y no es justo que en siglo de Gusmanes
       tenga cautiva en Londres mi poesía.
      ¡Muera yo entre Thenorios y Marbanes,
       que juro a Dios que estoy con poplexía
       de Contintones y de Boquinganes!
        (Bibl. Nac. ms. 10794, fol. 513v.)

    The above sonnet by Vélez Guevara, according to Gómez Ocerín, is an example of a type of poetry which without doubt appeared in abundance and was well accepted. The critic comments on various lines in the poem, citing possible meanings and background information for comprehension of the sonnet.

108. González López, Emilio. *Historia de la literatura española*, Vol. I: *Edad media y siglo de oro*. New York: Las Americas Publishing Company, 1962.

    González López says that in Vélez de Guevara's *El diablo cojuelo* the dominant feature is the *cuadro de costumbres;* the novel is a satire on Spanish society in general and *madrileñan* in particular. The critic points out that the playwright, inspired at times by Quevedo and at others by Cervantes, tends toward witty caricature in the depiction of characters as well as in his *cuadros de costumbres*. González López contends that Vélez' ingenious and keen-edged language, which is full of images, idioms, plays on words with unusual meanings for well-known terms, is a manifestation of *conceptismo*. In the opinion of the critic, Vélez' art reflects two sides: one, a tendency toward *lo culto*, the exquisite and delicate which leans toward *gongorismo*, expressed in the poetry of some of his *comedias;* the other, a satirical note, realistic, full of wit and vitality, disfigured at times by his inclination toward *conceptismo*, which is found in his prose and particularly in his novel, *El diablo cojuelo*.

109. Green, Otis H. *Spain and the Western Tradition,* Vol. II: *The Castilian Mind in Literature from El Cid to Calderón.* Madison: University of Wisconsin Press, 1964.

In his discussion of "Three Cosmological Problems" Green states that in 1641 a Spaniard (Luis Vélez de Guevara) could be lighthearted about Galileo's telescope (the revealer of "new stars"). A quotation is given from *El diablo cojuelo* in which the Limping Devil excuses himself for declining to discuss matters of astronomy:

Don Cleofás, our fall was so swift that we had no chance to observe anything; and I swear that if Lucifer had not brought with him a good third of the stars, as we constantly hear in the allegorical plays at Corpus Christi time, astrology would have even greater means than it now has to play tricks on you. I say this with all due respect for Galileo's telescope... for I speak with reference to things below the telescope and things below the roof tops, and with no less respect for the optics (and the whims) of those whimsical gentlemen who have discovered that the sun has a sunspot on its left side, have traced mountains and valleys on the moon and have seen horns on Venus.

Green says that these jesting remarks are very accurate and show unexpected familiarity with the significance of Galileo's telescopic discoveries — Galileo found, just as Vélez de Guevara's devil states that he did, hills and valleys on the moon; he found a spot on the sun, thus bringing into question the idea of the sun's incorruptibility and he showed that Venus had phases like those of the moon — hence the reference to that planet as having "horns."

110. Grillparzer, Franz. *Sämtliche Werke,* ed. by Reinhold Backmann, Vol. XV: *Spanische Studien.* Wein: Verlag von Anton Schroll & Co., 1937.

Grillparzer comments briefly on nine plays by Luis Vélez de Guevara in his *Spanische Studien.* In his opinion, *Los fijos de la Barbuda,* with the exception of the first act, appears rather poor and he adds that in contrast with Lope's dialogue, the above play is uneven and rather threadbare. Grillparzer believes that the main thought in *El espejo del mundo* is very superficially executed and that there is little good to be said of the details of the *comedia.* The German critic contends that nonsense is carried too far in *El embuste acreditado* and that *Los amotinados de Flandes* is infinitely mediocre, even half unintelligible.

Grillparzer does have something good to say about *La rosa de Alexandria:* a good play, good flowing verse, the lyric (not the action) is the whole poetic value of the drama in the eyes of the Spaniards.

111. Groult, P. Review of *El embuste acreditado,* by Luis Vélez de Guevara, ed. of Arnold G. Reichenberger, *Les Lettres Romanes,* XII (1958), 357-359.

   Groult says that *El embuste acreditado* is a farce but it is one which succeeds: "l'embuste est acreditado" which can be familiarly translated as "le truc a pris." The reviewer notes that Reichenberger defends the *comedia* against those who say that it lacks realism, contending that it is simply a farce; he uses the opinion of Spencer and Schevill that the play abounds in amusing situations, typical of the exuberant imagination of Luis Vélez de Guevara. Groult poses the question that if the play is a farce, isn't it an error to spend time studying the character of the personages? Doesn't Reichenberger put the drama on a level which was never intended? The reviewer points out that, in his opinion, the editor has been excessive with his notes and explanations.

112. Gutiérrez, Fernando. *El diablo cojuelo,* by Luis Vélez de Guevara, il. by Enrique C. Ricart. Barcelona: Editorial Orbis, 1943.

   The publication by Orbis of *El diablo cojuelo* in limited edition on fine paper, in excellent print with superb woodcut illustrations, is a tribute to Luis Vélez de Guevara. In the prologue, Fernando Gutiérrez briefly tells the story of Vélez' life, saying:

   > Vivió intensamente, alternando los juegos del corazón con los de la pluma, hiriéndose muchas veces con aquéllos y consolándose, como mejor podía, con éstos. Pasó por la vida un poco a la zaga de la prisa de Lope, con hambre muchas veces, con miseria todas, riéndose de sí mismo, de sus obras y de todo lo que le era propio, que todo esto es también una forma de vivir.

   Following the reproduction of *El diablo cojuelo,* there is a section containing a few brief notes.

113. Hämel, Adalbert. Review of *Ignez de Castro,* by H. Theodor Heinermann, *Literaturblatt für germanische und romanische Philologie,* XXXVII (1916), col. 303-306.

Hämel indicates that Heinermann's diligent study of the Inés de Castro dramas, by no means easy to obtain, shows that he has a clear insight into the development of the legend in Romance literature. The critic states that Heinermann discusses twenty-six plays; eight Portuguese, six Spanish, five French, seven Italian, and briefly mentions other dramas treating the theme of Inés de Castro. Hämel notes that Luis Vélez de Guevara's *Reinar después de morir* is the best Spanish drama on the subject and says that Vélez' *comedia*, along with that of La Motte, inspired works on the theme which followed.

114. ———. ———. *Zur Charakteristik des spanischen Dramas im Anfang des XVII. Jahrhs. (Luis Vélez de Guevara und Mira de Mescua)*, by Theodor G. Ahrens, *Literaturblatt für germanische und romanische Philologie*, XXXIV (1913), col. 154.

The reviewer is of the opinion that, in general Ahrens' study is of little importance in the advancement of our knowledge of Spanish drama of the seventeenth century. Hämel states that Ahrens offers no final judgment or conclusions concerning the *comedias* by Luis Vélez de Guevara which are discussed and that insufficient use is made of the investigations published prior to his study.

115. Hatten, Genell M. "A Comparative and Dramatic Analysis of Several Plays Utilizing the Inés de Castro Theme." Unpublished Master's thesis, Louisiana State University, 1968.

The purpose of the work, as stated by Hatten, is to study the treatment of the Inés de Castro theme in four plays: *Reinar después de morir* by Luis Vélez de Guevara, and *Corona de amor y muerte* by Alejandro Casona, both of which belong to the Spanish Golden Age tradition, and *Inés de Castro* by Houdar de La Motte, and *La reine morte* by Henri de Montherlant, written in the French classical tradition. The critic summarizes and analyzes the plays and says that both Vélez and Casona, following the vein of the Spanish Golden Age, have produced dramas in which the plots are difficult to follow because the authors are interested in giving a lyrical quality to the theme and have used theatrical devices and language to denote their emphasis. On the other hand, Hatten points out, the French dramatists, La Motte and Montherlant, have been more interested in creating an internal, psychological drama through character development. The critic indicates that even though *Reinar después de morir* suffers from a subordination of characters to plot, Vélez has managed to tell the story in an interesting manner and to evoke poetically the essence of the legend, an achievement of considerable merit. Hatten adds that since *Reinar después de morir* is written in the pastoral tradition, the action is encumbered by frequent references to the countryside, the hunt, shepherds and lyrical language exactly as required by the Siglo de Oro.

116. Heinermann, Heinrich Theodor. *Ignez de Castro. Die dramatischen Behandlungen der Sage im den romanischen Literaturen.* Ein Beitrag zur vergleichenden Literaturgeschichte. Inaugural-Dissertation zur Erlangung der Doktorwürde der Hohen Philosophischen und Naturwissenschaftlichen Fakultät der Kgl. Westfälischen Wilhelms-Universität zu Münster i. W. Borna-Leipzig: Noske, 1914.

Heinermann includes in his dissertation forty-four dramatic works in Romance literature which treat the Inés de Castro theme, and in addition lists German, English and Dutch plays on the subject. The historical basis of the story is given, Inés de Castro in *Romances* is considered (*Romances* from Durán's *Romancero General,* Madrid 1851, are reproduced), and dramas in Romance literature treating the Inés de Castro theme are discussed with summaries made of some of the plays. Heinermann indicates that the certain end for La Cerda's *Inés de Castro* was the appearance of Luis Vélez de Guevara's *Reinar después de morir,* which enjoyed great favor during Vélez' lifetime and continued to be effective on the stage long after his death. The critic mentions the florid, highflown and unnatural language used by Vélez and cites a passage from *Reinar* to illustrate his point.

117. Hendrix, W. S. "Notes on Collections of Types, a Form of *costumbrismo,*" *Hispanic Review,* I (1933), 208-221.

To illustrate the persistence of the "crippled devil" theme, Hendrix mentions numerous French works using the *Diable* as the center of interest and calls attention to a drawing by Henri Monnier for the frontispiece of the book, *Le livre des cent-et-un,* Paris, 1831 (the original title was *Le diable boiteux a Paris ou Paris et les mœurs comme elles sont),* in which a crippled devil is seated on a cask and on a scroll are the following names: Addison, Sterne, Fielding, Goldsmith, St. Fox, Dulaure, Mercier.

Hendrix adds that consciously or not, Monnier's drawing illustrates the fact that Spain, through France, and directly, influenced English *costumbristas* in the eighteenth century and that England in her turn influenced and revived *costumbrismo* in France in the late eighteenth and in the early nineteenth centuries.

118. ———. "Quevedo, Guevara, Lesage, and the *Tatler*," *Modern Philology*, XIX (1921-1922), 177-186.

> The aim of this article is to point out certain parallels in thought between the *Tatler* and the authors mentioned above. Hendrix indicates that apparently no one to this time has made a comparative study such as he has undertaken with emphasis on the importance in England of translations of Quevedo's *Sueños* (tr. 1709) and Lesage's *Le diable boiteux* (tr. 1708) based on Vélez de Guevara's *El diablo cojuelo*. According to the critic, Addison and Steele most likely would have read whatever was popular and probably examined the Spanish original of the *Diablo cojuelo*. Hendrix makes comparisons by quoting excerpts from the works of Quevedo, Vélez de Guevara and Lesage and similar ones from the *Tatler* papers.

119. Hernández, Francisco J. *El teatro de Montherlant, dramaturgia y tauromaquia.* Madrid: Editorial Prensa Española, 1969.

> Hernández discusses Montherlant and Spain, indicating that the French dramatist was influenced by Luis Vélez de Guevara's *Reinar después de morir* when he composed *La reine morte* and that his familiarity with the Spanish *comedia* by Vélez was not "simple lectura incidental." The critic states that Montherlant did not follow closely the Vélez play but rather artistically reworked the parts of the argument that suited his view of the dramatic conflict.

120. Hernández, J. M. Review of *Autos,* by Luis Vélez de Guevara, ed. by Ángel Lacalle, *Books Abroad,* VII (1933), 81.

> The reviewer indicates that there are three plays included in Lacalle's *Autos,* by Luis Vélez de Guevara: *Auto de la abadesa del cielo, Auto del nacimiento de Nuestro Señor,* and *Auto sacramental de la mesa redonda,* preceded by a prologue in which the editor gives in concise fashion the history of Vélez as a dramatist. Hernández states that the edition is not

very pretentious either in its bibliography or in its critical scope but it gives the reader an opportunity to become acquainted with the religious tendencies of the author of *El diablo cojuelo.*

121. Herrero García, M. *Ideas de los españoles del siglo XVII.* Madrid: Editorial Voluntad, S. A., 1930.

In his book on ideas of the Spaniards in the seventeenth century, Herrero García discusses traits of Spanish people from different parts of the country such as *gallegos, andaluces,* etc., as well as *italianos, judíos,* etc., and cites passages from literary works to illustrate his point. The section on the characteristics of the *andaluces* is particularly interesting in a study of Luis Vélez de Guevara. Herrero García lists as features of those from Andalucía: 1) *arrogancia,* 2) *ingenio,* 3) *locuacidad,* and 4) *amorosidad.*

122. H(errero) G(arcía), M. "Una fuente de *El diablo cojuelo,*" *Correo Erudito,* II (1941), 93.

Herrero García wonders if anyone has noted the close similarity between Vélez de Guevara's *El diablo cojuelo* and the "visión" found in *Amor con vista,* by Juan Enríquez de Zúñiga, Madrid, 1625. Herrero García believes that since Vélez' work was published in 1641, he probably was familiar with the little-popularized work, *Amor con vista.*

123. Hill, John M. "A *Romance* of Luis Vélez de Guevara," *Hispania,* V (1922), 295-297.

John M. Hill reproduces a *romance* of Luis Vélez de Guevara, in which *Lauro,* the poetic name of Luis Vélez, sings his sorrows and disillusions. The critic states that the *romance,* while contributing nothing to the literary fame of the playwright, is valuable as being an addition to the slowly accumulating fund of his work. Two manuscript versions of the *romance* are located in the Biblioteca Nacional in Madrid (Ms. 2856 and Ms. 3915).

124. ———. *Los novios de Hornachuelos, Revue Hispanique,* LIX (1923), 105-295.

The editor says that the reproduction of *Los novios de Hornachuelos* has no other object than that of presenting the text of the play. Hill indicates that the introductory remarks are, therefore, in no wise intended as a study and are limited to setting down the facts that are known in connection with the *comedia.* He gives information concerning the manuscripts of the work and authorship, pointing out that the drama has been attributed to Lope de Vega by Menéndez y Pelayo, La Barrera, Durán, Schack, and Hartzenbusch. Cotarelo believes the play was written by Lope de Vega and reworked by Vélez in 1629. Paz y Melia in his *Catálogo de las piezas de teatro que se conservan en el Departamento de Manuscritos de la Biblioteca Nacional,* Madrid, 1899, states that the *comedia* is ascribed to Vélez de Guevara in two manuscripts, one of which is incomplete; that a *suelta* indicates Lope as author. Hill's edition of *Los novios de Hornachuelos* is based on Ms. 15429 for acts I and II, on Ms. 16652 for act III. Variant readings of Ms. 16652, of the *suelta* and of the Hartzenbusch text, published from a modern manuscript copy furnished to him by Agustín Durán, are given for acts I and II, of the *suelta* and of Hartzenbusch for act III. Comparison of the Hartzenbusch text with that of the *suelta,* according to Hill, shows that the manuscript copy was taken from the latter and the attribution to Lope naturally followed.

125. ———. Review of *El conde don Pero Vélez y don Sancho el Deseado,* by Luis Vélez de Guevara, ed. by Richard Hubbell Olmsted, *The Modern Language Journal,* XXIX (1945), 167-168.

John M. Hill indicates that Olmsted, in his appreciation of the literary value of *El conde don Pero Vélez y don Sancho el Deseado,* may seem to some readers to be excessive in his praise and to rank the play more highly than it deserves. Hill points out that all will readily concede that the *comedia* is generally excellent and undeniably well executed, but in his opinion it is not equal to Vélez' best efforts nor is it especially superior to many another play of the period. The critic says that some readers may wish that the editor had been moved to comment upon various allusions, lines or passages that are hardly to be considered commonplace and unworthy of notice.

126. ———. ———. *The Dramatic Works of Luis Vélez de Guevara, Their Plots, Sources and Bibliography,* by Forrest Eugene Spencer and Rudolph Schevill, *Romanic Review,* XXX (1939), 84-89.

The reviewer is of the opinion that the critical estimates or judgments of individual plays expressed by the authors of *The Dramatic Works of Luis Vélez de Guevara* represent a distinct advance toward arriving at a true appreciation of Vélez' place in the history of the Spanish theater. Hill says that earlier critics have been disposed to dismiss Vélez as a servile imitator of Lope de Vega, but it now appears clear that the playwright's indebtedness was far less than has generally been supposed. The reviewer mentions a play not accessible to Cotarelo and not discussed by Spencer and Schevill, *El mejor Rey en rehenes*, which he feels exhibits many of the striking and peculiar characteristics of Luis Vélez' dramatic style and he would not hesitate to declare it a product of his pen. A copy of a *suelta* edition (extremely rare) is to be found in the Bibliothèque de l'Arsenal at Paris in a volume catalogued as *Quinque comedias famosas*, bearing the shelf number 12,286. In the same library, ascribed to Vélez in the catalogue is the *entremés, El hambriento*, Madrid, 1659, which, Hill says, apparently has escaped the attention of bibliographers. The reviewer adds information for several of the plays included in the work of Spencer and Schevill, giving the location of other copies or editions.

127. ———, and Frank O. Reed. *Los novios de Hornachuelos*, by Luis Vélez de Guevara, New York: The Century Company, 1929. (The Century Modern Language Series.)

The edition of *Los novios de Hornachuelos* is intended primarily for college students entering upon a study of Spanish drama of the Siglo de Oro, hence comprehensive notes and vocabulary are included. In the introduction, authorship of the play is discussed, an analysis of the *comedia* is given, and sources are indicated. The editors point out that Vélez shows much inequality in his dramatic work, at times attaining the highest levels, at others stooping to mere improvisation and even servile imitation. According to the critics, the playwright is a facile versifier, possessing imagination and dramatic instinct and at his best he does not suffer in comparison with the great Lope de Vega whom he used for his model. The editors state that Vélez shows a fondness for the spectacular, the heroic in action; in language for the declamatory, the sonorous and at times, the bombastic; his characters are nearly always well delineated and produce the effect of reality; in plot he shows invention and resourcefulness and in most of his plays the action holds the interest to the end. The critics conclude by saying that perhaps more exhaustive study of the dramatic output of Luis Vélez de Guevara may establish for him a place higher in the ranks of his contemporaries than previous incomplete and imperfect knowledge has accorded him.

128. Hohmann, L. *Studien zu Luis Vélez de Guevara.* Wissenschaftliche Beilage zum Jahresbericht der Oberrealschule und Realschule vor dem Holstenthore zu Hamburg. Hamburg: Lütcke & Wulff, 1899.

> Hohmann gives a biographical sketch of Luis Vélez de Guevara, indicating the pertinent facts about his life, expressions of praise by his contemporaries, and an overview of his literary production. An interesting statement made by the German critic is that one of Vélez' works is the novel, *Los tres hermanos,* included in a volume along with *El diablo cojuelo* published in 1733, in which Hohmann says Vélez imitated Alonso de Alcalá y Herrera. The critic studies in detail four *comedias* by Vélez: *Reinar después de morir, El diablo está en Cantillana, La luna de la sierra,* and *Más pesa el Rey que la sangre y blasón de los Guzmanes.*

129. Hurtado y Jiménez de la Serna, Juan, y Ángel González Palencia. *Historia de la literatura española.* 6th ed. Madrid: 1949.

> Juan Hurtado and Ángel González Palencia discuss aspects of the dramatic works of Luis Vélez de Guevara and give brief summaries of several of his plays. In their opinion, almost all of Vélez' *comedias* derive from others on the same subject by Lope de Vega, but they point out that Vélez' lack of originality and carelessness in the development of the action is compensated for by "la riqueza del caudal poético," and that "por el sentido de lo poético" he has been called the *Racine* of the Spanish theater.

130. Jones, Royston Oscar. *The Golden Age: Prose and Poetry, the Sixteenth and Seventeenth Centuries,* Vol. II of *A Literary History of Spain.* New York: Barnes and Noble, Inc., 1971.

> Jones says that the most noteworthy satirical fantasy after Quevedo's is *El diablo cojuelo* by Luis Vélez de Guevara. Vélez' story gives a satirical panorama of Spanish life as the adventures of Don Cleofás and the lame devil are related. The critic indicates that the book is written with a "sustained witty *éclat,*" and he quotes as an example several lines from the episode of Don Cleofás' midnight escape over the rooftops from the officers of justice pursuing him on a false charge of rape:

> ...no dificultó arrojarse desde el ala del susodicho tejado, como si las tuviera, a la buharda de otro que estaba confinante, nordesteando de una luz que por ella escasamente se brujuleaba, estrella de la tormenta que corría, en cuyo desván puso los pies y la boca a un mismo tiempo, saludándolo como a puerto de tales naufragios...

Jones believes that in spite of the fact that *El diablo cojuelo* is brilliant in style, its contents are the banalities of seventeenth-century satire, and the work as a whole must be judged superficial. The critic admits that the brilliance of the book made it popular; it was reprinted a number of times, translated into several languages and adapted by Lesage as *Le diable boiteux*.

131. José Prades, J. de. Review of *Reinar después de morir,* by Luis Vélez de Guevara, ed. of Giuseppe Carlo Rossi, *Revista de Literatura,* XXI (1962), 199.

The reviewer states that the "bello" drama by Vélez has merited this new edition, produced with great care by Professor Rossi. She mentions the introduction, in which the editor studies the Inés de Castro theme in the literature of the Peninsula and indicates that the notes at the foot of each page, "salvo leves reparos," are very useful to the Italian reader.

132. Juretschke, Hans. *Vida, obra y pensamiento de Alberto Lista*. Madrid: Consejo Superior de Investigaciones Científicas, Escuela de Historia Moderna, 1951.

Juretschke writes that Lista considered as the essence of "el teatro antiguo" Lope, Tirso, and Calderón, and that his articles in *El Censor* are practically limited to the three playwrights. One article cited by Juretschke as appearing in *El Censor* treats Vélez' *Reinar después de morir*. The author of Lista's biography says that the critic rated as writers of the second or third category Guillén de Castro, Vélez de Guevara, etc., and thought that there were six outstanding dramatists: after the three greats, Lope, Tirso and Calderón, Lista added Moreto, Rojas, and Ruiz de Alarcón.

133. Kennedy, Ruth L. "*Escarramán* and Glimpses of the Spanish Court in 1637-38," *Hispanic Review,* IX (1941), 110-136.

Kennedy points out that the play, *Escarramán*, provides amusing glimpses of the court of Philip IV with its literary academies, its rivalries between the different pressure groups, its political corruption, its mad search for diversion to escape the realities of the day. She indicates that the allusions, after three centuries, are elusive and that a thorough study should be made of the various *vejámenes* and burlesques of the period, together with the news letters. Kennedy adds that such an investigation is needed for full comprehension of such transition dramatists as Vélez de Guevara, Antonio Hurtado de Mendoza, Cáncer, etc. The critic notes that the burlesque, *Escarramán*, was published in 1671 without mention of an author's name but in the *Títulos de las comedias* in *Parte* XXXVII of the *Escogidas*, it is ascribed to Agustín Moreto. Kennedy says she has found nothing in *Escarramán* that would link this play with Moreto's name, but there is good reason to believe Vélez had a hand in it and she gives reasons to support her argument. Kennedy concludes by saying that in her opinion the author of the last scenes at least, and possibly the whole play, is Vélez de Guevara and that the date of the *comedia* is February 1638.

134. Kincaid, William A. "Life and Works of Luis de Belmonte Bermúdez (1587?-1650?)," *Revue Hispanique,* LXXIV (1928), 1-260.

In his study of Belmonte, Kincaid discusses the authorship of two plays which are of concern to a consideration of Luis Vélez de Guevara: *Darles con la entretenida (Diego García de Paredes) o el Valor no tiene edad y Sansón de Estremadura* and *El gran Jorge Castrioto y Príncipe Escanderbec,* the first attributed to Luis Vélez by Schaeffer, and a *suelta* in the Ticknor collection names Vélez, an ascription in which Durán concurs; to Belmonte by the author of this article and Sánchez-Arjona; the second play is ascribed to Luis Vélez and to Belmonte. Concerning *Darles con la entretenida,* Kincaid says that a realistic picture of the old soldier is drawn, the kind of man Belmonte had seen in America and Spain; Vélez' brave man would be superhuman in his courage; he would fight the wind or death itself. Kincaid says that the close similarity of the meter arrangement of *Darles con la entretenida,* which he believes written by Belmonte, and *El Príncipe Escanderbec,* convinces him that both plays were composed by the same author. Kincaid offers other evidence to bolster his argument, including a comparison of the metrical arrangement of seven plays by Luis Vélez with the two *comedias* mentioned above.

135. King, Willard F. *Prosa novelística y academias literarias en el siglo XVII.* Madrid: 1963. (Anejos del *Boletín de la Real Academia Española.* Anejo X.)

>The purpose of Willard F. King's study of literary academies of the seventeenth century is to show the extent of the influence of the academies on the novelistic prose of the time. Luis Vélez de Guevara figures prominently in "certámenes literarios," having presided over one of the most well-known academies of the seventeenth century, that of El Buen Retiro in 1637. The "certamen" in El Buen Retiro was part of the celebration taking place in Spain while the electors were meeting in Ratisbon to select the Holy Roman Emperor. Philip IV had hopes of being elected to the high post.
>Willard F. King cites *Trancos* IX and X of Vélez' *El diablo cojuelo* to illustrate how "interpolaciones académicas" were used in literary works of the time. Don Cleofás and his mentor, *el diablo cojuelo,* attend two meetings of an academy in Seville. Cleofás, using the pseudonym, *El engañado,* is president of the second session, while the devil, with the name *El engañador,* is the "fiscal." The humorous "premáticas" read by Cleofás in the second reunion and two sonnets read in the first are compositions by Vélez. One of the sonnets and all of the "premáticas" were read by Vélez in the "certamen literario" which took place in 1637 in El Buen Retiro.

136. ———. "The Academies and Seventeenth Century Spanish Literature," *PMLA,* LXXV (1960), 367-376.

>The vast number of literary academies in Spain in the seventeenth century and their importance is treated by Willard F. King. In her discussion she makes a special point of noting that everyone remembers the two academy sessions in *El diablo cojuelo.*

137. Kirk, Charles F. "A Critical Edition, with Introduction and Notes of Vélez de Guevara's Act I of *La Baltasara.*" Unpublished Master's thesis, The Ohio State University, 1940.

>Kirk says that in the seventeenth century Spanish theater, Lope de Vega overshadowed his contemporaries to such a degree that many have been completely forgotten and those who have been remembered have been subjected to misconceptions and frequently to undue criticism. The critic continues by stating that the realization has dawned that to fully understand *Siglo*

de Oro drama, second-rate writers need to be examined as carefully as those of top rank. Kirk believes that Luis Vélez de Guevara, the dramatist, has been neglected, that a writer whose theatrical production approaches the four hundred mark is worthy of extensive study.

La Baltasara is cited in the work by Spencer and Schevill as one of eight plays written by Vélez in collaboration with other writers. He wrote the first act of *La Baltasara*, Antonio Coello the second, and Francisco de Rojas the third. According to Kirk, one of the interesting phases of Vélez' act is the inclusion of the play within the play — *El Saladino*, attributed by Vélez to Damián Salucio del Poyo, a 112-line passage of extremely rhetorical and florid *octavas reales* dealing with the siege of Jerusalem by Saladino II. Kirk concludes that Vélez not del Poyo wrote the lines since the style is conceptistic and baroque, not in keeping with that of del Poyo. The reproduction of the first act of *La Baltasara* is followed by a section containing extensive notes to clarify the text, to point out syntactical and stylistic qualities of Vélez, and to present examples of similar ideology or phrasing used by the playwright elsewhere and by other Spanish writers.

138. ———. "A Critical Edition, with Introduction and Notes, of Vélez de Guevara's *Virtudes vencen señales*." Unpublished Ph. D. dissertation, The Ohio State University, 1957.

The author indicates a twofold purpose in writing his dissertation: One, to contribute to the small but ever increasing volume of critical analysis of the dramatic production of Luis Vélez de Guevara, and Two, to make available for American scholars the text of a play which, in some respects, is similar to Calderón's *La vida es sueño*. According to the critic, there is no doubt that a strong link exists between *Virtudes vencen señales* and *La vida es sueño*, for there are similarities and parallelisms, but there exist differences also. Kirk cites as a point of fact that Vélez' *Virtudes* assumes the tremendous power of natural heritage to overcome savage environment whereas Calderón's *La vida es sueño* supports with equal intensity a belief in the overpowering effect of such surrounding conditions. The critic contends that to call *Virtudes vencen señales* a great play would be a gross exaggeration, for while it has many qualities to recommend it, on the whole it is a rather pedestrian effort which never quite lives up to its potentialities.

139. Lacalle Fernández, Ángel. "Algunas poesías, en parte inéditas, de Luis Vélez de Guevara, sacadas de un manuscrito de

la Biblioteca Nacional Matritense," *Revista Crítica Hispano-americana,* V (1919), 53-58.

Lacalle includes seven poems by Luis Vélez de Guevara, found in an interesting manuscript in the Biblioteca Nacional in Madrid, which he believes, at least in part, are unpublished works. Lacalle calls Luis Vélez the famous author of *El diablo cojuelo,* an excellent dramatist in many of his innumerable *comedias,* and a witty poet whose humor Cervantes praised. According to Lacalle, the poems which he has brought into print justify Vélez' fame as a lyric poet for they are full of delicacy and charming poetic color.

140. ———. *Autos* de Luis Vélez de Guevara. Madrid: Librería y Casa Editorial Hernando, S. A., 1931. (Serie Escogida de Autores Españoles IX.)

Three *autos* by Luis Vélez de Guevara are included by Lacalle in his volume: *Auto de la abadesa del Cielo,* of the type which he says might be called "Autos de Nuestra Señora" with miracles and intercessions by the Virgin on behalf of the faithful; *Auto del nacimiento de Nuestro Señor,* typical example of the "Auto de nacimiento" or mystery play; and *Auto de la mesa redonda,* which Lacalle says belongs to the group of "Autos sacramentales" because of its more complex plot and allegorical form. According to the critic, the characters in the first of the above *autos* are excellently drawn and passages of the poetry reflect a vigorous splendor, at times with Biblical reminiscences. Lacalle points out that in the second of the *autos* is noted the popular element, even the use of "el habla antigua," and the last of the group offers a rare combination of the eucharistic allegory together with chivalric adventure — the conquest of Jerusalem by Charlemagne who is Christ and the twelve Peers who are the Apostles. The critic says of the latter *auto* that the development is somewhat confused but adds that the final scene where Flor de Lis, the church, describes the night in which the Crucified, Charlemagne, dies shows extraordinary lyrical qualities and force.

141. Leavitt, Sturgis E. "Some Aspects of the Grotesque in the Drama of the *Siglo de Oro,*" *Hispania,* XVIII (1935), 77-86.

In discussing the grotesque in drama of the *Siglo de Oro,* Leavitt says that deserving of fame is the lion that follows Guzmán el Bueno around in Vélez de Guevara's *Más pesa el*

Rey que la sangre. Leavitt indicates that some major playwrights of the century are almost able to refrain from shedding blood but Vélez de Guevara is not wholly free from this tendency. The critic notes that his efforts differ from those of all the rest in that he has in mind an artistic effect. Leavitt points out that in *Más pesa el Rey que la sangre,* after Pedro has been put to death his body appears under a black canopy, his throat cut and the bloody dagger sticking in the wound. The critic adds that this may not seem at first sight to be very artistic, but the arrangement of the other characters and the dialogue that follows emphasize not the horror but the father's sacrifice and his patriotism as a soldier. Leavitt states that in *Reinar después de morir,* it is necessary to the plot and legend to show the dead body of doña Inés and that the ensuing ceremony of obeisance and offering her the crown is an effective dramatic touch full of dignity and pathos.

142. Legarda, P. Anselmo de. *Lo "vizcaíno" en la literatura castellana.* San Sebastián: Biblioteca Vascongada de los Amigos del País, 1953.

 In the study of "lo vizcaíno" in Spanish literature, Legarda suggests that the insistence with which Vélez de Guevara refers to "Viscaya" in a number of his works may indicate that the poet had been to the lands of "Oñate" home of the "Guevaras" the family name he assumed in place of his real name, "Santander." References are made by Legarda to numerous passages in *El amor en vizcaíno, los zelos en francés y torneos de Navarra* to illustrate various aspects of his discussion. The critic points out that during the Golden Age, interest in "lo vizcaíno" coincided with "culteranismo," a baroque manifestation which was essentially obscure and unintelligible and that in Vélez' *El amor en vizcaíno,* the imperspicuity reaches great heights. According to Legarda, Dominga and her *doncella* use "esa fabla avizcainada ininteligible" from the beginning to the end of the *comedia* and that in *Los hijos de la Barbuda* if there is not "fabla" of the same style there is equal preoccupation with giving to the play archaic flavor.

143. Leonard, Irving A. "A Shipment of *comedias* to the Indies," *Hispanic Review,* II (1934), 39-50.

 Irving A. Leonard reproduces a document, dated May 16, 1713, Archivo General de las Indias, Sevilla, Sec. III, *Papeles de la Casa de Contratación,* legajo 674, which consists of four pages of titles of plays which were sent from Spain to the Indies. The list includes the following *comedias* by Luis Vélez de Guevara:

>*Reinar después de morir (Doña Inés de Castro — La Garza de Portugal)* Luis Vélez de Guevara
>
>*Atila, azote de Dios* (o *La silla de San Pedro*). Luis Vélez de Guevara
>
>*El Serco de Roma por el Rey Desiderio*. Luis Vélez de Guevara.

144. Lesage, Alain Rene. *Asmodeus, The Devil on Two Sticks*, from the French with a Memoir of the Author, embellished with two hundred engravings, from designs by Tony Johannot. London: Willoughby and Company.

>In the Memoir of the Author it is stated that Lesage's *Le diable boiteux* is confessedly imitated from a Spanish work of the same title by Vélez de Guevara, "but the original, it must be added, as compared with the imitation, was but a flimsy and time-serving pamphlet, extending to not more than a hundred and thirty-five pages, and utterly destitute of the wit and humour of 'Asmodeus'."

145. ———. *El bachiller de Salamanca o aventuras de don Querubin de la Ronda, El diablo cojuelo o El observador nocturno, seguidas de El diablo cojuelo, verdades soñadas y novelas de la otra vida traducidas a ésta por Luis Vélez de Guevara*. París: Baudry, Librería Europea, 1847. (Colección de los mejores autores españoles, Tomo XLI.)

>Lesage addresses the prologue to his *Diablo cojuelo o el observador nocturno* to Luis Vélez de Guevara to whom he dedicates his work. The French author says that the *Diablo cojuelo* of Vélez gave him the title and the idea for his story, thus he grants to him the honor of the invention, but that he cannot claim to be Vélez' translator for he had to change the text and to compose a new work following the same plan. According to Lesage, he has been considered in Paris as Vélez' imitator and thus praised second hand. The French author indicates that he is dedicating the new edition to the playwright as he had done nineteen years before with the first edition, noting the changes made in the work.

146. Lista y Aragón, Alberto. *Ensayos literarios y críticos,* con un prólogo por José Joaquín de Mora. 2 vols. Sevilla: Calvo-Rubio y Compañía, 1844.

> Three articles are devoted to Luis Vélez de Guevara by Lista in his *Ensayos literarios y críticos* (vol. II, pp. 144-151). The critic indicates that if the dramas by the playwright which he has not read resemble those he has examined, the praise accorded to him by Montalbán in *Para todos* is extravagant. Lista says that Vélez is inferior to Tirso "en la sal cómica," and description of characters; to Mira de Amescua in versification; and to Montalbán in the art of directing the action though perhaps he equals him in high-flown style and exaggeration. The critic states that Vélez disfigures the heroes of Spanish history depicted in his plays by having them use the language of ruffians and bullies, and that there are few traces in his works of the improvements in dramatic art advanced by Lope. Lista adds that Vélez' versification, generally, is "rastrera o gongorina," his style "débil y desmayado," but that the playwright is not lacking in talent although his taste is abominable. In the discussion of twelve *comedias* by Luis Vélez, Lista labels as one of the best scenes in the Spanish theater that in *Reinar después de morir* in which Inés begs the king not to kill her, finds no mercy and is delivered into the hands of the murderers after her children have been torn from her. Lista concludes by saying of Vélez:
>
> > ... Sus comedias no pueden en nuestros días sufrir la prueba aun de la crítica más moderada; pero hay en ellas un gran repertorio de argumentos, que animados por el genio pueden convertirse en dramas excelentes. Muchas de las ya citadas, *La romera de Santiago, El diablo está en Cantillana, y El espejo del mundo,* aunque ninguna se escape de la censura *Infelix operis summa,* tienen algunas situaciones y escenas muy apreciables, que conviene estudiar al hombre de gusto, y aun imitar al poeta dramático. (p. 151)

147. Lomba y Pedraja, José R. "El rey D. Pedro en el teatro," in *Homenaje a Menéndez y Pelayo en el año vigésimo de su profesorado. Estudios de erudición española,* con un prólogo de D. Juan Valera. 2 vols. Madrid: Librería General de Victoriano Suárez, 1899, pp. 257-339.

> Lomba y Pedraja presents a comprehensive study of "El rey Don Pedro," called by some "el cruel," by others "el justiciero," as he appears in dramatic works. Among the plays cited is

El diablo está en Cantillana by Vélez de Guevara, in which Don Pedro is pictured as "un mozo mujeriego y calavera, amigo de aventuras nocturnas." In pointing out the various ways used in the literary legend to foretell the death of Pedro, Lomba y Pedraja quotes the passage from *El diablo está en Cantillana* in which Esperanza curses the king in a semi-prophetic way for having banished the one with whom she is in love.

148. McCall, Johnston V. "The Doña Inés de Castro Legend in Spanish and French Literature." Unpublished Master's thesis, The University of North Carolina, 1926.

The history of the Inés de Castro theme is traced from the earliest known works in Portuguese literature based on historical fact, to Spanish versions which introduce the legendary element found in *romances,* and on to the French plays on the subject in which sweeping changes in the original story are noted. Also included in the discussion is Ramón de la Cruz' *sainete, Inesilla la de Pinto,* a parody on the French version by Antoine Houdar de La Motte. McCall compares Luis Vélez de Guevara's *Reinar después de morir* with the works of his predecessors and indicates that the Spanish playwright was more successful than they in the treatment of the Inés de Castro legend, which he developed with considerable skill. The critic points out that Vélez omitted the choruses used by Ferreira and Bermúdez, which was a carry-over from the ancient Greek theater, and eliminated some of the numerous scenes and details found in Cerda's work which made the story hard to follow. McCall says that Vélez' play has been considered by some critics as one of the best that has been written on the legendary story of Inés de Castro.

149. MacCurdy, Raymond R. *Spanish Drama of the Golden Age: Twelve Plays.* New York: Appleton-Century-Crofts, Educational Division, 1971.

In the introduction, MacCurdy states that the most important playwrights of Lope's generation were Tirso de Molina, Guillén de Castro, Mira de Amescua, Juan Ruiz de Alarcón, and Luis Vélez de Guevara. The critic indicates that Vélez, author of the *costumbrista* novel *El diablo cojuelo,* was better known to his contemporaries as a prolific dramatist (he is said to have written over four hundred plays) whose theater closely resembled that of Lope de Vega. MacCurdy includes in his anthology of plays *Reinar después de morir* by Luis Vélez, which is preceded by a biographical sketch of the playwright and a discussion of his dramatic works. According to the critic, Vélez showed little inclination to write *comedias de capa y espada,* which seemed too tame for his taste; he was fond of heroic and grandiose characters; bold, strongwilled men and women; and produced what MacCurdy calls "rousing productions" *(comedias de ruido).* The critic remarks that Vélez had a sense of humor and that no better satire on the extravagances of the *comedias de ruido* can be found than in *El diablo cojuelo,* tranco four, where the mad poet has written a play with the title *Tragedia Troyana, Astucias de Sinón, Caballo griego, Amantes adúlteros y Reyes endemoniados,* in which the cast includes "cuatro mil griegos por lo menos" and "once mil dueñas a caballo." MacCurdy contends that Vélez anticipated the Hollywood extravaganza by three centuries.

The historical basis for the Inés de Castro story is given and various works treating the legend are mentioned. MacCurdy says that whether the body of Inés de Castro was exhumed and crowned is not known, but what is certain is that in Portugal every year on April 24 the coronation of doña Inés de Castro is commemorated.

150. McKendrick, Melveena. "The *Bandolera* of Golden Age Drama, a Symbol of Feminist Revolt," *Bulletin of Hispanic Studies,* XLVI (1969), 1-20.

Included in McKendrick's study of the *bandolera* of Golden Age drama is Gila of Luis Vélez de Guevara's *La serrana de la Vera.* The critic indicates that although based on Lope de Vega's play with the same title, Vélez' *comedia* is quite different in mood and in details. McKendrick remarks that Vélez gives the tale an atmosphere of savagery and violence not found in Lope: Gila wrestles, shouts and swears like a man and even overcomes a bull barehanded. In an analysis of the character of Gila, the critic states that the *Serrana* accepts the captain's offer of marriage not out of love but because it satisfies her vanity and her desire for self-assertion; and when the blow falls, it strikes not so much at her ambitions or her honor but at the core of her supreme egoism. McKendrick contends that Vélez saw Gila as a rebel against her sex whereas other playwrights who treated the *bandolera* preferred to depict her as a rebel against society.

151. Marqués, E. F. Review of *Autos,* by Luis Vélez de Guevara, ed. of Ángel Lacalle, *Boletín de la Universidad de Madrid,* III (1931), 508-509.

Marqués says that Luis Vélez de Guevara, "autor popular por excelencia," lacks sufficient editions of his production for him to be considered in a complete manner, for there are aspects of his works which are completely unknown. The critic feels that Lacalle's publication of the three *Autos* by Vélez helps to fill part of the need for knowledge of the playwright's literary compositions. Marqués notes that *El Auto de la abadesa del cielo*, reproduced from an unpublished manuscript in the Biblioteca Nacional in Madrid, is another work on the legend of Sor Beatriz, *El Auto del nacimiento de Nuestro Señor* is a typical example of an *Auto de Navidad*, and *El Auto de la mesa redonda* belongs to the group of *Autos sacramentales* known as *Moralidades*.

152. Martínez, Enrique José. "Tragedy in the Spanish Theater of the Golden Age." Unpublished Ph. D. dissertation, The University of Pennsylvania, 1970.

Luis Vélez de Guevara is described by Martínez as one of the best representatives of the new school created by Lope de Vega. The critic states that Vélez' imitations are not so slavish as to be mere carbon copies of the master's, that Vélez shows poetic talent and imagination and even in the plays whose main themes are taken from Lope, displays a brilliant mastery of dramatic technique. Concerning *La serrana de la Vera*, Martínez says that Vélez does not seriously treat the problem of evil to the extent that the high tragedy does so the play is tragic only because the protagonist meets her death at the end. *Reinar después de morir*, according to the critic, is a drama where light and shadow are in constant interplay, where the playwright has captured in a beautiful manner many human emotions: love and fear — fear of losing the person who is loved as in the case of Inés and Pedro; fear of suffering insult and ridicule in the Infanta's position; even the king fears for the security of his throne if he is not sufficiently strong and severe in his judgment of the political repercussions. Martínez points out that what is more relevant and leads into the realm of tragedy is the fact that the shadow of Death permeates the entire play. The critic believes that the drama falls somewhat short of being high tragedy because Vélez does not question sufficiently the problematic Man in the Universe nor the Evil encountered therein but it is a tragedy if the term is not used within such a narrow definition.

153. Méndez Bejarano, Mario. "Lágrimas poéticas," in *Homenaje a Bonilla y San Martín,* Madrid: Imprenta Viuda e Hijos de Jaime Ratés, 1930, II, 601-613.

> Méndez Bejarano discusses the Inés de Castro theme in literature and says that perhaps the story might have been buried under the debris of the sixteenth and seventeenth centuries if Luis Vélez de Guevara had not exalted it with his superb drama, *Reinar después de morir.* Méndez Bejarano mentions the fact that a *refundición* of *Reinar después de morir* was made to inaugurate the season of the Teatro Español in 1902.

154. Menéndez Pidal, Ramón. *La epopeya castellana a través de la literatura española.* Buenos Aires: Espasa-Calpe Argentina, S. A., 1945.

> According to Menéndez Pidal, *romances novelescos y líricos* provided source material for Luis Vélez de Guevara in a number of *comedias,* notably: *El conde don Pero Vélez, La serrana de la Vera, El príncipe viñador, Reinar después de morir,* and *Los hijos de la Barbuda.* The critic remarks that Vélez de Guevara as a playwright still is not well known which is evidenced by the fact that it took a long, long time for such an important *comedia* as *La serrana de la Vera* to be published. A comparison is made between Lope's *Serrana* and that of Vélez, and Menéndez Pidal says that Vélez' play surpasses that of Lope in comprehension of the traditional theme: Vélez follows the tragic *romance* of the *serrana* whereas Lope has his play end with pardon and marriage. Menéndez Pidal indicates that Vélez' *El príncipe viñador* has special interest for the history of the *romancero* and the theater since it is based on a *romance* which does not appear in the collections of the sixteenth century but is a *romance* of oral tradition. He adds that the very old form is known only by the part of it found in *El príncipe viñador* and *Mientras yo podo las viñas* by Agustín de Castellanos, written also in 1610.

155. ———. *Romancero hispánico (hispano-portugués, americano y sefardí) teoría e historia.* 2 vols. Madrid: Espasa-Calpe, S. A., 1953.

> In Chapter XV (Vol. II) entitled "El romancero antiguo nacionaliza el teatro. Postrimerías (1587-1640)," Menéndez Pidal discusses *comedias* based on *romancero* themes, including six by Luis Vélez de Guevara. One of the plays, *La romera de Santiago,* Menéndez Pidal says now is attributed to Vélez as the

sueltas indicate, because Tirso did not write any dramas inspired by the *romance viejo*. The critic points out that the playwrights have passed on to posterity in their works *romances* that do not appear in the collections of the sixteenth century nor in the *pliegos sueltos*, as is true in the case of Vélez' *El príncipe viñador*. Menéndez Pidal states that the beginning of a *romance* — "Si el caballo vos han muerto, subid, Rey, en mi caballo" — serves as the long title and the argument of a play by Vélez, and from this can be seen how famous the *romances* were since the first line brought to mind a complete theatrical theme.

156. ——— y María Goyri de Menéndez Pidal. *La serrana de la Vera,* by Luis Vélez de Guevara. *(Teatro antiguo español,* Tomo I), Madrid: Imprenta de los Sucesores de Hernando Quintana, 1916.

The Señores Menéndez Pidal give as their reason for selecting *La serrana de la Vera* as the first of the series of unpublished plays which the Centro de Estudios Históricos proposed to publish: "... es una de sus (Vélez de Guevara) mejores concepciones dramáticas, injustamente inédita. Es también importante para la historia del teatro español por las relaciones que presenta esta obra con otras de Lope y de Tirso, viniendo a formar parte de un abundante ciclo de comedias." The critics state that the date 1603 found on the autograph manuscript in the Biblioteca Nacional is in error and they offer evidence to support their view. After giving historical sources, a comparison is made between Vélez' *La serrana de la Vera* and that of Lope with the same title, both *comedias* being based on a *romance popular* of which there are twenty-one versions. The Señores Menéndez Pidal are of the opinion that Vélez' *Serrana* excels in "vigor dramático." Other dramatic works treating the *serrana* theme are discussed, including Lope de Vega's *Las dos bandoleras* in which the critics presume Lope to be the imitator of Vélez.

157. Menéndez y Pelayo, Marcelino. *Estudios sobre el teatro de Lope de Vega,* ed. of Enrique Sánchez Reyes. 6 vols. Santander: Aldus, S. A. de Artes Gráficas, 1949.

Menéndez y Pelayo discusses plays by Luis Vélez de Guevara which he calls *refundiciones* of Lope's and indicates that Vélez is "dramaturgo insigne entre los de segundo orden y uno de los que mostraron cualidades más análogas a las de Lope..." (IV, 38). *El Hércules de Ocaña,* Menéndez y Pelayo considers to be an interesting *comedia* as is true in general of the plays by

Vélez, "que fue quizá el más excelente de los dramáticos de segundo orden, llegando a imitar con tal perfección el estilo de Lope de Vega, que muchas veces se confunde con él" (VI, 79).

158. ———. "Observaciones preliminares," in *Obras de Lope de Vega,* publicadas por La Real Academia Española, Vol. XII: *Crónicas y leyendas dramáticas en España.* Madrid: Sucesores de Rivadeneyra, 1901.

> Plays by Luis Vélez de Guevara which derive from others by Lope de Vega are analyzed briefly by Menéndez y Pelayo. In commenting on Vélez' *La serrana de la Vera,* the critic says:
>
>> ... Queda, pues, reducida la venganza de Gila a una de tantas catástrofes de amor y honor; pero la escena en que se consuma es de un efecto trágico extraordinario; y bastaría por sí sola para probar la injusticia del olvido que pesa sobre el teatro de Luis Vélez de Guevara, uno de los mejores poetas de segundo orden, que en momentos felices llega a hombrearse con los de primero (p. xxi).

159. Mérimée, Ernest. *A History of Spanish Literature,* tr., rev. and enlarged by S. Griswold Morley. New York: Henry Holt and Company, 1930.

> Mérimée says that although Luis Vélez de Guevara is better known today as a novelist he was nevertheless a most successful playwright and that some of his *comedias* such as *Reinar después de morir* occupy a distinguished place in the history of the drama of Spain. The critic indicates that Vélez' gaiety and animation earned for him the sobriquet *Quitapesares* (care-dispeller) from Cervantes, who was a connoisseur. Mérimée contends that Vélez' real title to fame is certainly *El diablo cojuelo,* which is witty and lively, the only fault being that the author's plays on words and far-fetched phrasemaking torture the reader's intelligence. The critic finds it strange that Vélez' novel, which in its French amplification by Lesage became the rage, seems not to have been very successful in Spain in its original form, and that it was in the wake of the imitation by Lesage that *El diablo cojuelo* found readers in its native land.

160. ———. *Précis d'histoire de la littérature espagnole,* ed. entièrement refondu. Paris: Librairie Garnier Frères, 1922.

> The French critic very briefly mentions Luis Vélez de Guevara in connection with his dramatic works, saying that his

success was great in the theater but today he is better known for his *Diablo cojuelo.* Mérimée notes that at the time that it was written, *El diablo cojuelo* was, without contradiction, the most celebrated of the "romans" which were very popular. The critic contends that the gravest reproach which can be addressed to the author is that sometimes he subjects the reader to torture by his play on words and search for expressiveness. Mérimée indicates that Vélez is one of the most difficult to understand of Spanish writers and that even Spaniards need extensive commentaries to interpret his meaning. The French critic points out that the version by Lesage was more popular in Spain than the original and the real *Cojuelo* was almost forgotten.

161. ———. Review of *La serrana de la Vera,* by Luis Vélez de Guevara, ed. of Ramón Menéndez Pidal and María Goyri de Menéndez Pidal, *Bulletin Hispanique, XVIII* (1916), 290-292.

According to Mérimée, *La serrana de la Vera* can scarcely pass as a masterpiece, but it does have some very dramatic scenes and interesting details. The French critic states that the *comedia* makes one think at times of the *Alcalde de Zalamea* of Calderón: the character of the rich farmer, Giraldo, is not unworthy of that of Pedro Crespo; the intrigue — that of a young girl deceived by a captain who promises to marry her — is the same in both plays; the appearance of royalty is a feature of each of the works; the two heroines are very different, for Isabel of the *Alcalde* has very little in common with Gila, who is an extraordinary type, a true phenomenon. Mérimée contends that the exploits of this ferocious virago in the *sierra* would be intolerable today in the theater, even the Spanish. The critic notes that the theme of the *serrana* was popular as evidenced by the fact that it was brought to the stage five times at least, by Lope before 1603 and Vélez in 1613, by Enciso around 1618, by Tirso *(La ninfa del cielo)* and was treated "a lo divino" by Valdivielso in 1619. Mérimée adds that the popularity of the subject is explained on the one hand by local tradition of the Vera de Plasencia and on the other by the survival of the old *Serranilla* which came into the stream of literature with the Archpriest of Hita and Santillana; the old tradition has been preserved in a *romance* of which there are said to be twenty-one versions, which accounts for the many variations of the story.

162. Mesonero Romanos, Ramón de. *Dramáticos contemporáneos a Lope de Vega.* Vol. XLV of *Biblioteca de Autores Españoles.* Madrid: M. Rivadeneyra, 1858.

Mesonero Romanos indicates that the theater of Luis Vélez de Guevara should not be scorned nor overlooked by modern critics and states that this playwright has not been studied as he deserves nor judged with impartiality. In the critic's opinion, if the only work by Vélez which had been preserved were *Reinar después de morir,* it alone would be enough to accord him a distinguished place among the best Spanish authors. Mesonero Romanos believes that Vélez knew how to invent an argument, develop it and bring it successfully to the stage, but he lacked skill in the denouement, taking away the interest created by the action and destroying the effect of the first acts. Six plays by Luis Vélez de Guevara are reproduced in this volume of *Biblioteca de Autores Españoles.*

163. ———. "Teatro de Vélez de Guevara," *Semanario Pintoresco Español,* (1852), 66-68.

A study of the theater of Luis Vélez de Guevara by Mesonero Romanos shows that the playwright shared public applause and acclaim with Lope de Vega, but that in all of Vélez' plays "a vueltas de bellezas y primores poéticos, de caracteres bien delineados, y de escenas de seguro y calculado efecto, hay, como no podía menos de suceder, enorme desarreglo, disparates increíbles, abuso, en fin, de la misma fecundidad y soltura del ingenio." In all the *comedias,* Mesonero Romanos adds, there appears the facile verse of the inspired and bold poet that Vélez was. The critic quotes "dos preciosos cuentos" spoken by the *graciosos* in *No hay contra un padre razón* and *El ollero de Ocaña,* and at the end of his article, Mesonero Romanos lists sixty-four dramas attributed to Luis Vélez de Guevara.

164. Michels, Ralph J. Review of *The Dramatic Works of Luis Vélez de Guevara. Their Plots, Sources and Bibliography,* by Forrest Eugene Spencer and Rudolph Schevill, *Hispania,* XXI (1938), 155-156.

The reviewer indicates that Schevill hopes that this book will serve "to further a truer appreciation of Luis Vélez' place in the theater of the Golden Age... The full significance of his dramatic contribution has never been adequately recognized or investigated in detail, and this study may be a step to a clearer understanding of his achievement."

165. Millé Giménez, Isabel. "Guzmán el Bueno en la historia y en la literatura," *Revue Hispanique,* LXXVIII (1930), 311-488.

Isabel Millé Giménez says that the first author to bring to the Spanish theater the story of Guzmán el Bueno was Luis Vélez de Guevara in his comedia, *Más pesa el Rey que la sangre, y blasón de los Guzmanes*. The critic states that Luis Vélez made an effort to remain faithful to history, or at least what was regarded as such during his time, and created personages which were not lacking in defects but neither were they without outstanding characteristics. Isabel Millé Giménez points out that Luis Vélez' influence is recognized in the later works treating the theme of Guzmán el Bueno.

166. Miller, Kenneth C. "A Partial Edition of *El lego de Alcalá, comedia famosa de Luis Vélez de Guevara*." Unpublished Master's thesis, The Ohio State University, 1946.

According to Kenneth C. Miller, *El lego de Alcalá* is a well written play which contains highly dramatic situations. The critic says that the drama belongs to the genre of *comedias de santos* and that except for a few scenes such as those in which the *demonios* fight and torture the protagonist, or when he is taken bodily to heaven, etc., it is not too far-fetched to be convincing. Miller makes a comparison of Vélez' *El lego de Alcalá* with two plays of similar subject matter by Lope de Vega, *El saber por no saber y vida de San Julián de Alcalá de Henares* and *El truhán del cielo y loco santo*. The critic believes that the dramatic unity of *El lego de Alcalá* is superior to that of *El saber por no saber* and that the characters in Vélez' play are better drawn than those in Lope's work. *El truhán* is only similar to *El saber por no saber* and *El lego de Alcalá* in that it is a *comedia de santos* and its protagonist, Junípero, is a character very similar to Julián in the plays of both Vélez and Lope. Miller suggests that in some respects Julián may be Vélez himself — that perhaps the extravagances which kept Julián constantly in trouble as a cleric may have been related to the excesses which caused Vélez to be relegated to the rank of a second rate dramatist.

167. Montesinos, José F. Review of *Ignez de Castro, Die dramatischen Behandlungen der Sage im den romanischen Literaturen* (Diss. Münster), by H. Theodor Heinermann, *Revista de Filología Española*, VIII (1921), 82-83.

The review by Montesinos of Heinermann's *Ignez de Castro* is of interest in the study of Luis Vélez de Guevara for it concerns thoughts on an Inés de Castro *comedia* supposedly written by Lope de Vega. Seemingly the play is lost since no one has been able to find it. Montesinos does not agree with Heinermann's reasoning that if Lope had composed a play on such a well-known and popular theme it would be strange for it to have been lost especially since a play as weak as Mejía de la Cerda's has been preserved, nor does the reviewer accept Heinermann's explanation that the title mentioned in *El Peregrino,* edition of 1618, refers to Mejía's drama published in 1612 in the third part of the *comedias* of Lope and other authors. According to Montesinos, the statement would imply that Lope had no direct intervention in the preparation of the lists for *El Peregrino,* which doesn't seem probable to him. The reviewer notes that the bibliography included with Heinermann's study makes the work useful for any one interested in "el teatro antiguo" of Spain.

168. Montoliu, Manuel de. *El alma de España y sus reflejos en la literatura del siglo de oro.* Barcelona: Editorial Cervantes, 1954.

Montoliu calls *El diablo cojuelo* a book which has remained eternally young because the cleverness and wittiness are coupled with the fluttering lightness of the style and with the sharp causticity of the satire which the author wields amidst that crowd of figures "demasiado reales para ser soñadas, demasiado soñadas para ser reales."

169. ———. *Manual de historia de la literatura castellana.* 5th ed. Barcelona: Editorial Cervantes, 1947.

The author indicates that up to one hundred *comedias* by Luis Vélez de Guevara are known but that the work which has given him universal fame is his ingenious and sparkling novel, *El diablo cojuelo.* The critic says that the *Diablo* is not strictly speaking a picaresque novel although there are points of similarity and he adds that "por su argumento es una obra de imaginación, una visión o un sueño en que el fondo eminentemente satíricorrealista que tiene de común con la novela picaresca, corre parejas con la invención radicalmente idealista de su plan." According to Montoliu, the *Diablo* is sprinkled throughout with little-used and picturesque words and with complex images and expressions, making the reading at times somewhat difficult. The critic points out that the work is basically one of realism but is enclosed in an idealistic plan: "el humorismo castellano, sin perder para nada su carácter genuino, traspasa en este libro los límites de la vulgar vida humana y aspira a hacerse trascendental y metafísico."

170. Morel-Fatio, Alfred. *L'Espagne au XVI*^{e} *et au XVII*^{e} *siècle, documents historiques et littéraires.* Paris: Librería Española de El Denne, 1878.

Beginning on page 603, Morel-Fatio reproduces documents concerning the "Académie Burlesque célébrée par les poetes de Madrid au Buen Retiro" in 1637 (February 15-25), at which Luis Vélez de Guevara presided. Vélez opened the Academy with a sonnet to Philip IV, followed by his *oración, memoriales, cédulas,* the "vejamen que dió Alfonso de Batres," "vejamen de Francisco de Rojas," poems of different types by poets of the day, Antonio de Solís, Antonio Coello, Gerónimo Cáncer, Luis de Benavente, Luis de Belmonte and others. Morel-Fatio found the manuscript which he reproduced in the Bibliothèque de l'Arsenal in Paris.

171. ———. Review of *El diablo cojuelo,* by Luis Vélez de Guevara, ed. of Adolfo Bonilla y San Martín, *Bulletin Hispanique,* V (1903), 307-314.

Commenting on Bonilla's edition of *El diablo cojuelo,* Morel-Fatio mentions the abundant notes included, saying that some of the explanations help to render more intelligible certain expressions used by Vélez while others seem useless since they involve terms which probably are understood by most readers. The French critic adds that there are omissions, pointing out a number of phrases which have not been explained satisfactorily; for example, "dar rocín por carnero y gato por conejo a los estómagos *del buelo.*" Morel-Fatio offers his observations suggested by reading the notes of Bonilla's edition and gives his own interpretations of certain expressions found in *El diablo cojuelo.*

172. Morley, S. Griswold. "El romance del *Palmero,*" *Revista de Filología Española,* IX (1922), 298-310.

Morley studies the *romance* of *Palmero* as an example of the enduring "tradición popular." He says that there are eight versions known before 1650:

    A. del *Cancionero* de Rennert
    B. del pliego aragonés
    C. del pliego suelto de Praga
    D. del pliego suelto de la Biblioteca Nacional de Madrid
    E. la impresa por Sepúlveda

Fragments introduced in:

F. Mejía de la Cerda, *La tragedia de doña Inés de Castro*
G. Guillén de Castro, *La tragedia por los celos*
H. Vélez de Guevara, *Reinar después de morir*

Morley believes that the dramatic versions lack intrinsic value, but they are of great importance for the history of the *romances*. The critic says that Vélez is the playwright who follows most closely the *romance* which begins "¿Dónde vas, el caballero?" He adds only "una cuarteta" to the *romance:*

> Las señas que ella tenía,
> bien te las sabré decir:
> su garganta es de alabastro
> y sus manos de marfil.

173. ———. "El uso de las combinaciones métricas en las comedias de Tirso de Molina," *Bulletin Hispanique*, XVI (1914), 177-208.

In his study of the metrical combinations in Tirso de Molina's plays Morley discusses *La romera de Santiago*, considered as a doubtful work by this playwright. The critic states that *La romera de Santiago* was printed in *Parte XXXIII de comedias nuevas escogidas de los mejores ingenios de España,* Madrid, 1670, as written by Tirso but in a "refundición suelta" of the eighteenth century, Luis Vélez de Guevara is designated as the author. Morley indicates that the long passages of *romance,* the style replete with *gongorismo* and various "discursos cuasi-filosóficos" which delay the development of the drama, make him believe that Tirso did not write the play. In addition, the critic points out that Tirso never used *romances viejos* for the argument of his *comedias* and *La romera de Santiago* is built completely around the theme of the "poemita épico." Morley concludes that there are many considerations which point to Luis Vélez rather than Tirso as the author. In *Apéndice I* at the end of the article, the critic reproduces the *Romance viejo de la Romera de Santiago.*

174. ———. "Judging Authorship and Chronology in the *comedia*," *Hispanic Review*, V (1937), 281-285.

In introducing a method for judging authorship and chronology, Morley cites the following as an example of the sort of test that could be applied to determine who wrote a play. *El niño diablo* is attributed to both Lope de Vega and Luis Vélez:

the ending of one version ascribes it to Lope, the other to *Lauro* (Vélez de Guevara). The critic points out that the word *diablo* was in the early language a trisyllable; nowadays it is a dissyllable. In the seventeenth century, the transition period, it was treated sometimes as three syllables, sometimes as two. A study by Robles Dégano showed that Vélez de Guevara, out of thirteen cases, made three syllables eleven times and two syllables but twice. In an examination of eleven autograph plays of Lope, eighteen examples of *diablo* were without exception a dissyllable. In the case of *El niño diablo,* the word occurs ten times in the course of the *comedia,* and of the ten cases, nine are three-syllabled; the *Lauro* ending contains the word used as three syllables; the Lope ending shows it as two. Morley says that obviously the odds are very strong that Vélez de Guevara wrote the play.

175. ———. Review of *El embuste acreditado,* by Luis Vélez de Guevara, ed. of Arnold G. Reichenberger, *Hispanic Review,* XXVI (1958), 79-81.

Morley believes that Reichenberger's *El embuste acreditado* is a most scholarly edition of a very minor text and wonders why the editor chose the *comedia* for so great an expenditure of time and research. The critic contends that the play is certainly no masterpiece; the suspense is null; all the interest lies in the twists of the action. Morley states that the *Embuste acreditado* had a number of editions, under various titles, in the seventeenth and eighteenth centuries, doubtless because the fantastic and improbable *embuste* amused the spectators like a class "B" western. The critic maintains that it is hard to find logical motivation in the plot and that today it is difficult to discern its attraction.

176. ———. ———. *El rey en su imaginación,* by Luis Vélez de Guevara, ed. of J. Gómez Ocerín, *Hispania,* V (1922), 115-117.

According to Morley, *El rey en su imaginación* in itself is commonplace enough, dealing with a familiar romantic folklore theme, and one can only regret that such a wealth of erudition and research in reproducing the text is lavished upon a mediocre work of art. He believes that the governing motive for the publication of this play was the fact that it exists in an autograph manuscript of a well-known author. Such a text, an authentic one as its author wrote it, affords the only sure basis for syntactical and metrical studies. Instead of emphasizing the linguistic side, Morley states, the editor expended the chief effort on vocabulary, a valuable contribution, and on parallels of the various themes. The reviewer contends that in the depiction of Carlos' madness, Luis Vélez does not distinguish himself in giving reality to a situation which is fundamentally false, although the audience is expected to take it seriously.

177. ———. ———. *La serrana de la Vera,* by Luis Vélez de Guevara, ed. of Ramón Menéndez Pidal y María Goyri de Menéndez Pidal, *Hispania,* I (1918), 185-188.

Morley states that *La serrana de la Vera* has an excellent first act, a second with some lively scenes, and an extravagant third, but only a preparation for something bigger (a first class Spanish dictionary?) can justify the expenditure of so much splendid erudition on plays of the second or fourth order when the best are not yet properly edited. Morley notes one passage in *La serrana de la Vera* worthy of mention, ll. 2298-2309, which the editors chose to leave without comment: "Cavallito, cavallito, el de las piernas de xerga,..." The critic indicates that these lines and the following are popular poetry beyond doubt; Vélez did not write them without inspiration from an outside source. Morley says he has not been able to put his finger on any other parallel than the two verses of the Asturian *romance* of *Conde Olinos:* "por la gracia de Dios Padre / comenzó el caballo a hablar," but feels that another *romance* nearer to the text exists.

178. ———, and Courtney Bruerton. *The Chronology of Lope de Vega's comedias, with a Discussion of Doubtful Attributions, the Whole Based on a Study of His Strophic Versification.* New York: The Modern Language Association of America, 1940.

A number of plays of doubtful attribution to Luis Vélez de Guevara and to Lope de Vega receive new consideration as Morley and Bruerton make a study of the *comedias* based on strophic versification. Among the works in question, *El niño |diablo* is believed by the authors not to be by [Lope and probably is a play of Vélez, and they conclude that *Los novios de Hornachuelos* may well be by Vélez. Morley and Bruerton are of the opinion that Lope did not write *El prodigioso príncipe transilvano* in spite of the attribution to Lope by Cotarelo, who says that Vélez was only fifteen years old in 1595 when the events recounted in the play took place. The critics believe that the *comedia* probably was written between 1595 and 1601 — Segismundo abdicated in 1602 and one of the last lines in the play refers to him: "que hoy tiene revuelto el mundo." Morley and Bruerton add that a *refundidor* whether Vélez or another would have changed that line if he were working after 1602.

179. Muñoz Cortés, Manuel. "Aspectos estilísticos de Vélez de Guevara en su *Diablo cojuelo*," *Revista de Filología Española*, XXVII (1943), 48-76.

Muñoz Cortés discusses charateristics of style in Vélez de Guevara's *Diablo cojuelo,* including the use of play on words, multiple meaning of terms, metaphors, similes, and images. Vélez is compared stylistically with Góngora and Quevedo, and Muñoz Cortés says that language for them is an art, not an instrument for simple expression. The critic states that the three writers all attempt to withdraw from reality: Góngora to soar to sublime heights, Quevedo, and Vélez in part, to sink to the lowest levels. Vélez at moments in *El diablo cojuelo* tends toward the idealistic which places him in between Góngora and Quevedo. Muñoz Cortés concludes by saying: "Caminos distintos para una misma huida. Huida de hombres con el alma helada por el desengaño, sin una tarea incitante en que quemar sus vidas."

180. ———. *Reinar después de morir y El diablo está en Cantillana.* Madrid: Espasa-Calpe, S. A., 1959. (Clásicos Castellanos, No. 132.)

In the prologue, Muñoz Cortés discusses in detail the historical basis of the doña Inés de Castro theme, as well as the *romances tradicionales* and the legend in its dramatic versions, and then gives an analysis of Vélez' *Reinar después de morir*. According to the critic, Vélez surpasses the playwrights who preceded him in writing on the topic in the composition of the work, in the action of the play, in the prophetic dream scene, and in the creation of the unfortunate feminine protagonist. A summary is given of the second play in this edition, *El diablo está en Cantillana,* which the critic says comprises comic elements and the supernatural, making it entirely different from *Reinar después de morir*. Muñoz Cortés states that the *Diablo está en Cantillana* is "graciosa, ágil, y de buenas situaciones," if the lengthy and boring dissertation on Seville be excepted. A metrical analysis for both plays is included.

181. Nercasseau y Morán, Enrique. "Discurso," in *Discursos leídos ante la Academia Chilena, correspondiente de la Real Academia Española en la recepción pública del señor don Enrique Nercasseau y Morán, el día 21 de noviembre de 1915,* Santiago de Chile: Imprenta de San José, 1915, pp. 1-21.

>The theme chosen by Nercasseau for his address before the Academia chilena is the error which he feels has been made in classifying Luis Vélez de Guevara's *El diablo cojuelo* as a picaresque novel. He avers that the characteristics of the literary genre, such as the autobiographical nature of relating the story, the *pícaro* who goes from master to master, etc., do not exist in *El diablo cojuelo.* Nercasseau makes the following statements concerning Vélez' *novela:*
>
>> Su origen debe buscarse en más alto ciclo, porque en algo participa de la alegoría o visión extra-humana, tan comunes en las derivaciones de la "Divina Comedia," y en parte se inclina originalmente a la invectiva, como en los "Sueños" de Quevedo. La novela toda de Vélez de Guevara es una sátira cortés de la sociedad de su tiempo, felicísima en la mayor parte de sus cuadros, y no afeada por la licencia y crudeza tan comunes en las novelas de la época. "El Diablo Cojuelo" sería una narración clásica de primer orden, y aun leíble hoy día, si no la deslustrara el conceptismo, y si no se hallara sobreabundante en equívocos y frases convencionales de difícil o imposible comprensión en nuestra era. Aun después del trabajo llevado a cabo por don Adolfo Bonilla y San Martín, en su edición de Madrid de 1910, la novela de Vélez de Guevara queda aguardando un comentario que la explique y la ponga al alcance general.
>
>In the second "Discurso," which is in answer to the first, Canon D. Manuel Antonio Román states that he is in complete agreement with Nercasseau that *El diablo cojuelo* should not be classed as a picaresque novel.

182. Northup, George T. *An Introduction to Spanish Literature.* 3rd ed., rev. by Nicholson B. Adams. Chicago: University of Chicago Press, 1960.

>Northup's opinion of Luis Vélez' *Diablo cojuelo* is that the idea is novel and the story begins well but is poorly sustained because the strained, equivocal style makes the reading difficult. The critic states that Lesage, recognizing the merits and defects

of *The Limping Devil*, rewrote the story and won for its French version a European vogue. Concerning Vélez as a playwright, Northup indicates that to Vélez is due the best dramatic version of the Guzmán el Bueno story, *Más pesa el Rey que la sangre*, and that Vélez' second famous play is *Reinar después de morir*, the best of a long series of dramas on the Inés de Castro legend.

183. ———. Review of *La serrana de la Vera*, by Luis Vélez de Guevara, ed. of Ramón Menéndez Pidal and María Goyri de Menéndez Pidal, *Modern Philology*, XV (1917), 447-448.

The opinion of Northup is that the Señores Menéndez Pidal made a good choice in *La serrana de la Vera* as the first in a series of critically edited Spanish plays of the classic period for the following reasons:

1) It is the unedited work of one of Spain's greatest dramatists and of high intrinsic merit.
2) It affords the editors a splendid opportunity to make valuable contributions in the fields of dialectology, lexicography, folklore, and balladry, in all of which subjects they are so proficient.
3) This is the first of a cycle of plays dealing with the same subject, the study of which is important to the history of the Spanish drama. It offers opportunity for a comparative study of works by Vélez, Lope de Vega, Tirso de Molina and others of lesser fame who have dealt with this same folklore theme.

184. Nozick, Martin. "The Inez de Castro Theme in European Literature," *Comparative Literature*, III (1951), 330-341.

Very briefly Nozick mentions Luis Vélez de Guevara's *Reinar después de morir*. He states that the *gracioso* Brito plays an important role for comic relief (one of the two or three light touches in all Inez literature) and he points out that it is Pedro's betrothed, Blanca, who overcomes the king's mercifulness by revealing to him the secret marriage of Inez and Pedro. Nozick adds that Blanca, on the other hand, balks at the idea of murder.

185. Ochoa, Eugenio de. *Tesoro del teatro español, desde su origen (año de 1356 hasta nuestros días), arreglado y dividido en cuatro partes,* Vol. IV: *Teatro escogido desde el siglo XVII hasta nuestros días.* Paris: Librería Europea de Baudry, 1838.

Ochoa states that *Reinar después de morir* is one of the "dramas más bellos de nuestro teatro" and since it is very superior, in his opinion, to the other works by Luis Vélez de Guevara, it alone is enough to give readers an appreciation of the dramatic talent of the playwright. The critic points out that Vélez' artistic skill is evident in the delineation of characters and in the expression of tenderness, the delicacy of feeling, the sad tone which prevails in the *comedia*, and in the impetuosity of love and affection. Ochoa indicates that Vélez knew well the heart of a woman in love who fears that she will be replaced by another. After the brief introductory summary, the play is reproduced.

186. Oliver, J. J. Review of *El rey en su imaginación*, by Luis Vélez de Guevara, ed. of J. Gómez Ocerín, *Revue Hispanique*, XLVIII (1920), 692-700.

The reviewer believes that Gómez Ocerín, in the "observaciones y notas" has pointed out terms in the play that are well-known and easy to understand, leaving unexplained many passages which are difficult to interpret. He says that Gómez Ocerín has failed to see the true theme of the drama, which is revealed by the critic stating that the addition of new lines by one of the proof readers changed substantially the figure of the protagonist and that the madness of Carlos turns out to be pretended, simple subterfuge to attain a purpose. The reviewer contends that if the loss of sanity of Carlos were real, the *comedia* would be an *esperpento* unworthy of the subtle skill of Vélez de Guevara. Oliver notes that the work deals with a young man (Carlos) who, being the offspring of a king, believes himself to be the son of peasants although he feels within his being a certain superioridad which impels him toward great undertakings. The reviewer adds that the apparent and "feigned" madness is a result of both the arrogance of Carlos and his violent passion for the queen, Diana, and that although the inclination to grandeur in Carlos is natural, the cause for "fingirse rey en su imaginación" is the love he feels for Diana. The critic contends that if this were not true, it would be absurd at the end for the queen to marry a mad man. Oliver ends his review with the following statement:

> ...El arte de Vélez (conocedor, como el primero de su tiempo, de los recursos escénicos) consiste en mantener suspensa la atención del que escucha la comedia, el cual queda sin saber a qué atenerse, hasta el final, acerca del carácter de la locura del protagonista. Carlos, loco, hubiera dado origen a una comedia bufa. "Fingido rey en

su imaginación" representa una creación dramática muy feliz, cuyo misterio no ha sabido desentrañar el Sr. G. O., que sólo alcanza a ver en él "al tipo del príncipe villano," superficial nota que no levanta el velo de su originalidad, ni se refiere especialmente a él, por lo cual no sirve para caracterizarle. (p. 700)

187. Olmsted, Richard H. *El conde don Pero Vélez y don Sancho el Deseado, comedia en tres actos de Luis Vélez de Guevara.* Minneapolis: The University of Minnesota Press, 1944.

The edition of Olmsted includes a list of the dramatic works by Luis Vélez de Guevara placed in two columns — those given in Cotarelo's study of Vélez and the ones found in La Barrera's *Catálogo*. A total of 105 *comedias* are cited as being written by Vélez, with *autos sacramentales, entremeses* and *bailes* as well as plays written in collaboration with others making up the number indicated. In several instances a *comedia* is mentioned in Cotarelo's list and not in La Barrera's and vice versa. Variations between Vélez' autograph and the manuscript attributed to Lope de Vega are noted, an analysis of *El conde don Pero Vélez y don Sancho el Deseado* is made, and sources used in composing the play are discussed. Olmsted says of the playwright: "Luis Vélez de Guevara es, a no dudarlo, uno de los grandes escritores del Siglo de Oro, y tanto por su teatro como por su novela merece uno de los primeros puestos en la historia de la literatura castellana." According to the editor, outstanding features of Vélez' theater are humor, variety of subjects, historical interest, "riqueza de inventiva" and well-delineated characters.

188. Palacín Iglesias, Gregorio B. *Historia de la literatura española*. 2nd ed., corrected and enlarged. México, D. F., 1958.

Among the principal dramatists of Lope de Vega's time, though of "segundo orden," Palacín Iglesias lists Antonio Mira de Amescua, Luis Vélez de Guevara, Juan Pérez de Montalván and Luis Quiñones de Benavente. The critic contends that Vélez tried to imitate Lope in almost all of his works. Palacín Iglesias considers as outstanding plays by Vélez *La hermosura de Raquel, Reinar después de morir,* and the *entremés, La burla más sazonada.* The critic's opinion of the *Diablo cojuelo* is that the work is original, clever and humorous but that the style is too obscure. He adds that *El diablo cojuelo* is a satirical story rather than a picaresque novel.

189. Palomo, María del Pilar. Review of *El embuste acreditado,* by Luis Vélez de Guevara, ed. of Arnold G. Reichenberger, *Revista de Literatura,* XI (1957), 239.

>The reviewer comments on the excellence of Reichenberger's edition of *El embuste acreditado,* which is representative of an important aspect of Luis Vélez de Guevara, "el cómico-burlesco," and of the national theater of Spain. Palomo says that the study of Merlín, a rather unique character, is interesting for the consideration of the *gracioso* in the theater of the *Siglo de Oro.*

190. Pavia, Mario N. *Drama of the Siglo de Oro. A Study of Magic, Witchcraft, and Other Occult Beliefs.* New York: Hispanic Institute of the United States, 1959.

>Pavia mentions in his study the role of Lope Sotelo as a phantom in Luis Vélez de Guevara's *El diablo está en Cantillana* and alchemists in *El diablo cojuelo.* Also included is the episode in *El diablo cojuelo* when the limping devil takes Cleofás on an aerial journey and shows him in one of the houses a witch smearing her body with an ointment in order to fly to a Witches' Sabbath between San Sebastián and Fuenterrabía. He regrets, however, that he cannot take him to the Witches' Sabbath, because the buck-goat devil who presides there is an enemy of his.

191. Paz y Melia, Antonio. "*El águila del agua,* representación española de Luis Vélez de Guevara," *Revista de Archivos, Bibliotecas y Museos,* X (1904), 180-200, 307-325; XI (1904), 50-67.

>According to Paz y Melia, Vélez put as the title of his autograph *comedia, El águila del agua* and another hand added the second part, *Batalla naval de Lepanto.* Durán is cited as believing that perhaps the play is a continuation of *El hijo del águila o el Señor Don Juan de Austria;* Barrera confuses *El hijo del águila* with *El águila del agua* and makes of the two one *comedia.* Paz y Melia contends that although Cervantes and Lope de Vega had already brought to the theater the celebrated battle: *La batalla naval* by Cervantes, which has not come down to us, and *La Santa Liga* by Lope, Vélez believed that he could treat the subject anew, counting on the resources of his creative ability to overcome the difficulty of introducing dramatic action into the historic fact of the battle, which lends itself so poorly to representation. The critic points out that if Vélez did not

succeed completely in writing a finished work according to our taste today, he satisfied the requirements of the theater of his time. The contrast between the character of Escamilla with that of D. Lope de Figueroa, the movement of the action, the realistic description of the galley slaves and the final scene of victory on board the *Real* make the reading of the play pleasing and justify publishing it to add one more work to the "preciada" collection of *comedias* by Vélez. After the introductory remarks, the play is reproduced.

192. ———. "Nuevos datos para la vida de Luis Vélez de Guevara," *Revista de Archivos, Bibliotecas y Museos*, VII (1902), 129-130.

Paz y Melia reproduces a letter written by Juan Vélez, Luis' son, to José de Pellicer, which throws light on the life of the author of *El diablo cojuelo,* although in Paz y Melia's opinion, there are errors in some of the information given. The document is in the Biblioteca Nacional in Madrid, Department of Mss., P. V. 4º, C. 23, Nº 58.

193. Pellicer de Ossau, Salas y Tovar, José. *Avisos históricos,* ed. E. Tierno Galván. Madrid: 1965. (This item could not be located. The following is cited in Barrera, *Catálogo bibliográfico y biográfico,* p. 465.)

José de Pellicer writes in his *Avisos históricos* the following lines after the death of Luis Vélez de Guevara:

Avisos de Madrid del 15 de noviembre de 1644. El jueves pasado murió Luis Vélez de Guevara, natural de Écija, ujier de cámara de su Majestad, bien conocido por más de cuatrocientas comedias que ha escrito, y su grande ingenio, agudos y repetidos dichos, y ser uno de los mejores cortesanos de España. Murió de setenta y cuatro años; dejó por testamentarios a los señores conde de Lemos y duque de Veragua, en cuyo servicio está don Juan su hijo. Depositaron el cuerpo en el monasterio de Doña María de Aragón en la capilla de los señores duques de Veragua, haciéndole por sus méritos esta honra. Ayer se le hicieron las honras en la mesma iglesia, con la propia grandeza que si fuera título asistiendo cuantos grandes, señores y caballeros hay en la corte. Y se han hecho a su muerte e ingenio muchos epitafios, que entiendo se imprimirán en libro particular, como el de Lope y Montalbán.

194. Penny, Carl O. "The Origins of Sebastianism in Three Spanish Plays of the Golden Age." Unpublished Master's thesis, Louisiana State University, 1964.

    The author compares three Golden Age *comedias* on the theme of Sebastianism: *El bautismo del Príncipe de Marruecos* by Lope de Vega, *El rey don Sebastián* by Luis Vélez de Guevara, and *La tragedia del rey don Sebastián* by Francisco de Villegas. Penny defines "Sebastianism" as a term used to refer not only to the documented history of the life of King Sebastian of Portugal (1554-1578), but also to a legend which developed after his death. The critic says that Luis Vélez de Guevara created the best of the Sebastianism plays simply by elaborating the framework provided by Lope.

195. Pérez de Guzmán y Gallo, Juan. "Representación de obras clásicas en el teatro español," *Boletín de la Real Academia de la Historia*, LX (1912), 247-255.

    Pérez de Guzmán indicates that the Real Academia was given an official order to determine whether or not the decorations, costumes, etc., which were provided for the representation by the Teatro Español of *La Celestina*, October 22, 1909, *El alcalde de Zalamea*, November 16, 1909, and *La luna de la sierra*, January 4, 1910, were faithful reproductions "arqueológicas" of those used in the period in which the action of each work takes place. Pérez de Guzmán's findings show that all the materials for the stage, principally the arms, armor, costumes of all the personages, etc., for *La luna de la sierra*, written by Luis Vélez de Guevara and reworked by Cristóbal de Castro for the representation of January 4, 1910, were perfectly suited to the time of the "Reyes católicos, Fernando e Isabel."

196. Pérez de Montalván, Juan. *Para todos, exemplos morales, humanos, y divinos, en que se tratan diversas materias, ciencias, y facultades, repartidos en los siete dias de la semana, y con algvnas adiciones nvevas en esta undecima impresion.* Lisboa: En la officina de Domingo Carnero, 1691. (First printing, 1632.)

    In the foreword to his *Auto sacramental de Escanderbech*, Montalván praises Luis Vélez de Guevara in the following terms:

        Esta es en suma toda la historia verdadera de Escanderbech, cuya vida escrivió en dos Comedias Luis Vélez de Guevara, ingenio el más claro, fértil, agudo, y floridíssimo destos tiempos.... (p. 342)

197. Pérez Pastor, Cristóbal. *Bibliografía madrileña o descripción de las obras impresas en Madrid*. 3 vols. Madrid: Tipografía de la "Revista de Archivos, Bibliotecas y Museos," 1906-1907.

    Pérez Pastor includes in his *Bibliografía madrileña* biographical documents relative to Luis Vélez de Guevara and members of his family which provide interesting glimpses of the private life of the playwright. Among the items listed is a "carta de poder" in favor of Luis Méndez de Carrión to collect from the Conde de Salinas the amount owed to Vélez as his "criado." Other official papers of significance, to mention only several of the many reproduced, are the following: the inventory of Vélez' possessions prepared before his marriage to María López de Palacios, a list of the property owned by the prospective bride, and the last will and testament of Luis Vélez de Guevara, in which he enumerates various debts owed by him.

198. ———. "Noticias y documentos relativos a la historia y literatura españolas," *Memorias de la Real Academia Española*, X (1911), 289.

    Several documents of interest to the biography of Luis Vélez de Guevara are included in the above work. One of these papers dated 1608 has the title "Escritura de los Marqueses de Alcañices en favor de Luis Vélez de Guevara de 500 ducados. Madrid, 23 de septiembre de 1608."

199. Pérez y González, Felipe. *El diablo cojuelo. Notas y comentarios. Nuevos datos para la biografía de Luis Vélez de Guevara*. Madrid: "Sucesores de Rivadeneyra," 1903. (Colección de artículos publicados en *La Ilustración Española y Americana*.)

    Pérez y González indicates that his purpose in writing the articles included in this volume is to point out what he considers to be "deslices" in Bonilla's edition of *El diablo cojuelo*. According to the author, Bonilla relied too heavily on the information gathered by Agustín Durán, at the request of the Real Academia Española, to clarify points in question made by Nicolas Pianitzky, a Russian who was endeavoring to translate the *Diablo cojuelo*. Lengthy commentaries are made to correct what the critic considers to be errors in Durán's explanations of obscure expressions. Included in Pérez y González' work is a section entitled "Nuevos datos para la biografía de Luis Vélez de Guevara," in which he reproduces the letter written by Juan Vélez to José Pellicer y Tovar, giving biographical information about his father, the baptismal record of Luis Vélez, the last will and testament of the playwright, and other pertinent data concerning the author of the *Diablo cojuelo*.

200. ———. "La 'cuestión' de Albania en el teatro antiguo español," *La Ilustración Española y Americana*, XLVII (1903), 95, 98-99, 118-119.

A study is made of the Escanderbey theme in the *teatro antiguo español* with emphasis on the *comedias*, *El gran Jorge Castrioto y Príncipe Escanderbeg* and *El Príncipe esclavo y hazañas de Escanderbeg*, both of which Pérez y González attributes to Luis Vélez de Guevara. The critic does not believe that Belmonte wrote *El gran Jorge Castrioto y Príncipe Escanderbeg*, to whom La Barrera says the *comedia* generally is ascribed, and avers that Lope de Vega's *Loa para una égloga* grants to Vélez the authorship of both plays:

>   Por no cansar los señores
>   Solicité los poetas;
>   ....
>   Luis Vélez Escanderbecas;
>   ....

Pérez y González is of the opinion that the plural *Escanderbecas* leaves no doubt that Vélez wrote two plays in which Escanderbey figures as the protagonist. He further cites Pérez de Montalván in *Para todos:* "Esta es, en suma, toda la historia verdadera de Escanderbech cuya vida escribió en dos comedias Luis Vélez de Guevara...." The other "comedia escanderbeca" of Vélez, *El Príncipe esclavo,* is as La Barrera indicates, the second part of *El gran Jorge Castrioto y Príncipe Escanderbeg*. Pérez y González remarks that the "comedias escanderbecas" of Vélez must have been very successful when represented, judging not only by Lope de Vega's line about it but by the various theatrical works written later based on the same subject, including several operas which were performed in Paris in the eighteenth century.

201. Pfandl, Ludwig. *Historia de la literatura nacional española en la Edad de Oro,* tr. del alemán por Jorge Rubio Balaguer. Barcelona: Sucesores de Juan Gili, S. A., 1933.

According to Pfandl, in writing *El diablo cojuelo,* Luis Vélez de Guevara followed in the footsteps of Cervantes and Quevedo. The critic contends that the playwright resembles Quevedo in the force of the satire which is not lacking in bitterness nor cynicism, and is like Cervantes in his conception of the satirical novel as a work of art. Pfandl indicates that *El diablo cojuelo* is similar to *El coloquio de los perros* in that the attractiveness of the composition lies not so much in interest in the episodes but rather in the ideas and thoughts of the author. Pfandl advises that only a person who knows the language at first hand should read *El diablo cojuelo* because of the double meanings of words, the daring metaphors, the proverbs, etc. The German critic says that the work is only intelligible for the Spaniards themselves in editions with abundant notes and commentaries and is almost impossible to translate successfully into a foreign language.

202. ———. Review of *El Rey en su imaginación,* by Luis Vélez de Guevara, ed. of J. Gómez Ocerín, *Archiv für das Studium der neuerem Sprachen und Literaturen,* CXLIV (1922), 132-133.

Pfandl says that the theme of *El rey en su imaginación* by Luis Vélez de Guevara is unusually involved because the story of the make-believe king is varied and enlarged by the comedy motive, but that Gómez Ocerín has followed the complicated train of thought of the dramatic action and has placed it in the context of the "comedias Technik" in general. The German critic points out that Gómez Ocerín recognizes the influence of Cervantes, and also identifies common characteristics with Amadís and Palmerín. Pfandl adds that he only wishes that Gómez Ocerín had been inclined to write a monograph on the problem of *El rey en su imaginación* comparable to that of Ramón Menéndez Pidal on *El condenado por desconfiado.*

203. ———. ———. *The Dramatic Works of Luis Vélez de Guevara. Their Plots, Sources and Bibliography,* by Forrest Eugene Spencer and Rudolph Schevill, *Deutsche Literaturzeitung,* LIX (1938), col. 1453-1455.

The German critic praises the work of Spencer and Schevill as a valuable source for the study of the dramatic works of Luis Vélez de Guevara, an author about whom there is need for further research. Pfandl considers that the grouping of the works according to subject matter, *autos,* doubtful works, and those written in collaboration with other playwrights, information on the location of manuscripts, *sueltas*, etc.; an analysis of each play: bibliographic material; and a short criticism of each *comedia* provide a wealth of data for further investigation. The critic remarks that the work in question makes one wish that a similar study could be made of a dozen other Spanish dramatists.

204. Place, Edwin B. "A Note on *El diablo cojuelo* and the French Sketch of Manners and Types," *Hispania*, XIX (1936), 235-240.

Place supplements and amplifies certain phases of W. S. Hendrix's article, "Quevedo, Guevara, Lesage and the *Tatler*" (*Modern Philology*, XIX, 177-186), in which he deals with the influence of Vélez de Guevara's *Diablo cojuelo* (1641) upon the English essay of manners. Place says that the tradition of the "Crippled Devil" as an observer and satirist of manners, a theme which traveled from Spain to France through Lesage's brilliant adaptation and later to England, came to be a sort of exemplar for the early nineteenth century sketch of manners. The "Crippled Devil" theme, according to Place, apparently exercised quite as much influence in France as the *Spectator* and *Tatler*, and to illustrate his point, the critic discusses several French works treating the theme.

205. Profeti, Maria Grazia. "Note critiche sull'opera di Vélez de Guevara," in *Miscellanea di studi ispanici* (Università di Pisa), No. 10 (1965), 47-174.

A comprehensive study of the life, art, and works of Luis Vélez de Guevara is made by Maria Grazia Profeti, in which she includes his *comedias, entremeses,* and *El diablo cojuelo.* The critic comments on aspects of *La serrana de la Vera, Reinar después de morir, La luna de la sierra* and other Vélez dramas, studies the playwright's style and use of the language, including the "fabla arcaica" and "el sayagués" in some of his plays, and considers the use of the "romancero" and popular themes. A chapter is devoted to *El diablo cojuelo,* in which observations are made on the style and language, noting phrases used in the work which have been discussed by other critics, including Rodríguez Marín, Bonilla, and Rosselli. Profeti indicates her interpretation of a number of the expressions, for example: "Adanes del baratillo," "Antojos de la preñez," "ciuilidades," "Doncella chanflona," etc.

206. ———. *Virtudes vencen señales,* by Luis Vélez de Guevara. Università di Pisa, 1965. (Instituto di Letteratura Spagnola e Ispano-Americana. Collana di studi diretta da Guido Mancini.)

> Profeti indicates the texts of the *Virtudes* used for her edition: that of Zaragoza, 1640, with copies in Göttingen and Florence, and the *suelta* without date in the Palatina Library of Parma, and notes omissions in one and another of the texts and also the variants. Her conclusion is that the *suelta* is more correct and has fewer variants than the 1640 edition of Zaragoza. The critic discusses sources used by Vélez and mentions the element of astrology which appears in this work as well as in others of the period, for example, *La vida es sueño, Barlaán y Josafat,* etc. In the eighty pages of notes and commentaries following the text, Profeti considers the syntax, archaic terms, *cultismos,* the rustic language, etc., a valuable contribution to the study of Luis Vélez de Guevara.

207. Quevedo y Villegas, Francisco de. *Perinola,* in Vol. II of *Obras de D. Francisco de Quevedo y Villegas, Colección completa,* corregida, ordenada e ilustrada por D. Aureliano Fernandez-Guerra y Orbe (*Biblioteca de Autores Españoles,* Vol. XLVIII), Madrid: Imprenta de los Sucesores de Hernando, 1921, p. 478.

> In *Perinola,* which is a bitter attack on Pérez de Montalbán's *Para todos,* Quevedo says that Montalbán should leave the writing of *comedias* to Lope, to Luis Vélez, to Pedro Calderón and others. Quevedo's statement is included in this bibliography to show the place that Luis Vélez apparently enjoyed among his contemporaries — he is ranked along with Lope de Vega and Pedro Calderón.

208. Reas, Marjorie V. "Three Thematically Similar Plays Attributed to Luis Vélez de Guevara, Together with a Critical Annotated Edition of *La obligación a las mvgeres.*" Unpublished Ph. D. dissertation, Wayne State University, 1968.

> The author compares as to plot, theme sources, characters, style and staging, and metrical system, three thematically similar plays associated with the name of Luis Vélez de Guevara: *La obligación a las mvgeres, Cumplir dos obligaciones,* and *Cumplir dos obligaciones y Duquesa de Sajonia,* to determine whether

they are all from the pen of Vélez. Reas explains that *La obligación a las mvgeres* was not selected for editing because of its literary merits but for the reason that it is the only one of the three plays which all critics agree was written by Vélez de Guevara. From the evidence presented, the critic concludes that all three plays are the work of Vélez: *Cumplir dos obligaciones* is identical in theme and plot to *La obligación a las mvgeres*, differing only in a slight change of meter, introduction of two new characters, expansion of comic scenes and addition, deletion or transposition of words, lines and passages; *Cumplir dos obligaciones y Duquesa de Sajonia* manifests all the characteristics of the theater of Vélez: propensity for combining themes, meters almost identical with meters used in other plays by Vélez, characters cast from the same mold as those considered typical of Vélez, style — "agilidad expresiva" found in his original and plastic metaphors, competitive imagery, repetition of words, etc. Reas believes that all evidence points directly to Vélez de Guevara as far as authorship is concerned.

209. Recoules, Henri. "Les allusions au théâtre et a la vie théâtrale dans le roman espagnol de la première moitié du XVIIe siècle," in *Dramaturgie et Société*, ed. by Jean Jacquot, with the collaboration of Elie Konigson and Marcel Oddon, 2 vols., Paris: Centre National de la Recherche Scientifique, 1968, pp. 133-148.

In his study of allusions to the theater and to stage life found in the Spanish novel of the first half of the seventeenth century, Recoules includes Luis Vélez de Guevara's *Diablo cojuelo* along with fourteen other prose works of the period. The critic believes that the opinion of the authors of the novels concerning dramatic art and their reactions to the theater of their time deserve to be considered. A passage is cited from Tranco X (*Clásicos cast.*, p. 215) of the *Diablo cojuelo*, in which Vélez criticizes certain abusive details of the *comedia* of his time, and Recoules notes that Vélez addresses the prologue of his *Diablo* to the "mosqueteros de la comedia de Madrid." The critic says that the authors of the novels cited used their works to express their opinions and in most cases to pay homage to the theater and to the actors.

210. Reed, Frank O., and Esther M. Dixon. *La Estrella de Sevilla*, introd. by John M. Hill. Boston: D. C. Heath and Company, 1939.

Concerning the authorship of *La Estrella de Sevilla*, there is a point of interest for the study of Luis Vélez de Guevara, in this edition by Reed and Dixon. In a footnote on p. xix, Hill modestly voices the suspicion that it may some day be discovered that the author of *La Estrella de Sevilla* is Luis Vélez de Guevara.

211. Reichenberger, Arnold G. "Currency Inflation Reflected in Luis Vélez de Guevara's *El embuste acreditado,*" *Modern Language Notes,* LXXVI (1961), 34-35.

Reichenberger is concerned with the following passage from *El embuste acreditado* (ll. 1843-46 in his edition of the work):

¡Sacad tesoros! ¡Alerta!
Que todo el oro y la plata
es como esta patarata
que en mi embuste se concierta.

which Merlín exclaims when it has become evident that the "embuste" planned by him had convinced Rosimunda that she was actually flying through the spheres exposed to the heat of the sun. Reichenberger believes that the point of comparison between "el oro y la plata," i.e. currency, and Merlín's "embuste" is exactly the element of trickery. According to the critic, the joke implies that the money in circulation is nothing but a "patarata," nonsense concretized in a fraud *(embuste),* and the fraud is the devaluated "vellón." Reichenberger gives historical facts to back up his statement and adds that if the interpretation of Merlín's ironic remark is correct, it would strengthen considerably the probability of the conjectured years 1617-1618 as the most likely date of composition of *El embuste acreditado* (the proposed date is based on literary and metrical grounds). The critic says that Merlín's *redondilla* could be a reflection of the unpopularity of the revival of the coinage of *vellón* to which the opposition was so great that the Crown in 1619 was induced to commit itself to refrain from minting *vellón* of any kind for any purpose during the next twenty years and subsequently to coin only *vellón* containing the mixture of silver required by law.

212. ———. *El embuste acreditado,* by Luis Vélez de Guevara. Granada: Universidad de Granada, 1956. (Colección Filológica XII.)

A scholarly study is made by Reichenberger of *El embuste acreditado,* in which he gives various versions of the play, considers the date, and discusses *El embuste* in relation to three other *comedias* by Vélez: *El caballero del Sol, La niña de Gómez Arias,* and *El conde don Pero Vélez.* The critic contends that there are certain points of similarity between the three dramas by Vélez and some of the works of Cervantes published between 1614 and 1615. He cites the resemblance between Rosimunda's flight through the heavens to Sicily in *El embuste acreditado* and the Clavileño episode in the second part of *Don Quijote.* Both constitute a hoax — in each of the works the eyes of the protagonist are bandaged and a torch lighted to make the victims believe they are traveling through the fire of heaven. Reichenberger lists three reasons for the literary value of *El embuste acreditado:*

> 1) Nuestro autor logra crear una trama en la que hay equilibrio, variación y movimiento.
>
> 2) Varios de los caracteres están trazados con habilidad —Merlín y Rosimunda entre los protagonistas y Livia y Fabricio entre los personajes secundarios.
>
> 3) Aunque el humor de esta comedia tiene un tinte satírico, no llega a la amargura ni a la mordacidad. (p. 87)

213. ———. "The *Quinta parte* of *Comedias nuevas escogidas,*" *The Library Chronicle,* XVII (1951), 115-128.

   Reichenberger indicates that the *Quinta parte* of the Ticknor collection (*Quinta parte* of the great forty-eight volume series known under the general title *Comedias nuevas escogidas de los mejores ingenios de España 1652-1704*) is not, and was not, even in its original state a copy of the genuine *Quinta parte,* Madrid, 1653, "por Pablo de Val, a costa de Juan de San Vicente, mercader de libros," but is a "tomo variante." The critic points out that of the *comedias* in the Ticknor volume, the first, third, ninth, and eleventh have been inserted in place of four others whose authors and titles in the index have been defaced with ink and replaced by others. Reichenberger believes that this fact has not been known to bibliographers. He gives a bibliographical description of the volume and reproduces a facsimile of the page listing the *comedias,* which includes *El embuste acreditado* and *Los amotinados en Flandes* by Luis Vélez de Guevara. The two Vélez plays appeared in the genuine *Quinta parte* and had not been defaced and replaced by others.

214. ———. "The Uniqueness of the *comedia,*" *Hispanic Review,* XXVII (1959), 303-316.

An enlightening analysis of the *comedia* is made by Reichenberger, in which he explains the reasons for its uniqueness. He says that the individualizing, autobiographical element is almost completely absent in Spanish dramatic literature. If it exists it has to be laboriously reconstructed by modern scholarship, or it can only be surmised as in the case of the alleged scorn for nobility on the part of Luis Vélez de Guevara. The critic adds that one could almost say there is only one protagonist in the Spanish *comedia*, the Spanish people; from king to peasant each person exists primarily as a member of his community, to whom are assigned definite duties — a king acts as a king should, the nobleman as his position demands, and so on down the line. Reichenberger states that if the code-bound Spanish theater made the development of individual character difficult and rare, by the same token, faith made tragedy nearly impossible. The critic cites several real tragedies, among them *La Estrella de Sevilla*. He says that doña Inés de Castro in Vélez' *Reinar después de morir* is a pitiful, even pathetic figure, but too passive to be tragic.

215. Rennert, Hugo A. Review of *El diablo cojuelo*, by Luis Vélez de Guevara, ed. of Adolfo Bonilla y San Martín, *Modern Language Notes*, XIX (1904), 181-183.

Rennert notes that even though Bonilla has provided an excellent edition of *El diablo cojuelo*, with commentaries and explanations, there still remain passages in the text which are not entirely clear and upon which no observations are found. According to the reviewer, *El diablo cojuelo* is by no means easy to read and he wishes that Bonilla had given more interpretation though he admits that the editor has cleared up a number of obscure passages and allusions and thrown light on many others.

216. ———. ———. *La serrana de la Vera*, by Luis Vélez de Guevara, ed. of Ramón Menéndez Pidal and María Goyri de Menéndez Pidal, *Romanic Review*, IX (1918), 238-239.

The reviewer believes that the Señores Menéndez Pidal conclusively prove the date of the composition of *La serrana de la Vera* to be 1613 or later and that this date is of importance for the study of the origins of the play and its imitations. Rennert finds especially interesting in the *Observaciones* by the editors, the chapter devoted to a comparison of the plays by Lope and by Vélez de Guevara. The reviewer says that both poets have written much better *comedias*.

217. ———. *The Life of Lope de Vega.* New York: Benjamin Blom, Inc., 1968.

    Scattered throughout the book are brief notices about Luis Vélez de Guevara. In a footnote (p. 231), two letters are cited which are concerned with Vélez' ability to write "a lo divino," an indication of a play to be written by various dramatists including Vélez (p. 330), a "copla" by the playwright that pleased Lope (p. 172), and a number of other references to Luis Vélez de Guevara.

218. ———. *The Spanish Stage in the Time of Lope de Vega.* New York: 1909. (Reprinted with the permission of the Hispanic Society of America by Kraus Reprint Corporation, 1967.)

    Of interest to the study of Luis Vélez de Guevara is the citation on pages 102-103 that in 1618 the playwright's *comedia, El caballero del Sol* was performed by the company of Baltasar Piñedo in the house of Juan Gaytán de Ayala, in the Calle de Atocha, "with the same *invenciones* and stage arrangement with which this play was represented in the garden of his Excellency the Duke of Lerma." Rennert notes that the latter representation was, doubtless, intended solely for the delectation of the Duke's friends but that the performance in the house of Gaytán de Ayala is the only one he has found recorded in which an admission fee was charged and from which other profits accrued to the person giving the *comedia*. The details are so curious that Rennert transcribes them.

219. Revuelta, Luisa. *La luna de la sierra,* by Luis Vélez de Guevara. 3rd ed. Zaragoza: Editorial Ebro, S. L., 1958. (Biblioteca Clásica Ebro. Clásicos Españoles.)

    In the commentary to her edition of *La luna de la sierra,* Luisa Revuelta compares Vélez' *La luna* with Lope de Vega's *Peribáñez y el Comendador de Ocaña,* which she indicates are similar in many respects. The critic states that in both *comedias* the theme of honor is treated, revealing the sturdy spirit of independence and "pundonor" of the old Spanish peasantry as shown in the characters of Peribáñez and Antón. Revuelta points out that the two plays are different in that the Comendador de Calatrava in Lope's *Peribáñez* pays for his audacity with his life whereas Vélez in *La luna de la sierra* avoids bloodshed perhaps to give a surprise ending to a public accustomed to death at the end when the play was concerned with honor. Revuelta says that the reputation of Vélez as a great dramatist was undisputed among his contemporaries and that his "gracia de ecijano en el trato de las gentes" mixed with certain traces of "quevedesca" satire came to be proverbial.

220. Reyes, Alfonso. *Capítulos de literatura española*. México: La Casa de España en México, 1939.

In the section called "Tres siluetas," in which Reyes writes about Ruiz de Alarcón, he mentions Luis Vélez de Guevara in connection with the visit of the Prince of Wales to Spain when wedding negotiations were taking place for the Prince with the Infanta of Castile, María de Austria. The critic says that the visit of the Prince of Wales to Spain left its trace in the poetry of the time and that in the midst of the court festivities there were rivalries which were not well concealed. Reyes cites the fact that Luis Vélez, who was "ujier de la cámara del Príncipe," was not afraid to displease the Conde-Duque de Olivares, complaining of the annoyance of the guests and the pretensions of the Prince:

> Yo nasí en el rinión de Andalucía,
> y no es justo que en siglo de Guzmanes
> tenga cautiva en Londres mi poesía.
> Muera yo entre Tenorios y Marbanes,
> que juro a Dios que estoy con poplexía
> de Contintones y de Boquinganes.
>
> (p. 194)

Reyes quotes the following words that Vélez had to say about Ruiz de Alarcón: "... Por más que te empines, —camello enano con loba—, es de Soplillo tu trova." (p. 171)

221. Río, Ángel del. *Historia de la literatura española*, Vol. I: *Desde los orígenes hasta 1700*. Rev. ed. New York: Holt, Rinehart and Winston, 1963.

Ángel del Río states that among the dramatists who followed the fundamental lines of Lope de Vega's dramatic art, there are two of first rank: Tirso de Molina and Alarcón. Two others: Guillén de Castro and Mira de Amescua were outstanding for composing a particular type of *comedia*. Among the other playwrights, the critic mentions Luis Vélez de Guevara, whom he labels as "dramaturgo fino, cercano en cualidades artísticas al maestro." Ángel del Río indicates that Vélez excels in dramatic works based on early legends: *Reinar después de morir*, or in "comedias de ambiente rústico-popular": *La serrana de la Vera* and *La luna de la sierra*. The critic adds that Vélez de Guevara was also famous for *El diablo cojuelo*. He says that Vélez' prose work is not strictly speaking a picaresque novel because it lacks the basic element, "el autobiografismo literario." In Ángel del Río's words, *El diablo cojuelo* "es más bien una sátira social con elementos fantásticos."

222. Rodríguez Cepeda, Enrique. *La serrana de la Vera*, by Luis Vélez de Guevara. Madrid: Ediciones Alcalá, 1967. (Colección Aula Magna.)

Rodríguez Cepeda studies the characters, the themes, the structure and the versification of *La serrana de la Vera*. He indicates that in writing the play Vélez created a great work in which almost everything leaves an impression and even vengeance represents deep justice. Rodríguez Cepeda states that Vélez availed himself of the drama to express veiled criticism of various elements of society: the "donjuan" type soldier, the weak father who abandons his daughter and assists in her capture, the Santa Hermandad, "el pueblo," a character in the play and the conscience of the whole work. The critic says that by means of a simple argument (the *romances populares*, dishonor, and the tragic vengeance of a woman), Vélez produced a work of transcendental themes. According to Rodríguez Cepeda, the playwright treats the conflicts of the society in which he lived and includes the beliefs, customs, honor, love, lack of harmony in moral values, tragic fate, etc. In the Appendix, the editor reproduces the following: *Carta de Juan Vélez*, *Poemas de Luis Vélez*, and *Romances de La serrana de la Vera*.

223. ———. Review of *Diavolul schiop (El diablo cojuelo), Domnie dupa moarte (Reinar después de morir)*, tr. by Theodor Enescu, with introd. and notes. Bucharest (Romania), Editura Pentru Literatura Universala, 1968, *Revista de Filología Española*, LI (1968), 294-295.

The reviewer indicates that *El diablo cojuelo* is "obra clave" for understanding the Spanish novel up to Galdós and is one of the most frequently published books in the world (Moscow 1964). Rodríguez Cepeda says that the same applies to *Reinar después de morir* as far as popularity, for it has had constant representations since the seventeenth century, and in the twentieth century influenced Montherlant in writing his *La reine morte*. The critic does not agree with Enescu that *El diablo cojuelo* is a descendant of the picaresque novel, for he says that Vélez left that form behind to write a "novela de costumbres," which was to influence not only Lesage but many other writers as well.

224. ———. ———. "Note critiche sull'opera di Vélez de Guevara," by Maria Grazia Profeti, *Segismundo*, II (1966), 214-217. (The same article appears in *Revista de Literatura*, XXVIII (1965), 252-254.)

Rodríguez Cepeda praises Maria Grazia Profeti for her excellent study, in which she has brought to light facts overlooked in the past that in part may contribute to the creation of a new image of Luis Vélez de Guevara, the true one. The reviewer notes that the playwright is a much more complex person in both his nature and his works than is realized at first sight and that there are many facets of his life which have not been explored adequately. Rodríguez Cepeda discusses a number of questions concerning the poet which Profeti does not consider, for example: "la ascendencia judía" of Vélez, his change of name, the mystery about the time spent as a soldier, his years in the service of the Conde de Saldaña, the negative idea of Vélez toward the Inquisition as revealed in *La serrana de la Vera*, and other questions concerning the life of the playwright.

225. ———. ———. *Virtudes vencen señales*, ed. of Maria Grazia Profeti, *Segismundo*, II (1966), 212-214. (The same review appears in *Revista de Literatura*, XXVIII (1965), 280-283.)

The reviewer calls the edition of *Virtudes vencen señales* "magnífica" and says that the commentaries and notes at the end of the *comedia*, eighty pages in length, are indispensable for any study of Luis Vélez de Guevara. Rodríguez Cepeda points out that the Italian critic studies the syntax, *culto* vocabulary, "sayagués" language, archaic expressions, as well as the sources of the play, date of the work, etc. The critic arranges in order the ninety *culto* words studied by Profeti which already appear in the indexes of "la lengua poética de Góngora" compiled by Dámaso Alonso. Rodríguez Cepeda indicates that in the last fifty years there have been eight "ediciones sueltas de valor considerable" of Vélez' works since Ramón Menéndez Pidal made his study of *La serrana de la Vera*, "tragedia clave para la interpretación del arte y pensamiento del poeta de Éciia."

226. ———, and Enrique Rull. *El diablo cojuelo,* by Luis Vélez de Guevara. Madrid: Ediciones Alcalá, 1968. (Colección Aula Magna.)

> In the introduction to their edition of *El diablo cojuelo,* Rodríguez Cepeda and Rull discuss possible sources of Vélez' work, including a detailed comparison with *Los antojos de mejor vista* by Rodrigo Fernández de Ribera. According to the critics, *El diablo cojuelo* is an *esperpento* — the theme is "desengaño," with a grotesque perception of reality, a negative vision of fortune, a scoffing at double truth, chaos and confusion in a degraded society, "una estética" systematically deformed. In considering the structure of *El diablo cojuelo,* Rodríguez Cepeda and Rull treat the work from three perspectives ("temporal, espacial o irreal") and outline by *tranco* the perspective and "visión" in each. The critics give background information on "la Fortuna" in literature before presenting Vélez' view — "la Fortuna" for Vélez is a "visión degradada de la sociedad." In the Appendix, p. 233, the editors include fragments of the *Orazión que oró Luis Vélez en el zertamen del Buen Retiro (21 de Febrero 1637) siendo pressidente.* (Ms. de la Biblioteca Nacional de Madrid, pp. 509 y ss.), *Los motivos literarios, La Fortuna en Quevedo,* and *La fábula de la Fénix en Quevedo y Villamediana.*

227. Rodríguez Marín, Francisco. "Cervantes y la Universidad de Osuna," in *Homenaje a Menéndez y Pelayo,* prologue by Juan Valera, Madrid: Librería General de Victoriano Suárez, 1899, pp. 757-819.

> On page 804, Rodríguez Marín lists the following statement which is of interest for the biography of Vélez:
>
>> Vélez de Guevara (Luis) natural de Écija.
>> En 31 de julio de 1596 se graduó de bachiller en artes, *gratis* por ser pobre, con otros diez y ocho estudiantes, todos ecijanos.

228. ———. "Cinco poesías autobiográficas de Luis Vélez de Guevara," *Revista de Archivos, Bibliotecas y Museos,* XIX (1908), 62-78.

> Rodríguez Marín puts into print again four poems by Luis Vélez de Guevara which Bonilla brought to light in the *Revista de Aragón,* 1902, to which he adds a sonnet by the playwright, also autobiographical in nature. The *poesías* reproduced are from

manuscripts in the Biblioteca Nacional in Madrid, for each of which the Ms. number is given. In commenting on the *Memoriales* by Vélez, Rodríguez Marín says that it makes one sad to read such extravagant praises of people who, with very few exceptions, were of much less worth than the needy Vélez.

229. ———. *El diablo cojuelo,* by Luis Vélez de Guevara. Madrid: Espasa-Calpe, S. A., 1969. (Clásicos Castellanos, No. 38.)

In the prologue to his *Diablo cojuelo,* Rodríguez Marín states that in presenting this edition his purpose is to provide a more understandable version for readers who are unfamiliar with the intricacies of the language. In commenting on Vélez' *novela,* the critic mentions similarity between the *Diablo cojuelo* and the comic and satirical works of Quevedo and says that Vélez' story is "de agradable lectura" and would be more so without "la pesada y adulatoria enumeración de todo aquel inacabable señorío que el autor, en el tranco VIII, hace pasar por el espejo de Rufina María, dispuesto *ad hoc* por el redomando desenredomado." Rodríguez Marín points outs aspects of the *Diablo* which add to the ingenious invention: the interesting variety of scenes, the liveliness of the dialogue and especially "el chispeante gracejo" of Vélez de Guevara. The critic adds that the literary expression tends to be "descuidadilla" by the excessive use of gerunds among other things which Rodríguez Marín does not enumerate.

230. Rodríguez Padrón, Jorge. Review of *El teatro de Montherlant,* by Francisco J. Hernández, *Cuadernos Hispanoamericanos,* CCXXXVI (1969), 509-513.

The reviewer states that perhaps the most pertinent fact concerning the French dramatist, Henri de Montherlant, and Spain is his contact with *Reinar después de morir* by Luis Vélez de Guevara and the possible influence of the drama on *La reine morte.* Rodríguez Padrón indicates that the controversy stirred up among French critics as to the paternity of Vélez in this work caused Hernández to assume the importance of Montherlant's reading of the Spanish author's *comedia.* The reviewer notes that from what Hernández has presented it may be considered that Montherlant made use of Vélez' play but that he reworked artistically the part of the theme which seemed to him in agreement with his dramatic trajectory.

231. Rojas, Agustín de. *El viaje entretenido,* in *Nueva Biblioteca de Autores Españoles,* Vol. IV: *Orígenes de la novela,* by Marcelino Menéndez y Pelayo, introd. by Adolfo Bonilla y San Martín. Madrid: Casa Editorial Bailly/Bailliére, 1915.

At the beginning of Agustín de Rojas' *Viage entretenido,* published for the first time in Madrid, 1603, there appear stanzas of praise written by Luis Vélez de Santander. The poem is mentioned because it was printed in 1603, which was before the playwright changed his name to "Guevara" in 1608.

232. Romera-Navarro, Miguel. *Historia de la literatura española.* 2nd. ed., corrected and enl. Boston: D. C. Heath, 1949.

Romera-Navarro indicates that Luis Vélez de Guevara was a fertile and excellent lyric poet in addition to being a dramatic poet, and that he also wrote in prose. The critic points out that Vélez' *Diablo cojuelo* differs from picaresque novels in that it does not treat the adventures of a *pícaro* but those of a student traveling through the air with the *diablejo* observing the way of life of the different social classes of Madrid. Romera-Navarro says it is a satire of customs, very ingenious in thought and written in a bold, dense, and obscure style. In discussing Vélez' dramatic works, the critic states that the playwright was not very original in his arguments nor profound in his conception of the drama but that he was outstanding in delineation of characters. Romera-Navarro agrees with Menéndez y Pelayo that Vélez was the best of the playwrights of "segundo orden," who imitated Lope de Vega with such perfection that in some instances the *comedias* of the two are confused.

233. ———. *La preceptiva dramática de Lope de Vega y otros ensayos sobre el Fénix.* Madrid: Ediciones Yunque, 1935.

On page 86, note 2, of *La preceptiva dramática,* Romera-Navarro quotes what he calls one of the wittiest gibes at the copiousness of some poets, which was composed by Luis Vélez de Guevara for the Academia burlesca en Buen Retiro which took place in 1637:

Un poeta buratin ha llegado a esta corte que hace grandes pruebas y axilidades de su persona, entre las quales escrive una comedia en una ora con la mano çurda y anda por la maroma con un entremes en un pie y un baile de a doze en esotro y una loa de çinquenta colunas en la boca.... (Acad. burlesca, ed. Morel-Fatio, *L'Espagne au XVI*ᵉ *et au XVII*ᵉ *siècle,* Heilbrome, 1878, p. 618.)

234. ———. "Querellas y rivalidades en las Academias del Siglo XVII," *Hispanic Review,* XI (1941), 494-499.

Romera-Navarro states that the literary Academies of the *siglo de oro* in most instances were short lived, but the Academia Poética de Madrid (1616-1622) was an exception. Members of this Academy included such brilliant writers as Lope de Vega, Góngora, Quevedo, Pérez de Montalbán, Antonio Hurtado de Mendoza, Guillén de Castro, Ruiz de Alarcón, Tirso de Molina, Vélez de Guevara, Salas Barbadillo, Castillo Solórzano and Calderón. Romera-Navarro tells about one occasion in which Salas Barbadillo presented a symbolical academy with animals which could be identified with some of the literary men who attended the Academia as members. The title is *La peregrinación sabia,* first published in his *Coronas del Parnaso y Platos de las musas* (Madrid, 1635), but probably written in his youth. (The Clásicos castellanos edition, Madrid, 1924, pp. 54-59, is cited.) In this fable, there is a cat: "El gato sazonaba la risa de la Academia por su desvergüenza y audacia, porque los más de sus trabajos eran hurtados de los ingenios que estaban presentes." Romera-Navarro says that there was a poet among the group who was always writing *memoriales* in verse asking for money and whose "sales y gracias" earned for him the nickname "quitapesares" (the cat in the fable is called "quitabolsones"). According to Romera-Navarro, Luis Vélez de Guevara is very probably the cat portrayed by Salas Barbadillo.

235. Roscoe, Thomas. *The Spanish Novelists: A Series of Tales from the Earliest Period to the Close of the Seventeenth Century,* tr. from the originals, with critical and biographical notices, 3 vols. London: Richard Bentley, late Colburn and Bentley, 1832.

Included in *The Spanish Novelists* is the story *Modern Miracles; or Spirits of the Other World,* by Luis de Guevara, "natural de Segura," whom Roscoe considered to be Luis Vélez de Guevara. The introductory notice does apply to Vélez and for that reason Roscoe's work is listed in this bibliography. According to the English critic, Vélez de Guevara was designated by French writers as the "Spanish Scarron," probably because of his brilliant wit, which Roscoe says infused life and spirit into the court and palace of Philip IV of Spain. The critic states that Vélez' fame as a lively writer both in prose and in verse was little inferior to that of Lope de Vega himself. Roscoe contends that Vélez' name occupies a high place among the dramatic writers of his time but the work on which rests his chief claim to popularity and applause is *El diablo cojuelo; verdades de la otra vida, The Devil upon Two Sticks; Tidings of the other World*, the earliest and most remarkable among the productions in Spanish literature entitled *La novela alegórica satírica*. The critic indicates that *El diablo cojuelo* is full of originality and admirable traits of nature, combined with an ease and vividness of style which make it universally popular. (The introductory remarks on Luis Vélez de Guevara are found in Vol. III of *The Spanish Novelists*, pp. 131-132.)

236. Rosen, Harold E. "A Critical Edition, with Introduction and Notes, of Vélez de Guevara's *El amor en vizcaíno, los celos en francés y torneos de Navarra.*" Unpublished Ph. D. dissertation, The University of Oregon, 1966.

According to the author, his purpose in presenting a critical edition of *El amor en vizcaíno, los celos en francés y torneos de Navarra* is to make available an authentic, readable copy of this *comedia*, which is not accessible to the majority of readers for consideration in the judgment of the playwright's art. Rosen indicates that *El amor en vizcaíno* is something of a *tour de force* in which Vélez shows his ability to write verse in the tradition of dramatic poetry created by Lope de Vega, demonstrates his clever wit as he experiments with the figurative language which was the prevailing taste in lyric as well as dramatic poetry, and displays his capacity for effecting ingenious subtleties with his parody and his puns. The critic notes that in Vélez' *comedia* there exist traces of the *cultismo* of Góngora, the *conceptismo* of Quevedo, the warm-hearted, playful satire of Cervantes, and the lyrical versatility of Lope de Vega. Rosen points out that while Vélez cannot be classed as the equal of any of the masters of Spanish Golden Age literature in their personal and superbly developed style, it would be an error to disregard the contribution made by Luis Vélez de Guevara to the era of splendor in the literature of Spain which was celebrated for its many stylistic achievements.

237. Rosselli, Ferdinando. "Alcune integrazioni ai glossari del *Diablo cojuelo*," in *Miscellanea di studi ispanici (Università di Pisa)*, No. .6 (1963), 178-222.

Rosselli lists in alphabetical order some of the controversial expressions and terms used in Luis Vélez de Guevara's *El diablo cojuelo,* indicating interpretations given by Adolfo Bonilla y San Martín and Francisco Rodríguez Marín, to which he adds his own observations. A few of the debatable terms included are: "alfaneque," "chinche en el ojo," "dar las aceitunas carta de pago a la cena," "hidalgo a quatro vientos," "mula de Liñán," "nites gut," etc. There are words listed which presumably have not been explained previously by other critics since no mention is made of them, so that Rosselli's contribution is worthy of note.

238. Rossi, Giuseppe Carlo. *Reinar después de morir,* by Luis Vélez de Guevara. Napoli: R. Pironti e Figli editori, 1961. (Collana di testi romanzi.)

In the introduction to his edition of *Reinar después de morir* by Luis Vélez de Guevara, Giuseppe Rossi discusses the Inés de Castro theme in literature. Among the peninsula writers on the subject, he includes Resende, Camoens, Ferreira, Jerónimo Bermúdez, Mejía de la Cerda, and others. French playwrights treating the Inés de Castro story mentioned are Houdar de La Motte, Victor Hugo, and Henri de Montherlant. Rossi's opinion is that Vélez' tragedy, *Reinar después de morir,* is the best of the many dramatic works written about Inés de Castro. The critic notes the interplay of pain and pleasure in Vélez' *comedia* and says that the opening of the play with a song affords a lyrical beginning which accentuates the contrast between the first part of the work, the dramatic development and the tragic conclusion.

239. Rozzell, Ramón. "Facistol," *Modern Language Notes,* LXVI (1951), 155-160.

Rozzell cites a number of plays by Luis Vélez de Guevara to explain the figurative usage of the term "facistol" as it occurs in Lope de Vega's *El caballero de Olmedo.* He explains that the root-idea of the imagery comes from an instrumental or functional concept of "facistol" and not from some aspect of its shape or design. But, Rozzell asks, what underlying reality has been caught in a poetic moment to accommodate the logic of this dramatic metaphor? He quotes the following lines from *La niña de Gómez Arias:*

GÓMEZ ARIAS: ......
      le hice facistol la infame cara
      aunque se precia de jayán robusto
......

"He made a choir-desk of the man's infamous face." Rozzell says that formerly the leader audibly tapped the lectern, but that Gómez as "choir master" conducting his antagonist "the choir" uses his face as a lectern, that is he tapped firmly, struck or beat his face.

240. ———. *La niña de Gómez Arias,* by Luis Vélez de Guevara. Granada: Universidad de Granada, 1959. (Colección Filológica XVI.)

In the introduction, Ramón Rozzell mentions the three different *sueltas* of Vélez' *La niña de Gómez Arias* that are known and where they are located (two in the British Museum and one in the Schaeffer Library of the University of Freiburg, Germany). The critic discusses at length the theme of Gómez Arias, stating that the first important work based on the legend is *La niña de Gómez Arias* by Vélez and that the origin of the story and the old *cantar*

> Señor Gómez Arias
> doleos de mí
> soy niña y muchacha
> y nunca en tal me vi.

still is not known — Vélez could have been familiar with the theme first-hand since he was a native of Andalusia. A comparison of the drama by Vélez with that of the same title by Calderón is presented and Rozzell remarks that the *comedias* are different in many ways, noting in particular the ending: Calderón has Gómez Arias put to death while Vélez lets him live. In the opinion of the critic, Vélez' work is a better reflection of the legend and the *cantar* than Calderón's, for in the later play, there is a series of amorous intrigues which are too complicated. According to Rozzell, Vélez' drama is a picaresque *comedia* which abounds in gibes and satire of the society of his time and herein lies the key to Vélez' worth — he is an author imbued with greater social conscience than other dramatists of the seventeenth century. Rozzell notes that of the two authors, Calderón is the better poet and a more careful writer than Vélez.

241. ———. "The Song and Legend of Gómez Arias," *Hispanic Review,* XX (1952), 91-107.

According to Rozzell, the matter of origin of the legend of Gómez Arias and the song from which it sprang remains an unfinished task for modern scholarship. His purpose in writing this article is to discuss the literary function of both the *cantar* and the legend and to review the problem of their genesis. The critic says that the first major work based on this subject was *La niña de Gómez Arias* by Luis Vélez de Guevara, probably written within the first two decades of the seventeenth century though the date of the *comedia* is unknown. Rozzell indicates that Ochoa seems to be unaware of Vélez' work or any other material antecedent to Calderón's *La niña de Gómez Arias,* as he avers that Calderón was inspired by Tirso de Molina's *El burlador de Sevilla,* for Gómez Arias is a true "Don Juan." The critic contends that Ochoa, by his very innocence, has unwittingly pointed out the importance of the Gómez Arias tradition, especially Vélez' *comedia,* in the development of Spanish "donjuanismo." Rozzell notes that despite all efforts to find historical basis for the story, "la tradición de Gómez Arias" is known solely through the medium of creative literature. He concludes by saying that Calderón might have known the legend only from Vélez and that Vélez perhaps knew it at first hand, being an Andalusian born in 1579.

242. Rull, Enrique. Review of *La serrana de la Vera,* by Luis Vélez de Guevara, ed. of Enrique Rodríguez Cepeda, *Segismundo,* II (1966), 390-392.

The reviewer indicates that since the edition of *La serrana de la Vera* by Menéndez Pidal and María Goyri de Menéndez Pidal in 1916, there has not been a carefully edited text of the *comedia* until now. Rull notes that the text of the Menéndez Pidal edition has been followed rather closely but that the important study which precedes the play reveals new thought on the matter of Vélez. The critic points out that the editor presents a new vision of the playwright as "cristiano nuevo" and quotes Rodríguez Cepeda's opinion of Vélez: "Aseguramos que la vida conflictiva del poeta de Écija no fue nada caprichosa y que verdaderamente respondió a una honda motivación." Rull states that other innovations include the interpretation of the protagonist, Gila, as "vengadora de mujeres," as "reformadora de su propia honra" and above all the study of her "actitud amorosa"; don Lucas as a "donjuán" type; and another character in the play, "el pueblo," a kind of chorus of the *comedia,* which is also the conscience of the work.

243. Sáinz de Robles, Federico Carlos. *El teatro español, historia y antología desde sus orígenes hasta el siglo XIX,* Vol. IV:

El Siglo de Oro. Dramaturgos de segundo orden de los ciclos de Lope y de Calderón. Madrid: Aguilar, 1943.

Sainz de Robles considers Luis Vélez de Guevara to be one of the most outstanding figures of the Spanish theater of the Golden Age and says that for many critics he is more than a brilliant second rate dramatist and should be ranked with Moreto, Rojas and Ruiz de Alarcón. The author points out that although Vélez' works may lack originality and may contain faults in technique, these defects are compensated by "el torrente de poesía, con la gracia íntima, con el humorismo melancólico, con la deliciosa objetividad y el hondo sentido patético que Vélez lleva a sus producciones." The critic indicates that Luis Vélez was perhaps the only playwright of the *siglo de oro* about whom his contemporaries had only good things to say, and he includes quotations from Claramonte, Cervantes, Quevedo, and others to back up his statement. Sainz de Robles states that Vélez' *Reinar después de morir, La luna de la sierra,* and *La serrana de la Vera* are "piezas primorosas" which compete with others by Lope, Tirso and Alarcón and even surpass them in some respects.

244. ———. *Ensayo de un diccionario de la literatura,* Vol. II: *Escritores españoles e hispanoamericanos.* Madrid: Aguilar, 1949.

The author calls Luis Vélez de Guevara "magnífico poeta, novelista y autor dramático... un ingenio chispeante y chisporroteante." Sainz de Robles contends that *El diablo cojuelo* is a novel which reveals "mucho de satírica y algo de picaresca," and that ever since the first copy appeared in 1641 its success has increased with time and the editions are innumerable. He further states that the *Diablo* has been translated into all the "idiomas cultos." Sainz de Robles considers Vélez to be one of the most significant figures of the Spanish theater of the Golden Age and refers to him as "El gran simpático Vélez de Guevara."

245. Salcedo Ruiz, Ángel. *La literatura española, resumen de historia crítica,* Vol. II: *El siglo de oro.* Madrid: Casa Editorial Calleja, 1916.

Salcedo Ruiz finds that the argument of *El diablo cojuelo* could not be more ingenious: flying through the air, rooftops raised showing different social types in intimate life, and to this pleasing story is added the exactitude of the descriptions. The critic believes that the only detraction is that Vélez sought rare words and little-used phrases which make the work unintelligible, and he contends that nobody could understand the rich novelistic content of Vélez' invention until Lesage put the story into standard French prose. Salcedo concludes: "¡Justo castigo al pecado de excederse en el cincelado del léxico y del régimen!"

246. Samonà, Carmelo. "L'esperienza cultista nel teatro dell'età di Lope: appunti ed esempi," in *Studi di letteratura spagnola,* Rome: 1964, pp. 99-168.

    The Italian critic discusses "culteranismo" and the influence of Góngora in the theater at the time of Lope de Vega. Samonà points out passages in *Reinar después de morir* which illustrate Luis Vélez' use of "culto" expressions, metaphors and gongoristic comparisons. *Reinar después de morir* is considered somewhat in detail and the critic says that the drama is essentially lyrical and pathetic with the *gracioso* offering the only light element in the *comedia*.

247. Sánchez, José. *Academias literarias del siglo de oro español.* Madrid: Gredos, 1961.

    José Sánchez considers the "Academias literarias de España" and the important part they played in the development and evolution of the golden age literature and he indicates that there were many of the academies in Spain, especially in Madrid. The critic points out that burlesques were put on by the writers for Felipe IV such as the one cited by the Portuguese writer, Pedro José Suppico in his *Apotegmas políticos y morales*. José Sánchez cites the passage in which Calderón plays the part of *Adán* and Vélez the *Padre eterno*. Calderón had stolen some pears from Vélez and speaks at length excusing himself and blaming Vélez for other thefts. Vélez, tired of the long-winded improvisation and of holding the heavy globe, symbol of the role he was playing, threw it to the floor and said angrily:

> ¡Por Cristo Crucificado
> que, como soy pecador,
> me pesa de haber criado
> un Adán tan hablador!

Of particular interest for this bibliography is *La Academia del buen Retiro,* called *La Academia burlesca de Felipe IV,* 1637, at which Vélez presided. Sánchez gives the organization and structure of the Academy, including the "Oración que oró

Vélez" and "el vejamen que leyó en la misma Francisco de Rojas y Zorrilla."

248. Sánchez Mogul, Antonio. *Reparaciones históricas: Estudios peninsulares.* 1st series. Madrid: Imprenta y Litografía de los Huérfanos, 1894.

> One of the fifteen studies in Sánchez Mogul's *Reparaciones históricas* is entitled "La coronación de Inés de Castro," pp. 131-143. In discussing the coronation, the author asks the question, "Where did the crowning episode originate?" He says that there is no mention of it in the early chronicles and Portuguese literature but that Spanish authors, beginning with Bermúdez, followed by Mejía de la Cerda and Luis Vélez de Guevara, all include the coronation of Inés de Castro. Sánchez Mogul considers the crowning of the dead body the most original part of the legend and the episode which has lived most vividly in the imagination of the people. The critic believes that it all came about as a result of mixing and confusing the exhumation of the body of Inés, declaring her queen and burying her with pomp in Alcobaza in a marble sarcophagus, on top of which appears a statue dressed in royal garments and wearing a crown. All of these facts apparently led to the coronation of the body itself, according to Sánchez Mogul's explanation. In the study entitled "Nuño Álvarez Pereira en la poesía castellana," the critic includes a *romance* written by Luis Vélez de Guevara in praise of the famous Portuguese hero, "El Condestable Nuño Álvarez Pereira, el vencedor de Aljubarrota."

249. Sánchez Pérez, José A. *El diablo cojuelo, El asombro de Turquía y valiente toledano, El ollero de Ocaña,* by Luis Vélez de Guevara. Madrid: Aguilar, 1956. (Colección crisol, no. 168.)

> According to Sánchez Pérez, Luis Vélez de Guevara is "una gloria" not discussed in Spanish literature, because he had the misfortune to be a contemporary of Lope de Vega, Guillén de Castro and Tirso de Molina and for that reason modern literary critics place Vélez on a secondary level within the dramatic school of Lope de Vega. Sánchez Pérez contends that Vélez showed great ability in the development of his *comedias,* depicted characters of astonishing naturalness, was very knowledgeable of life and social customs, very skillful in the use of language, and possessed great facility for versification. The critic lists the poems by Vélez that are known, gives titles of sixty-two of his

comedias, and points out that none of these gave him the fame that he enjoyed from his satirical novel of customs, *El diablo cojuelo.*

250. Santos, Francisco. *El Arca de Noé y Campana de Belilla,* ed., prologue and notes by Fernando Gutiérrez. Barcelona: Selecciones Bibliófilas, Segunda serie, 1959. (First published, Zaragoza, 1697.)

> Francisco Santos is not very complimentary to Luis Vélez de Guevara in the following lines quoted from *El Arca de Noé y Campana de Belilla:*
>
>> Tocó la Campana y desaparecieron todos los Autores de viejo, siguiéndolos vno que avia venido tarde y tambien llevava vn libro en las manos que, preguntando a Noé quién era, me dixo: el libro se intitula el Diablo Cojuelo, Aventuras de Don Cleofas Leandro Perez Zambullo, digno de que le consumiera vn Polvorista: está sin ensenança buena, ni moralidad y esto sobre acabar como la nieve..." (p. 157)

251. Saz, Agustín del. Review of *Autos,* by Luis Vélez de Guevara, ed. of Ángel Lacalle, *Revista de la Biblioteca Archivo y Museo del Ayuntamiento de Madrid,* IX (1932), 102-103.

> The reviewer states that Lacalle has published three important *autos* by one of the great figures of the Golden Age in Spain, forgotten in the midst of the great masters of the period but nonetheless an author of great merit. According to Saz, two of the *autos* were printed in the seventeenth century, *Auto del nacimiento de Nuestro Señor* and the *Auto sacramental de la mesa redonda,* while the *Auto de la abadesa del cielo* makes its first appearance in Lacalle's edition. The reviewer notes that Lacalle has reproduced an *auto de nacimiento,* another of *Nuestra Señora,* and a third a *sacramental,* making a valuable contribution to the history of the literature of Spain.

252. Schack, Adolf Friedrich von. *Historia de la literatura y del arte dramático en España,* tr. from the German into Spanish by Eduardo de Mier. 3 vols, Madrid: M. Tello, 1887. (First German ed. 1846, 2nd greatly enlarged 1854.)

> Chapter XXI of Schack's *Historia* is devoted to Luis Vélez de Guevara. A passage from *Tranco* IV of *El diablo cojuelo* is

quoted, and the paragraphs are followed by a discussion of Vélez' dramatic works. Schack states that the playwright stands among the most distinguished poets of his time; that perhaps he should not be counted as one of the Spanish dramatists of the first order but should have a place of top rank among those of secondary importance. The German critic adds that Vélez' style is more superficial than that of the great masters of the Spanish theater and that most of his *comedias* seem to have been written for the purpose of making a great impression — they are spectacular in nature. Schack believes that Vélez' best dramas are those based on national history and considers the following to be the most outstanding by this author: *Si el caballo vos han muerto, Más pesa el Rey que la sangre, Cumplir dos obligaciones y Duquesa de Sajonia, La desdichada Estefanía, Reinar después de morir,* and *La romera de Santiago.*

253. Schaeffer, Adolf. *Geschichte des spanischen Nationaldramas,* Vol. I: *Die Periode Lope de Vega's. Leipzig:* F. A. Brockhaus, 1890.

Schaeffer devotes pages 283 to 303 of his *Geschichte* to a discussion of thirty-six plays by Luis Vélez de Guevara, including some that are considered doubtful works, such as *Dalles con la entretenida* and *Don Pedro Miagro*. Schaeffer says that Luis Vélez' talent, unlike that of Lope de Vega, was a supple one which adapted to the prevailing tendencies, a characteristic which most writers of second rank share with him. According to the critic, Vélez was never guilty of literary piracy as were most later writers,, and when he did borrow from Lope *(La desdichada Estefanía, El Hércules de Ocaña, El Rey Don Sebastián)*, he adapted the material in his own independent manner. Schaeffer concludes with the statement that Luis Vélez, resembling Lope, was a source from which later dramatists drew without hesitation.

254. ———. *Ocho comedias desconocidas de don Guillén de Castro, del Licenciado Damián Salustio del Poyo, y de Luis Vélez de Guevara, etc., tomadas de un libro antiguo de comedias nuevamente hallado.* 2 vols. Leipzig: F. A. Brockhaus, 1887. (Colección de Autores Españoles, tomos XLVII y XLVIII.)

Eight of the rarest plays of the twelve included in a very old volume of Spanish dramas which had come into the possession of Adolf Schaeffer are reproduced in the *Ocho comedias.*

The book lacked the title page and preliminary pages but according to Schaeffer's calculations was printed between 1612 and 1616. There are four plays by Luis Vélez de Guevara among those published in the *Ocho comedias,* three of which are considered by Schaeffer to be *completamente desconocida.* The German critic's comment on *El capitán prodigioso, Príncipe de Transilvania* is that it is an historical drama of "gran estilo" and very different from the absurd play by Montalván, *El Príncipe prodigioso y defensor de la Fe.* Schaeffer indicates that the subject of *El Hércules de Ocaña* is the same as that of Lope's *Valiente Céspedes* but that Vélez treated it in a different way. Two other plays by Vélez found in Schaeffer's volume are *La devoción de la misa* and *El Rey don Sebastián.*

255. Schäpers, Roland. "La mula de Liñán,' eine Bermerkung zu Guevaras *Diablo cojuelo,*" *Romanische Forschungen,* LXIX (1957), 133-135.

According to Schäpers, the phrase "la mula de Liñán" in the *Diablo cojuelo* does not mean "air" as Rodríguez Marín states in his edition of Vélez' story but rather is a mule, an invisible mule, for the devil to ride on horseback through the air as Liñán does through the world of the "pícaros." The German critic cites *La vida de los pícaros,* attributed by some to Hurtado de Mendoza and by others to Pedro Liñán de Riaza, indicating that the story appears in a volume of the works of Liñán. Schäpers quotes lines from poetry by Liñán which he believes suggested to Vélez the use of the term "la mula de Liñán." Parallels are drawn between Liñán's imaginary trip through the world of the "pícaros" and the devil's ride on an invisible mule, but Schäpers adds, there is a difference: Cienllamas arrives at his destination while Liñán's journey is pure fantasy.

256. Schevill, Rudolph. "*Virtudes vencen señales* and *La vida es sueño,*" *Hispanic Review,* I (1933), 181-195.

Schevill compares *Virtudes vencen señales* by Luis Vélez de Guevara with *La vida es sueño* by Calderón, indicating similarities with quotations cited from each of the plays to illustrate the point in question and mentioning differences, especially between the protagonists: Filipo, the typical Vélez superman, a model of virtue and nobility of character, as opposed to Segismundo, who shows his savage instincts and acts the tyrant upon his accession to royal power. Schevill says that *Virtudes vencen señales* is one of Vélez' finest efforts and that judging from the language and style it belongs to the poet's middle period before the use of *culto* became prominent in his works. The critic notes that the natural descriptions in this *comedia novelesca* possess an unusual simplicity and directness. According to Schevill, Vélez' *gracioso*, Clarín, is superior to Calderón's; his humorous dialogue, together with the amusing scenes provided by the *labradora* Tirrena, add much to the dramatic work in which is found some of the poet's finest verse.

257. Sená, Jorge de. "Inês de Castro ou literatura portuguesa desde Fernão Lopes a Camões e historia político social de D. Alfonso IV a D. Sebastião e compreendo especialmente a analise estrutural da *Castro* de Ferreira e do episodio camoniano de Inês," in *Estudos de Historia e Cultura* (1ª serie), vol. I, Lisboa, Edição da Revista Occidente, 1963, pp. 123-618.

A comprehensive study of the Inés de Castro theme in literature is made by Jorge de Sená. He treats principally Portuguese works but does discuss others, including Vélez' *Reinar después de morir*. The Portuguese critic believes that the *romance Doña Isabel de Liar* was used by both Vélez and Mejía de la Cerda in writing their *comedias*. The critic quotes lines from the *romance*: ... / por los campos de Monvela / caballeros vi asomar / and says that Vélez and Mejía changed "Monvela" to "Mondego." According to Sená, Vélez' *Reinar después de morir* is historical fantasy.

258. Serrano y Sanz, Manuel. Review of *El diablo cojuelo, notas y comentarios* by Felipe Pérez y González, *Revista de Archivos, Bibliotecas y Museos*, IX (1903), 388.

The reviewer states that Felipe Pérez y González examines various difficult passages in the *Diablo cojuelo*, correcting with judicious criticism based on his vast store of knowledge the errors made by Durán in the notes he compiled to aid the Russian, Nicolas Pianitzky, who requested assistance from the Academia Española in attempting to understand some of the obscure passages in *El diablo*. Serrano y Sanz adds that Felipe Pérez y González has filled a void in the literary history of Spain with a book so worthy of applause because of the many "novedades" that it contains.

259. Simón Díaz, José. "La inquisición prohibe *Los tres portentos del cielo,* de Vélez de Guevara," *Aportación Documental para la Erudición Española,* Madrid: Consejo Superior de Investigaciones Científicas, 1947, pp. 3-4. (Supplement no. 2, first ser., vol. I of *Revista Bibliográfica y Documental.*)

    Díaz discloses that Luis Vélez de Guevara's *Los tres portentos del cielo* was censured by the Inquistion and could not be performed. The "calificadores" said: "...no se puede permitir representar por estar en ella profanada toda la Sagrada Escritura i mezclar muchas cosas contrarias a la verdad de la Historia Sagrada."

260. ———. "Textos dispersos de clásicos españoles. XII. Vélez de Guevara," *Revista de Literatura,* XXI (1962), 89-103.

    Simón Díaz indicates that through the efforts of Bonilla y San Martín, Rodríguez Marín, Gómez Ocerín, Lacalle, and others, the "obra poética" of Vélez is gradually becoming known. Simón Díaz reproduces twenty-two poems by Vélez, giving the work in which each appeared, where published, and the date.

261. Sims, E. R. Review of *El diablo cojuelo,* by Luis Vélez de Guevara, ed. of Francisco Rodríguez Marín, *Modern Philology,* XVIII (1920-1921), 620-622.

    According to the reviewer, Rodríguez Marín has explained most of the difficult passages in *El diablo cojuelo* in copious notes which contain a wealth of detailed description that cannot be found elsewhere. The critic points out that Rodríguez Marín scarcely mentions Vélez' sources, one of these being Lucian, and another Quevedo to whom the debt is far greater. Sims contends that generally it may be said that there are few characters satirized in *El diablo cojuelo* for whom parallels may not be found in either the *Sueños* of Quevedo or in some of his verses.

262. Sloman, Albert E. Review of *El embuste acreditado,* by Luis Vélez de Guevara, ed. of Arnold G. Reichenberger, *Bulletin of Hispanic Studies,* XXXV (1958), 102-103.

    Sloman indicates that *El embuste acreditado y el disparate creído* was first published in the *Quinta parte de comedias escogidas de los mejores ingenios de España* in 1653. Apart from reprintings of this version, the play survives in two other forms:

in the *Parte treinta y quatro de comedias nuevas escritas por los mejores ingenios de España* (Madrid 1670) under the title *El disparate creído* and attributed to Zabaleta, and in an undated manuscript in the Biblioteca Palatina at Parma as *La comedia de otro demonio,* "de tres ingenios." Sloman says that Reichenberger uses the 1653 text as the basis for his critical edition, on the grounds that it is by some seventeen years the earliest which is extant and one which ascribes the play, rightly in his view, to Vélez de Guevara. The reviewer states that when so few of Spain's major plays are available in satisfactory edition, Vélez de Guevara and the mediocre *comedia* which is attributed to him are fortunate to have so scrupulous and scholarly an edition.

263. ―――. *The Dramatic Craftsmanship of Calderón, His Use of Earlier Plays.* Oxford: The Dolphin Book Co., Ltd., 1958.

Sloman examines eight plays written by Calderón which derive directly from other plays, sometimes the work of earlier dramatists like Lope de Vega, Tirso de Molina and Vélez de Guevara, sometimes works in which Calderón himself had collaborated with his contemporaries like Pérez de Montalbán and Antonio Coello. The critic makes a detailed comparison between Luis Vélez de Guevara's *La niña de Gómez Arias* and Calderón's play with the same title. Sloman indicates that though there are differences in the two works, it is apparent that Calderón's debt to Vélez is considerable. However, the critic adds, Calderón reverses the outcome of Vélez' play to provide a denouement both dramatically and morally appropriate. Gómez' crimes are the rebellion of an individual, but he has rebelled against not only "la niña" but her family and society as a whole. It is a complete evasion of the moral problem to allow Gómez to survive unscathed, and, Sloman continues, this is a serious weakness of Vélez' play. The critic avers that Calderón transformed the play of Vélez de Guevara into a work which is artistically superior and thoroughly his own.

264. Spencer, Forrest E., and Rudolph Schevill. *The Dramatic Works of Luis Vélez de Guevara. Their Plots, Sources, and Bibliography.* Berkeley, Calif.: University of California Press, 1937. (University of California Publications in Modern Philology, Vol. XIX.)

Ninety-four dramatic works by or attributed to Luis Vélez de Guevara are discussed by Spencer and Schevill. The *comedias* are not listed in chronological order but are grouped into classifications assigned by the authors. For each play, Spencer and Schevill have quoted the first and final lines, the date of the first printed text, together with the library in which it may be found, the number of the play in Cotarelo's list, the cast of characters, and a well condensed resume of each *comedia*. Following the plot summary, the authors discuss bibliographical problems, indicate possible sources, and mention imitations and related plays by other dramatists. Manuscripts and the more important *sueltas* are also cited and available evidence as to date of composition is added. Generally, though not always, a brief critical comment is given regarding the literary merits of the play in question. According to Spencer and Schevill, Luis Vélez de Guevara deserves a prominent place among the chief playwrights of the seventeenth century — he derives from Lope de Vega and points unmistakably to Calderón.

265. Suppico de Moraes, Pedro Joseph. *Collecçam politica de apophthegmas memoraveis.* Parte I dedicada a Augusta, E Real Magestade de ElRey de Portugal D. Joaõ OV. Nosso Senhor. Lisboa Occidental: No Officina de Antonio Pedrozo Galraõ, 1720.

Suppico mentions a number of "dichos agudos" of Luis Vélez de Guevara in his *Apophthegmas.* In *Livro* III, page 70, is found the following "copla" composed by Vélez upon seeing a funeral procession on a hot day when members of the cortège were clothed in flannel robes:

> Con calores excessivos
> Van de baeta cubiertos:
> Gran traça hallaron los muertos
> De vengarse de los vivos!

266. Ticknor, George. *History of Spanish Literature.* 6th American ed., corrected and enl. 3 vols. New York: Gordian Press, Inc., 1965.

Ticknor discusses Vélez de Guevara as a dramatist and comments on a number of his plays. One of these *comedias, Más pesa el Rey que la sangre,* he labels as "King before Kin," adding that a good deal of skill is shown in putting the subject into a dramatic form. The critic says that Vélez' religious dramas show the disturbing element of love adventures mingled with what ought to be very spiritual and above human passion. Ticknor cites several works dealing with Biblical characters, among them *La corte del demonio,* in which are depicted atrocities at the court of Nineveh that Ticknor feels should not have been so much as hinted at before any respectable audience in Christendom. Another play mentioned is *El pleito que tuvo el diablo con el Cura de Madrilejos,* written by Vélez in collaboration with Rojas and Mira de Amescua, in which an account is given of the case of a poor mad girl who was treated as a witch and escaped death only by confessing that she was full of demons, who are driven out of her on the stage, before the audience, by conjurations and exorcisms. According to Ticknor, the whole subject of witchcraft belonged to the Holy Office and Vélez' drama was forbidden to be represented or read and soon disappeared quietly from public notice.

267. Triwedi, Mitchell D. "Inés de Castro, 'cuello de garza': Una nota sobre el *Reinar después de morir* de Luis Vélez de Guevara," *Hispanofila,* V (1962), 1-7.

The author notes that "colo de garça," the "sobrenombre tradicional" of Inés de Castro is not found in the earliest versions of the story and does not appear until the sixteenth century. According to the critic, it is to be supposed that the alleged "mote" was invented in the period following the earliest chroniclers. Triwedi finds it strange that there are no references to "colo de garça" in the *Trovas* of Resende nor in other works up to the two *romances* of Gabriel Lasso de la Vega: Camões refers to Inés' neck as "colo de alabastro." The critic points out that in Vélez' *Reinar después de morir* the poetic possibilities inherent in "cuello de garza" are developed fully for the first time. Triwedi discusses the symbolism connected with the "garza" and how Vélez weaves the idea into the plot until the transformation of the real heron into the figurative "garza" (Inés) becomes evident.

268. Turkiainen, V. Review of *El rey en su imaginación,* by Luis Vélez de Guevara, ed. of J. Gómez Ocerín, *Neuphilologische Mitteilunger,* XXIV (1923), 184-186.

The German critic indicates that *El rey en su imaginación* follows the spirit and motif of the romances of chivalry derived from national Spanish tradition, thus is reminiscent of Lope de Vega and other dramatists of the Golden Age as well as Cervantes in *Don Quijote.* Turkiainen believes that Lope's *El cuerdo loco,* which bears similarity to Vélez' *El rey en su imaginación,* surpasses the *comedia* by Vélez in versification.

269. Umbral, Francisco. Review of *El diablo cojuelo,* by Luis Vélez de Guevara, ed. of María del Pilar Palomo Velázquez, il. by Goñi. Barcelona: Marte, 1965. (Col. Pliegos de Cordel), *Estafeta Literaria,* No. 338 (1966), pp. 21-22.

   Of the author of *El diablo cojuelo* Umbral says that great is the literary formula of Vélez de Guevara, which in its diversity and harmonious absurdities corresponds exactly "con la riqueza confusa e impura de aquella humanidad imperial, de aquel nutrido grupo español; su novela nos sigue sonando a pueblo y a verdad de España." The reviewer states that the edition alternates between the modern and the archaic and indicates that it is not possible to edit "en rústica." Umbral adds that the art of Goñi happily interprets the prose of Vélez.

270. Valbuena Prat, Ángel. *El teatro español en su Siglo de Oro.* Barcelona: Editorial Planeta, 1969.

   Valbuena Prat considers Luis Vélez de Guevara as a playwright (pages 160-167 in his *Teatro español en su Siglo de Oro*) and says that Vélez is "una de las primeras figuras de nuestro teatro y el dramaturgo del ciclo de Lope de Vega que tuvo más potencialidad trágica y un sentido más comprensivo de los temas nacionales y populares." Seven plays by Vélez are mentioned with a short discussion given to *Reinar después de morir* and *Auto del nacimiento de Cristo.*

271. ———. *Historia de la literatura española.* 3rd ed., corrected and enl. 3 vols. Barcelona: Editorial Gustavo Gili, S. A., 1950.

   Volume II contains a readable and scholarly analysis of the works of Luis Vélez de Guevara, including an evaluation of the playwright's theater. Three *comedias* Valbuena Prat calls the most outstanding: *La luna de la sierra, La serrana de la Vera,* and *Reinar después de morir* — "la más fina y trágica a la vez"; others he labels as having "gran fuerza dramática y variedad de personajes": *El águila del agua, El Hércules de Ocaña, La devoción de la misa, El rey en su imaginación,* and *Más pesa el Rey que la sangre.* The critic says there is still another group which does not fail to interest either for the ideas put forth, some character or episode, beautiful verse, or the caricature of the *gracioso.* Concerning *El diablo cojuelo,* Valbuena Prat notes that at times the text of this ingenious satire is very difficult to understand and he contends that "todo lo extraño y caótico del libro, entre graciosas sátiras costumbristas y desaforadas imágenes y retorsiones de pensamiento" can be explained by the change-over late in life to writing prose for which Vélez had not developed a skill.

272. ———. *Historia del teatro español.* Barcelona: Editorial Noguer, 1956.

Valbuena Prat says that Vélez de Guevara gives universality to the theme of doña Inés de Castro in one of the most beautiful tragedies, *Reinar después de morir,* in which "lo femenino e infantil transcurre con la fluidez de un río, entre las peñas adustas del asesinato por razón de Estado," and that *Reinar después de morir* reaches heights in the theater comparable to the greatness of the "octavas" of Camoens in his great epic poem, *Os Lusíadas.* According to the critic, Vélez in *Reinar después de morir* and other powerful dramas continued to justify his place at the side of the six most famous Spanish playwrights of the Golden Age: Lope, Tirso, Alarcón, Calderón, Rojas and Moreto. Valbuena Prat states that perhaps Vélez' *La serrana de la Vera* may equal and even surpass *Reinar después de morir* in vigor and originality but is inferior to it in the delicate lyrical tension which envelops all of the historical-legendary action.

273. ———. *La novela picaresca española.* Madrid: Aguilar, 1943.

According to Valbuena Prat, *El diablo cojuelo* by Luis Vélez de Guevara is an ingenious work full of keen-edged satire with the theme based on "motivos folklóricos." The critic points out that it is not unusual to find invocations to the devil in "popular" verses: "Diablo cojuelo tráemele luego," "con el diablo cojo que corre más que todos." Valbuena Prat indicates that for Vélez the devil is "el diablillo travieso," "las pulgas del infierno, la chisme, el enredo," and says that all the novel abounds in this "picante ironía." The critic contends that Vélez was influenced by Quevedo's *Sueños,* which served as a model for the social satire as well as for the style and use of the language.

274. ———. *Reinar después de morir. La luna de la sierra,* by Luis Vélez de Guevara. (Teatro escogido I). Madrid: Compañía Ibero-americana, S. A., 1930? (Biblioteca populares

Cervantes, ser. 1. Las cien mejores obras de la literatura española, vol. LXXVII.)

Valbuena Prat states that among the followers of Lope de Vega, Luis Vélez de Guevara is the dramatist who best knew how to interpret the emotional value of the popular legends, *romances* and *canciones*. In the opinion of the critic, Vélez' masterpieces are *Reinar después de morir, La luna de la sierra,* and *La serrana de la Vera,* in each of which there is some historical basis and in which "cantares populares" either give origin to the work as in *La serrana de la Vera:* "Allá en Garganta la Olla / en la Vera de Plasencia..." or are sung during the most dramatic moment in the play as in *La luna de la sierra,* the "cancioncilla" "Ay, luna que reluces — toda la noche me alumbres," and in *Reinar después de morir,* "el romance de la aparición": "¿Dónde vas, el caballero?"

275. Vega Carpio, Lope Félix de. *Epistolario de Lope de Vega Carpio* que ... publica Agustín G. de Amezúa. 4 vols. Madrid: 1935-43.

In a letter dated Madrid, November 9, 1608, to the Conde de Saldaña, Lope asks the nobleman to forgive Vélez for the "carta descomedida" he had written to him, indicating that the playwright loved the Conde and would humble himself at his feet. Included in the letter is the following poem (Lauro was the pen name of Vélez):

> Saliçio a Lauro enamora,
> Lauro a Saliçio recrea,
> Saliçio a Lauro dessea,
> Y Lauro a Saliçio adora.
> Si, desconformes agora,
> Pide el mexor de los buenos
> Consejo a libros agenos,
> Belardo, assí le dirás:
> Qvien es más, perdone más,
> Qvien menos, offenda menos.
>
> (III, 10)

In another letter written in Madrid, probably in the summer of 1618 to the Duque de Sessa, Lope asks in verse for "una sotana nueva" and at the end of the poem he says, "Parece cossa de Luis Vélez," (IV, 17), referring, no doubt, to the numerous *Memoriales* of Vélez in which he was always asking for something.

276. ———. *El jardín de Lope de Vega*, in *Colección escogida de obras no dramáticas de Fray Lope Félix de Vega Carpio* by D. Cayetano Rosell. Madrid: M. Rivadeneyra, 1856. (*Biblioteca de Autores Españoles*, vol. XXXVIII.)

    Lope praises Luis Vélez de Guevara, in *El jardín de Lope de Vega* with the following words:

> De Luis Vélez florido y elocuente
> La lira, que ya fue del dulce Orfeo
> ....
> (p. 423b)

277. ———. *Epístola a don Juan de Arguijo*, in *Colección escogida de obras no dramáticas de Fray Lope Félix de Vega Carpio*, by D. Cayetano Rosell. Madrid: M. Rivadeneyra, 1856. (*Biblioteca de Autores Españoles*, vol. XXXVIII.)

    In an *Epístola a don Juan de Arguijo*, Lope de Vega says of Luis Vélez de Guevara:

> Y al famoso Luis Vélez, que tenía
> en éxtasis las musas, que a sus labios
> Iban por dulce néctar y ambrosía.
> (p. 427z)

278. ———. *Laurel de Apolo*, in *Colección escogida de obras no dramáticas de Fray Lope Félix de Vega Carpio*, by D. Cayetano Rosell. Madrid: M. Rivadeneyra, 1856. (*Biblioteca de Autores Españoles*, vol. XXXVIII.)

    In Silva II of *Laurel de Apolo*, Lope de Vega praises Luis Vélez de Guevara in the following manner:

> Ni en Ecija dejara
> El florido Luis Vélez de Guevara
> de ser su nuevo Apolo.
> Que pudo darle solo,
> y solo en sus escritos,
> Con flores de conceptos inauditos,
> Lo que los tres que faltan;
> Así sus versos de oro
> Con blando estilo la materia esmaltan.
> (p. 195)

279. Vélez de Guevara, Luis. *El diablo cojuelo, verdades soñadas y novelas de la otra vida traducidas a estas, añadido al fin con ocho Enigmas curiosos y dos novelas.* Madrid: Imprenta de Ramón Ruiz, 1797.

> The above edition of *El diablo cojuelo* is included in this bibliography because of the "ocho enigmas" and the two "novelas" included after the *Diablo*. The title page of the book bears no name other than that of Luis Vélez de Guevara, which would seem to indicate that he is also the author of the "enigmas" and the two "novelas." The "Octavo enigma" is reproduced below because in some respects it could apply to Vélez:
>
>> Yo soy redondo, ya largo,
>> de breve y luenga estatura,
>> trágico en suerte y ventura,
>> pues que sin hacerme cargo
>> me previene sepultura:
>> mi inocencia en roncas voces
>> clamorea, y de la tumba
>> sale en acentos feroces:
>> tanto mi quexa retumba,
>> mas va que no me conoces.
>>
>> (p. 208)
>
> Following the "enigmas" is the *Novela de los tres hermanos*, "escrita sin el uso de la A." The last item in the book is the *Novela del caballero invisible*, "compuesta en equívocos burlescos." The works in this volume are not necessarily by Luis Vélez. The *Novela de los tres hermanos* is included in the *Biblioteca de Autores Españoles*, XXXIII, 369-373, and is attributed to Francisco Navarrete y Ribera. The *Novela del caballero invisible* appears in the same volume of the *Biblioteca de Autores Españoles*, 375-376, as an anonymous work.

280. Vera y Mendoza, Fernando de. *Panegírico por la poesía,* published by Manuel Pérez de Guzmán. 2nd ed. Seville: Imp. de E. Rasco, 1886. (First published in Seville, Jan. 9, 1627, and though the author does not give his name, the work generally is attributed to Fernando de Vera.)

> In the *Panegírico,* the author has the following to say about Luis Vélez de Guevara: "De Luys Velez, solo digo que es el Rey de Romanos...." (p. 54)

281. Veynar, Eva B. "Mythological and Other Classical Allusions in the Theater of Ruiz de Alarcón and Luiz Vélez de Guevara." Unpublished Master's thesis, The University of Tennessee, 1940.

>The intention of the author of the thesis is to include all those allusions which Ruiz de Alarcón and Vélez might have discovered in the Greek and Roman writers. The allusions were taken from forty-two plays (fifteen by Vélez were examined, which represents only a small part of the *comedias* attributed to his pen by Spencer and Schevill). The allusions, three hundred and fourteen in all with sixty-two duplicates, are listed in alphabetical order, followed by the abbreviation of the titles of those books from which Vélez and Alarcón received their information about the item; after a colon further abbreviations represent those reference volumes in which the item was identified by the thesis writer. The English form is given and then a brief statement which explains and identifies it. The exact location in Vélez or Alarcón is given by letters and numbers which represent volume and page. In the Appendix, a Table of Allusions lists in alphabetical order the allusion showing the number of times used by Alarcón, Tirso, and Vélez. Veynar made use of a previous thesis, "Mythological and Other Classical Allusions in the Theater of Tirso de Molina" (Master's thesis, The University of Tennessee, 1938, by Jessie V. Davis), for the information on Tirso. Veynar feels that a catalogue of classical allusions in Spanish Golden Age literature might serve a number of purposes: 1) to indicate how widely the author who used the allusions had read, 2) to show how much the audience of the day seemed to know about the classic tales, and 3) to determine authorship of doubtful plays.

282. Vic, Jean. "La Composition et les sources du *Diable boiteux* de Lesage," *Revue d'Histoire Littéraire de la France*, XXVII (1920), 481-517.

>In citing "Les sources espagnoles" Vic mentions *El diablo cojuelo* by Luis Vélez de Guevara which Lesage himself recognizes in the dedication of his work. The French author says that he owed "au très illustre auteur Luis Vélez de Guevara" the idea and the title of his story. Vic makes a comparison between Lesage's *Diable boiteux* and the *Diablo cojuelo*, adding that Vélez' work was inspired by Quevedo's *Sueños*. The French critic labels *El diablo cojuelo* as "un roman d'allégories et d'aventures."

283. Viel-Castel, Louis de. *Essai sur le théâtre espagnol.* 2 vols. Paris: G. Charpentier, editeur, 1882.

    Viel-Castel believes it to be something extraordinary that among the dramatic poets who imitated Lope de Vega, there were a number who attained brilliant success. Most of these, the French critic contends, are completely forgotten today, even in Spain. Viel-Castel indicates that Luis Vélez de Guevara is one of the playwrights who was admired by his contemporaries but who is today regarded with less indulgence by the few readers of the works by him which remain.

284. Wade, Gerald E. "Mythological and Other Classical Allusions in the Theaters of Tirso, Alarcón and Vélez," *Bulletin of the Comediantes,* X (1958), 6-9.

    The author discusses two theses in which mythological and other classical allusions in the theaters of Tirso, by Jessie V. Davis, and Alarcón and Vélez, by Eva B. Veynar, are studied and catalogued showing the frequency with which certain names found in Greek and Roman men of letters from the earliest days to the time of later emperors of the west are used. In the fifteen plays by Vélez which were examined, there appeared one hundred and forty-one different allusions, with *fortuna* occurring forty-eight times. Wade raises the question of how the Spaniard of the Golden Age could reconcile the pagan quality of classic lore with the orthodox religious belief that was so much a part of him. The critic explains that Spanish religious men and writers had no trouble in reconciling pagan and Christian ideology, as can be noted in the great artist, Calderón, as well as in other writers — the study of classical grammar was necessary to understand the language of God, the scriptures.

285. ———. Review of *La niña de Gómez Arias,* by Luis Vélez de Guevara, ed. of Ramón Rozzell, *Modern Language Notes,* LXXV (1960), 719-721.

    Wade indicates that Rozzell finds it impossible, as does he the reviewer, to decide with finality just how *La niña de Gómez Arias* was played in Vélez' time. According to Wade, the play has elements of broad farce and also pathos. That is, he says, for us it has pathos, but did it for Vélez? The reviewer raises the question as to whether the *comedia* might have been played purely as farce, stressing the several *burlas* of the drama, even that of the "niña's" enslavement. Wade concludes by stating that *La niña de Gómez Arias* is not a good play, whether judged by the standards of our time or by those of Vélez' day.

286. ———. "The Orthoëpy of the Holographic *comedias* of Vélez de Guevara," *Hispanic Review*, IX (1941), 459-481.

A study is made by Gerald E. Wade of the four *comedias* from the pen of Luis Vélez de Guevara which have survived in holographic form: *El águila del agua, La serrana de la Vera, El rey en su imaginación,* and *El conde don Pero Vélez y don Sancho el Deseado*. The first part of the examination of Vélez' orthoëpy is a tabulation which considers the individual word with its combination of vowels, weak and strong, tonic and atonic, in pretonic, tonic or post-tonic syllables; in diphthong, dieresis, syneresis or bi-syllabism. In Part II of the investigation there is presented a compilation of the words in hiatus or synalepha. In order that the interested reader may examine in their context the various items of the compilation, the author has given their location in the plays in which they occur. Wade points out that the four plays range in composition date from 1613 for *La serrana de la Vera,* through 1615 for *El conde don Pero Vélez y don Sancho el Deseado,* and 1620-25 for *El rey en su imaginación,* to 1627-32 for the *Águila del agua*. The conclusion reached by Wade is that Vélez' orthoëpy, as far as he has been able to determine, shows no tendency toward change in any feature due to the lapse of years.

287. Wardropper, Bruce W. *Introducción al teatro religioso del Siglo de Oro (Evolución del Auto Sacramental: 1500-1648)*. Madrid: Revista de Occidente, 1953.

Wardropper includes Luis Vélez de Guevara in the chapter "Otros precursores de Calderón" in the writing of religious drama and lists the only *autos* by Vélez that are easily accessible: the three treated by Ángel Lacalle in his edition of *Autos* by Luis Vélez de Guevara published in 1931. Wardropper contends that the *Auto de la abadesa del cielo* is not an allegorical work nor is it related to the Eucharist so should not be claimed as forming part of the cycle which might be called *Autos de Nuestra Señora*. The critic states that the *Auto del nacimiento* is an insignificant "seudo-misterio navideño," and he adds that the only true *auto sacramental* is the *Auto famoso de la mesa redonda*. Wardropper indicates that the allegory in *La mesa redonda* deals with the seizure of Jerusalem by Charlemagne, or Christ, with parallels drawn between the twelve Peers and the Apostles, in which the analogy although complicated is plausible but the play lacks coherence — the relation between the different episodes is not always clear.

288. Willers, Hermann. "*Le Diable boiteux* (Lesage), *El diablo cojuelo* (Guevara), Ein Beitrag zur Geschichte frankospanischer Literaturbezeihungen," *Romanische Forschungen,* XLIX (1935), 215-316.

   The German critic states that Luis Vélez de Guevara has been characterized as an emulous follower of Lope de Vega in a great number of his plays but that he owes nothing to Lope for the popularity of *El diablo cojuelo,* which sixty-six years after its appearance inspired a French imitation. A detailed comparison is made between *Le diable boiteux* and *El diablo cojuelo* with passages quoted from each to illustrate similarities and differences.

289. Wilson, Edward M. "*La iglesia sitiada* — a Calderonian Puzzle," *Modern Language Review,* LIX (1964), 583-594.

   Wilson presents evidence for and against Calderón's authorship of *La iglesia sitiada* and concludes that although Calderón may have possessed a copy of it and studied it, the parodied *romance* resembles others in works by Luis Vélez (acted in 1633) and by Juan Pérez de Montalbán (acted in 1635). This fact, according to Wilson, seems to be the most relevant clue to the problem of authorship. The critic considers that the play was probably the work of one or the other of these two men, Vélez or Montalbán, both of whom at times collaborated with Calderón and who were as famous in 1636 as he was.

290. ———. Review of *El embuste acreditado,* by Luis Vélez de Guevara, ed. of Arnold G. Reichenberger, *Modern Language Review,* LIII (1958), 445-446.

   The reviewer considers Reichenberger's work a good edition of a very poor play, indicating that although Vélez wrote four or five masterpieces and a larger number of agreeable dramas, *El embuste* is pretty feeble. He says that the tricks are too childish to amuse and the verse of too little distinction to be memorable. The critic contends that the play is almost certainly incomplete: the editor observes on p. 315 a loose end in the third act and there are others. Wilson believes that Reichenberger treats the characters too realistically and that his notes are too copious — notes should illuminate, not distract, but he does admit that there are useful clarifications on some syntactical complications, on obscure plays upon words and some difficult legal allusions. Wilson states that he is sorry Reichenberger did not find a better play to edit.

291. ———. "The *Cancionero* of don Joseph del Corral," *Hispanic Review*, XXXV (1967), 141-160.

The *Cancionero* of don Joseph del Corral is of interest to scholars concerned with problems of the transmission of poetry during the early years of the reign of Philip IV. Fifty-eight poems and poetical fragments are included in a list which was taken from a collection of manuscripts belonging to Sir Thomas Phillipps. Wilson indicates two poems attributed to Luis Vélez de Guevara, one questionable and one certain to be his, which were found among the manuscripts.

292. ——— and Duncan Moir. *The Golden Age: Drama, 1492-1700,* Vol. III of *A Literary History of Spain.* London: Ernest Benn Limited, 1971.

Wilson and Moir state that one of Lope de Vega's most successful contemporaries, and one of the closest to him in poetic and dramatic spirit, was Luis Vélez de Guevara. The critics add that nowadays Vélez is remembered above all for his satirical novel *El diablo cojuelo* but he was a fertile dramatist, especially given to historical and heroic themes, treated often with the same satirical spirit which is admired in his novel. *Reinar después de morir* is cited as the most celebrated of Vélez' plays. Wilson and Moir indicate that one of Vélez' most attractive qualities as a dramatist is his healthy exploitation of melodrama, savagery, and violence. They name as one of his most remarkable plays in this vein *La serrana de la Vera.* According to the critics, the protagonist of Vélez' drama, Gila, is an extraordinary example of an interesting type of character in the Golden Age drama, the *mujer varonil.* Other good plays by Luis Vélez mentioned by the critics are: *El rey en su imaginación; La luna de la sierra, Más pesa el Rey que la sangre, El privado perseguido, El ollero de Ocaña,* and *El diablo está en Cantillana.*

293. Wurzbach, Wolfgang. Review of *El rey en su imaginación*, ed. of J. Gómez Ocerín, *Zeitschrift für romanische Philologie*, XLI (1921), 627-629.

    The reviewer contends that *El rey en su imaginación* does not offer any particular interest as it is a rather mediocre work and is not one of the precious jewels of Spanish dramatic literature. According to Wurzbach, the enthusiastic praise of Cervantes in *El viaje del Parnaso* ("escogido entre millares" — "quitapesares" — "poeta gigante") appears to later critics to be something of an exaggeration. The reviewer remarks that among the manuscripts in the Biblioteca Nacional no doubt there could have been another *comedia* more worthy of publication than *El rey en su imaginación*.

294. Ynduráin, Francisco. *Reinar después de morir*, by Luis Vélez de Guevara. 4th ed. Madrid: Editorial Ebro, 1958. (*Biblioteca Clásica Ebro, Clásicos Españoles.*)

    Ynduráin says in the introduction to his edition of *Reinar después de morir* that an acceptable critical evaluation of the dramatic works of Luis Vélez de Guevara as yet has not been made but that modern critics little by little are bringing out of obscurity the *comedias* of Vélez and are claiming for him a place at the side of the great dramatists of the *Siglo de Oro:* Lope, Tirso, Alarcón, Calderón, Rojas, Moreto. Ynduráin adds that two of Vélez' *comedias* have been performed in recent years and with great success: *Reinar después de morir*, reworked by F. Fernández Villegas, 1902, was presented in El Español de Madrid and continues to figure in the repertory of theatrical companies; Cristóbal de Castro adapted for representation *La luna de la sierra*, proof of the lasting value of these dramas which continue to move the audience by the force of their dramatic qualities and the charm of their poetry. Ynduráin indicates that critics censure in the greater portion of Vélez' *comedias* his lack of skill in the denouement which is abrupt and not logical, but he notes that the playwright knew how to create characters, especially feminine figures, from the implacable Gila of *La serrana de la Vera* to the sweet unfortunate doña Inés de Castro. According to Ynduráin, Vélez exceeds himself to vie with Lope de Vega and to surpass him in the creation of Inés, amorous, innocent, feminine, who is the defenseless victim of the traitorous murderers.

295. Z[amora], A[lonso]. "Vélez de Guevara, Luis," *Diccionario de literatura española,* by Germán Bleiberg and Julián Marías. 3d ed., corrected and enl. Madrid: Revista de Occidente, 1964, pp. 815-817.

Alonso Zamora states that Vélez de Guevara "es un ejemplo de poesía desbordada, de gran finura de matices, delicada, al servicio de un talento dramático de primer orden." The critic indicates that Vélez was a follower of Lope de Vega, from whom he took ideas for many of his *comedias,* and that Vélez, resembling Lope, knew how to interject *romances* and *cantarcillos* at the most propitious moment. Alonso Zamora discusses *El diablo cojuelo,* which he calls "una novela crítico-picaresca," and mentions briefly a number of dramatic works by Vélez. *Reinar después de morir* receives more attention from the critic as he lists some of the works on the Inés de Castro theme which preceded that of Vélez. Alonso Zamora says that in *Reinar después de morir* "Vélez ha sabido mezclar con una finura sin rival en nuestro teatro el escalofrío de la tragedia con una atmósfera lírica, musical, suave, de una ternura extraordinaria."

SOURCES

The items for this bibliography have been derived in part from an examination of the following resources, indices, bibliographical works and journals:

Indices and Bibliographies

Barrera y Leirado, Cayetano de la. *Catálogo bibliográfico y biográfico del teatro antiguo español desde sus orígenes hasta mediados del siglo XVIII.* Madrid: 1860.
Bibliographie hispanique, 1905-17. 13 vols. New York: Hispanic Society, 1909-19.
Bleiberg, Germán, and Julián Marías. *Diccionario de literatura española.* 3d ed., corrected and enl. Madrid: Revista de Occidente, 1964.
British Museum Catalogue of Printed Books. Photolithographic ed. to 1955. London: Published by the Trustees of the British Museum, 1965.
Chatham, James R., and Enrique Ruiz-Fornells, with the collaboration of Sara Matthews Scales. *Dissertations in Hispanic Languages and Literatures. An Index of Dissertations Completed in the United States and Canada 1876-1966.* University Press of Kentucky, 1970.
Coe, Ada M. *Catálogo bibliográfico y crítico de las comedias anunciadas en los periódicos de Madrid desde 1661 hasta 1819.* Baltimore, Md.: The Johns Hopkins Press, 1935. (The Johns Hopkins Studies in Romance Literature and Language, Extra Volume IX.)
Delk, Lois Jo, and James Neal Greer. *Spanish Language and Literature in the Publications of American Universities; A Bibliography.* Austin, Texas: University of Texas Press, 1952. (University of Texas Hispanic Studies, vol. IV.)
Dissertation Abstracts: *A Guide to Dissertations and Monographs Available in Microfilm.* Ann Arbor, Mich.: University Microfilms, 1952- .
Fitzmaurice-Kelly, James. *Spanish Bibliography.* Oxford: 1925.
Foulché-Delbosc, R., and L. Barrau-Dihigo. *Manuel de l'hispanisant.* 2 vols. New York: The Hispanic Society of America, 1920, 1925.
Gallardo, Bartolomé José. *Ensayo de una biblioteca española de libros raros y curiosos.* 4 vols. Madrid: Rivadeneyra, 1863-89.
Golden, Herbert H., and Seymour O. Simches. *Modern Iberian Language and Literature: A Bibliography of Homage Studies.* Cambridge, Mass.: Harvard University Press, 1958.

Grismer, Raymond L. *A Bibliography of Articles and Essays on the Literature of Spain and Spanish America.* Minneapolis: Perine Book Company, 1935.

Index translationum. Répertoire international des traductions. Paris: UNESCO, 1949- .

Kayser, Christian G. *Vollständiges Bücher-Lexicon.* 1750-1910. Leipzig: Verlag von Ludwig Schumann, 1834-1912.

Laurenti, Joseph L. *Ensayo de una bibliografía de la novela picaresca española, años 1554-1964.* Madrid: Consejo Superior de Investigaciones Científicas, 1968.

Library of Congress and National Union Catalog, Author Lists 1942-1962; A Master Cumulation, compiled by the editorial staff of the Gale Research Company. Detroit: Gale Research Company, 1969-1971.

McCready, Warren T. *Bibliografía temática de Estudios sobre el Teatro Español Antiguo.* Toronto: University of Toronto Press, 1966.

Medel del Castillo, Francisco. *Índice general alfabético de todos los títulos de comedias.* Madrid: Imprenta de Mora, 1735. (Reprinted by John M. Hill in *Revue Hispanique,* Vol. XXXV, 1929.)

Mesonero Romanos, Ramón de. "Índice alfabético de las comedias, tragedias, autos y zarzuelas del teatro antiguo español, desde Lope de Vega hasta Cañizares (1580-1740)," in *Dramáticos posteriores a Lope de Vega* (Vol. XLIX of *Biblioteca de autores españoles*), Madrid: 1924.

Modern Language Association of America. *Annual Bibliography.* Published in the April issue of PMLA. New York: 1921- .

———. *MLA International Bibliography of Books and Articles in the Modern Languages.* New York: 1963- .

Palau y Dulcet, Antonio. *Manual del librero hispanoamericano, inventario bibliográfico de la producción científica y literaria de España y de la América desde la invención de la imprenta hasta nuestros días con el valor comercial de todos los artículos descritos....* Barcelona: 1923-27. 7 vols. (2.ª ed. corregida y aumentada, Barcelona: 1948-62. 14 vols.)

Pane, Remigio Ugo. *English Translations from the Spanish 1484-1943.* New Brunswick, N. J.: Rutgers University Press, 1944.

Parker, J. J., and A. G. Reichenberger. "A Current Bibliography of Foreign Publications Dealing with the *Comedia.*" *Bulletin of the Comediantes,* 1942- .

Paz y Melia, A. *Catálogo de las piezas de teatro que se conservan en el departamento de manuscritos de la Biblioteca Nacional.* Madrid: Imp. del Colegio Nacional de Sordomudos y de Ciegos, 1899.

Penny, Clara Louisa. *List of Books Printed 1601-1700 in the Library of the Hispanic Society of America.* New York: Printed by Order of the Trustees, 1938.

Sainz de Robles, Federico. *Ensayo de un diccionario de la literatura.* 2nd ed., corr. y aumentada con más de 1.000 artículos. 3 vols. Madrid: Aguilar, 1953.

Salvá y Mallen, Pedro. *Catálogo de la biblioteca de Salvá.* 2 vols. Madrid: Carlos Bailly-Bailliere, 1872.

Serís, Homero. *Bibliografía de la literatura española.* 2 vols. Syracuse, N. Y.: Centro de Estudios Hispánicos, 1948-54.

Simón Díaz, José. *Bibliografía de literatura hispánica.* 7 vols. Madrid: Consejo Superior de Investigaciones Científicas, 1950-1967.

Simón Díaz, José. *Manual de bibliografía hispánica.* Madrid: Editorial Gustavo Gili, S. A., 1963.
Union List of Serials in Libraries of the United States and Canada. 3d ed. New York: H. W. Wilson Company, 1965.
Whitney, James Lyman. *Catalogue of the Spanish Library and of the Portuguese Books Bequeathed by George Ticknor to the Boston Public Library.* Boston: Boston Public Library, 1879.
Year's Work in Modern Language Studies. London: Oxford University Press, H. Milford, 1931-

Periodicals

Atenea (Concepción, Chile)
Archiv für das Studium der neueren Sprachen und Literaturen
Boletín de la Real Academia de Buenas Letras de Barcelona
Boletín de la Real Academia de la Historia
Boletín de la Real Academia Española
Boletín de la Universidad de Madrid
Books Abroad
Bulletin Hispanique
Bulletin of Hispanic Studies
Bulletin of the Comediantes
Comparative Literature
Correo Erudito
Cuadernos Hispanoamericanos
Deutsche Literaturzeitung
Estafeta Literaria
Filología (Buenos Aires)
Hispania
Hispanic Review
Hispanófila
Ilustración Española y Americana, La
Lettres Romanes, Les
Library Chronicle, The
Literaturblatt für germanische und romanische Philologie
Memorias de la Real Academia Española
Modern Language Journal
Modern Language Notes
Modern Language Review
Modern Philology
Neuphilologische Mitteilungen
Nueva Revista de Filología Hispánica
PMLA — Publications of the Modern Language Association of America
Quarterly Review, The
Revista Crítica Hispanoamericana
Revista de Aragón
Revista de Archivos, Bibliotecas y Museos
Revista de Bibliografía Nacional
Revista de Dialectología y Tradiciones Populares
Revista de Filología Española
Revista de la Biblioteca Archivo y Museo del Ayuntamiento de Madrid

Revista de las Indias
Revista de Literatura
Revue Critique d'Histoire et de Littérature
Revue d'Histoire Littéraire de la France
Revue Hispanique
Romance Philology
Romanic Review
Romanische Forschungen
Segismundo
Semanario Pintoresco Español
Symposium
Zeitschrift für romanische Philologie

INDEX

(Numbers refer to bibliographical entries, not pages)

"A propos du *Diablo cojuelo* aperçus de stylistique comparée," 68
Academia burlesca en Buen Retiro a la Magestad de Philippo Quarto el Grande, 38, 170
"Academias literarias del siglo de oro español," 247
academies, 30, 38, 135, 136, 170, 233, 234, 247
"Academies and Seventeenth Century Spanish Literature, The," 136
Ackerman, Stephen H., 1
Adams, Nicholson B., 2, 182
"Aesthetic Treatment of *Romancero* Material in the *comedias* of Luis Vélez de Guevara, The," 86
Águila del agua, El, 52, 191, 271, 286
Ahrens, Theodor G. 3, 114
Alarcón, Juan Ruiz de. See Ruiz de Alarcón y Mendoza, Juan.
Alba y el sol, El, 2
Alborg, Juan Luis, 4
Alcalde de Zalamea, El, 161, 195
"Alcune integrazioni ai glossari del *Diablo cojuelo*," 237
Alguacil alguacilado, El, 70
"Algunas poesías, en parte inéditas, de Luis Vélez de Guevara," 139
"Algunas poesías inéditas de Luis Vélez de Guevara sacadas de varios manuscritos," 39
"Allusions au théâtre et à la vie théâtrale dans le roman espagnol de la première moitié du XVIIe siècle," 209

Alma de España y sus reflejos en la literatura del siglo de oro, El, 168
Alonso Cortés, Narciso, 5
Álvarez y Baena, Joseph Antonio. 6
Amescua, Mira de, 1, 3, 12, 32, 47, 58, 114, 146, 149, 188, 221, 266
Amezúa, Agustín G. de, 275
Amor con vista, 122
Amor en vizcaíno, los zelos en francés y torneos de Navarra, El, 142, 236
Amorós, Andrés, 7
Amotinados de Flandes, Los, 110, 213
Anales de la literatura española (Años 1900-1904), 42
Anderson, Carleton Q., 8
Anibal, Claude E., 9, 10, 11, 12, 36
Anonymous, 13
Antojos de mejor vista, Los, 226
Antonia y Perales, 77
Antonio, Nicolás, 14, 93
Apophthegmas, 247, 265
Apraiz y Buesa, Ángel, 15
Aprobación, 77
Arca de Noé y campana de Belilla, El, 250
Arrom, José Juan, 16
Arte nuevo de hacer comedias, El, 33
Ashcom, Benjamin B., 17, 18, 19, 20
Asmodeus, The Devil on Two Sticks, 144
Asombro de Turquía y valiente toledano, El, 249

"Aspectos estilísticos de Vélez de Guevara en su *Diablo cojuelo*," 179
Astrana Marín, Luis, 21
Atarantados, Los, 77
Atila, azote de Dios o La silla de San Pedro, 143
Atkinson, William C., 22
Aubrun, Charles V., 7, 23, 24, 25, 26
"Aubrun y el teatro español," 7
Auto de la abadesa del cielo, 120, 140, 151, 251, 287
Auto de la mesa redonda, 120, 140, 151, 251, 287
Auto del nacimiento de Nuestro Señor, 120, 140, 151, 251, 270, 287
Auto sacramental de Escanderbech, 196
"Autor del *Príncipe transilvano*, El," 67
"Autos de Luis Vélez de Guevara," 140
Avalle-Arce, Juan Bautista, 27
Aviso y guía de forasteros, 68
Avisos históricos, 193

Bachiller de Salamanca o aventuras de don Querubin de la Ronda, El, 145
Baltasara, La, 137
"*Bandolera* of Golden Age Drama, A Symbol of Feminist Revolt, The," 150
bandoleras (comedias de), 47, 150
Barlaán y Josafat, 206
Barrantes y Moreno, Vicente, 28, 29
Barrera, Isaac J., 30
Barrera y Leirado, Cayetano A. de la, 31, 124, 187
Batalla naval, La, 191
"Bâtard Don Juan d'Autriche, personnage de théâtre, Le," 52
Batres, Alfonso de, 170
Bautismo del Príncipe de Marruecos, El, 194
Bell, Aubrey F. G., 32
Belmonte Bermúdez, Luis de, 2, 18, 134, 170
Benavente, Luis de, 170

Bermúdez, Jerónimo, 148, 238
Berndt, Robert J., 33, 34
Bibliografía madrileña o descripción de las obras impresas en Madrid, 197
Biblioteca de autores españoles, 93, 162, 276, 277, 278
Bibliotheca Hispano Nova, 14
Bienaventurada Madre Teresa de Jesús, monja descalza de Nuestra Señora del Carmen, La, 91
Bininger, Robert J., 35, 36
Blanco, Noemí Campos, 37
Blecua, José M., 38
Bonilla y San Martín, Adolfo, 39, 40, 41, 42, 43, 44, 61, 94, 101, 153, 171, 199, 205, 215, 228, 237, 260
Brenan, Gerald, 45
Bruerton, Courtney, 46, 47, 48, 49, 178
Buchanan, Milton A., 50, 105
Burla más sazonada, La, 77, 188
Burlador de Sevilla, El, 241
Buscón, (Vida del), 40

Caballero de Olmedo, El, 239
Caballero del Sol, El, 36, 212, 218
Calderón de la Barca, Pedro, 2, 27, 132, 138, 161, 207, 240, 241, 256, 263, 272, 289
Camoens, Luis de, 15, 103, 238, 267, 272
Cáncer, Gerónimo, 133, 170
"*Cancionero* de don Joseph del Corral, The," 291
"Cantar de *La niña de Gómez Arias*, El," 27
Capdet, Françoise, 51, 52
Capitán prodigioso, Príncipe de Transilvania, El, 254
Capítulos de literatura española, 220
Caro Baroja, Julio, 53
"Carta abierta al Sr. D. Manuel Serrano y Sanz (observaciones acerca de *El diablo cojuelo*)," 40
"Cartas de D. Gerónimo Dalmao y Casanate a los diputados del Reino de Aragón...," 54
Casona, Alejandro, 115
Castellanos, Agustín de, 34, 154
Castilian Literature, 32

Castro, Américo, 55, 56, 57, 58
Castro, Cristóbal de, 195, 294
Castro, Guillén de, 132, 149, 221, 249, 254
Catalán Menéndez Pidal, Diego, 59
Catalán Serrallonga y vandos de Barcelona, El, 16, 102
Catálogo bibliográfico y biográfico del teatro antiguo español, 31
Cejador y Frauca, Julio, 60
Celestina, La, 195
Censor, El, 132
Cerco de Roma por el Rey Desiderio, El, 16, 143
Cervantes Saavedra, Miguel de, 13, 61, 62, 68, 97, 108, 159, 191, 201, 212, 236, 243, 268, 293
"Cervantes y el *Persiles:* un aspecto de la difusión de esta novela," 97
"Cervantes y la Universidad de Osuna," 227
Cervantinas y otros ensayos, 21
Chabás, Juan, 63
Chandler, Frank W., 64
Chandler, Richard E., 65
Chrónica de El-Rei, Dom Pedro I, 8
Chronology of Lope de Vega's comedias..., The, 178
Cilley, Melissa A., 66
"Cinco poesías autobiográficas de Luis Vélez de Guevara," 228
Cioranescu, Alejandro, 67, 88
Cirot, Georges, 68, 69, 70, 71
Cirre, José F., 72
Claramonte y Corroy, Andrés de, 12, 73, 243
Clark, Fred M., 74
classical allusions, 281, 284
Coello, Antonio, 102, 137, 170
Colección de entremeses, loas, bailes, jácaras, y mojigangas desde fines del siglo XVI a mediados del XVIII, 77
Colección escogida de obras no dramáticas de Fray Lope Félix de Vega Carpio, 276, 277, 278
Collecçam politica de apophthegmas memoraveis, 265
Colmeneruela, La, 77
Coloquio de los perros, El, 201

Comedia de otro demonio, La, 262
Comedia española 1600-1680, La, 24
Comedias y entremeses de Miguel de Cervantes Saavedra, 61
"Comparative and Dramatic Analysis of Several Plays Utilizing the Inés de Castro Theme, A," 115
"Composition et les sources du *Diable boiteux* de Lesage, La," 282
conceptismo, 4, 5, 9, 45, 108, 137, 156, 160, 169, 178, 180, 181, 199, 227, 234, 236, 237, 238, 243, 269
"Concerning 'La mujer en hábito de hombre" in the *comedia*," 17
Conde de Saldaña (ballad), 92
Conde don Pero Vélez y don Sancho el Deseado, El, 10, 36, 44, 59, 63, 92, 125, 154, 187, 212, 286
Conde don Sancho niño, El, 35, 36
Conde Olinos, El (romance), 177
Conde preso, El (romance), 59
Conde Vélez y el rey Sancho el Deseado, El, 92
Condenado por desconfiado, El, 202
Condesa bandolera, La, 47
Cornil, Suzanne, 75
Corona de amor y muerte, 115
Corte del demonio, La 1, 36, 266
Corte del rey-poeta (recuerdos del Siglo de Oro), La, 95
Coster, Adolphe, 76
Cotarelo y Mori, Emilio, 36, 77, 78, 124, 187
Crawford, J. P. Wickersham, 79
"Critical Edition, with Introduction and Notes, of Vélez de Guevara's Act I of *La Baltasara,* A," 137
"Critical Edition, with Introduction and Notes, of Vélez de Guevara's *El amor en vizcaíno, los celos en francés y torneos de Navarra,* A," 236
"Critical Edition, with Introduction and Notes, of Vélez de Guevara's *El conde don Sancho niño,* A," 35

"Critical Edition, with Introduction and Notes, of Vélez de Guevara's *Virtudes vencen señales*, A," 138
Criticón, El, 68
Crónica de Alfonso XI, La, 27
Cruz, Ramón de la, 148
Cuerdo loco, El, 268
" 'Cuestión' de Albania en el teatro antiguo español, La," 200
culteranismo, 4, 22, 70, 71, 80, 108, 142, 159, 160, 168, 169, 171, 179, 205, 206, 225, 229, 236, 245, 246, 250
Cumplir dos obligaciones, 208
Cumplir dos obligaciones y Duquesa de Sajonia, 208, 252
"Currency Inflation Reflected in Luis Vélez de Guevara's *El embuste acreditado*," 211

Dalmao y Casanate, Gerónimo, 54
Darles con la entretenida, 134, 253
"Date of Schaeffer's *Tomo antiguo*, The," 49
Davis, Jessie V., 281
Delano, Lucile K., 80
Dellepiane de Martino, Ángela Blanco, 81
Desdichada Estefanía, La, 252, 253
Devoción de la misa, La, 46, 254, 271
Devoto, Daniel, 82
Día de fiesta por la tarde, El, 68
Diable boiteux, Le, 23, 32, 41, 45, 70, 93, 117, 118, 144, 145, 282, 288
"*Diable boiteux* (Lesage), *El diablo cojuelo* (Guevara), Ein Beitrag zur Geschichte frankospanischer Literaturbeziehungen, Le," 288
Diablo cojuelo, El, 4, 5, 23, 30, 32, 40, 41, 42, 45, 56, 57, 60, 64, 68, 69, 70, 84, 89, 90, 93, 94, 96, 97, 99, 108, 109, 112, 118, 122, 130, 135, 136, 139, 144, 145, 149, 159, 160, 168, 169, 171, 179, 181, 182, 188, 190, 199, 201, 204, 205, 209, 215, 221, 223, 226, 229, 232, 235, 237, 244, 245, 249, 250, 252, 255, 258, 261, 269, 271, 273, 279, 282, 288, 295

Diablo cojuelo, El asombro de Turquía y valiente toledano, El ollero de Ocaña, El, 249
"*Diablo cojuelo et Le Diable boiteux:* Deux définitions du roman, El," 23
Diablo cojuelo, verdades soñadas y novelas de la otra vida traducidas a estas, añadido al fin con ocho Enigmas curiosos y dos novelas, El, 279
Diablo está en Cantillana, El, 26, 81, 100, 128, 146, 147, 180, 190, 292
Diavolul schiop, 223
Díaz de Escovar, Narciso, 83
Díaz-Plaja, Guillermo, 84
Discursos leídos ante la Academia chilena, 181
Disparate creído, El, 262
Diverses Avantures de France et d'Espagne, Nouvelles Galantes et Historiques, 96
Dixon, Esther M., 210
Domnie dupa moarte, 223
Don Pedro Miagro, 253
Don Quijote, 68, 212, 268
Doña Inés de Castro, 16, 143
Doña Inés de Castro en el teatro castellano, 15
"Doña Inés de Castro Legend in Spanish and French Literature, The," 148
donjuanismo, 241, 242
Dos bandoleras, Las, 47, 156
Drama of the Siglo de Oro: A Study of Magic, Witchcraft and Other Occult Beliefs, 190
Dramatic Craftsmanship of Calderón, The, 263
Dramatic Works of Luis Vélez de Guevara: Their Plots, Sources, and Bibliography, The, 11, 22, 126, 164, 203, 264
Dramáticos contemporáneos a Lope de Vega, 162
Dramaturgie et Société, 52, 209
Dugdale, B. E. C., 85
Durán, Agustín, 116, 124, 134, 199, 258

"Eight Plays of Vélez de Guevara," 46
Elogio del juramento del serenissimo Príncipe don Felipe Domingo, Qvarto deste nombre, 89
Embuste acreditado, El, 20, 36, 110, 111, 175, 189, 211, 212, 213, 262, 290
Encantos de Merlín, Los, 2
Enciso, Jiménez de, 78
Endres, Valerie F., 86
Enescu, Theodor, 223
Enríquez de Zúñiga, Juan, 122
Ensayo de un diccionario de la literatura, 244
Ensayos literarios y críticos, 146
Entrambasaguas, Joaquín de, 87, 88, 89, 90, 91
Entwistle, William J., 92
Epístola a don Juan de Arguijo, 277
Epistolario de Lope de Vega Carpio, 275
Epopeya castellana a través de la literatura española, La, 154
"¿Es de origen mítico la 'leyenda' de la serrana de la Vera?", 53
Escanderbey, 18, 58, 80, 134, 196, 200
"Escarramán and Glimpses of the Spanish Court in 1637-38," 133
Esclavo del demonio, El, 1, 47
Espagne au XVIe siècle, documents historiques et littéraires, L', 170
Españoles: cómo llegaron a serlo, Los, 55
Espejo del mundo, El, 46, 110, 146
"Esperienza cultista nel teatro dell'età di Lope: appunti ed esempi, L'," 246
Espinel, Vicente, 68
Essai sur le théâtre espagnol, 283
Estebanillo González, 93
Estrella de Sevilla, La, 9, 12, 210, 214
Estrella de Sevilla and Claramonte, The, 12
Estudios de literatura castellana: El siglo de oro, 30
Estudios de literatura española y comparada, 67, 88
Estudios sobre el teatro de Lope de Vega, 157
Estudios sobre Lope de Vega, 87
Estudos de Historia e Cultura, 257
Etimologías españolas, 40
"Evolution of the Inés de Castro Story in Drama, The," 8

fabla arcaica, 140, 142, 205, 206, 225
"Facistol," 239
Fernández de Navarrete, Eustaquio, 93
Fernández de Ribera, Rodrigo, 226
Fernández Villegas, F., 294
Ferreira, Antonio, 85, 148, 238
Fitzmaurice-Kelly, James, 94
"Flamenco en algunos textos españoles antiguos, El," 101
Flecniakoska, Jean-Louis, 52
Flores García, Francisco, 95
Fonseca, Gondin da, 8
fortuna, 226, 284
Foulché-Delbosc, R., 96
"Fragment de traduction française du Diablo cojuelo, Un," 96
"Fuente de El diablo cojuelo, Una," 122

García Blanco, Manuel, 97
García del Castañar, 24
Garza de Portugal, La, 143
Gassier, Alfred, 98
Geschichte des spanischen Nationaldramas, 253
Gil y Zárate, Antonio, 99
Gili Gaya, Samuel, 100
Gillet, Joseph E., 101
Givanel Mas, J., 102
Glaser, Edward, 103
Golden Age: Drama, 1492-1700, The, 292
Golden Age: Prose and Poetry, the Sixteenth and Seventeenth Centuries, The, 130
Gómez Ocerín, J., 13, 57, 71, 104, 105, 106, 107, 176, 186, 202, 260
Góngora, Luis de, 73, 179, 225, 234, 246
González López, Emilio, 108
González Palencia, Ángel, 129

Goyri de Menéndez Pidal, María, 43, 50, 76, 105, 156, 161, 177, 183, 216, 242
Gracián, Baltasar, 68
"*Gracioso* Continues to Ridicule the Sonnet, The," 80
Gran Iorge Castrioto y Príncipe Escanderbey, El, 18, 200
Green, Otis H., 109
Grifos Lombardo, 59
Grillparzer, Franz, 36, 110
Groult, P., 111
Guevara, Antonio de, 68
Gutiérrez, Fernando, 112, 250
"Guzmán el Bueno en la historia y en la literatura," 165

Hämel, Adalbert, 113, 114
Hambriento, El, 126
Hartzenbusch, Juan Eugenio, 124
Hatten, Genell M., 115
Heinermann, H. Theodor, 113, 116, 167
Hendrix, W. S., 117, 118, 204
Hércules de Ocaña, El, 3, 49, 157, 253, 254, 271
Hermosura de Raquel, La, 46, 103, 188
Hernández, Francisco J., 119, 230
Hernández, J. M., 120
Herrero García, M., 121, 122
Hijo del águila, El, 51, 52, 191
Hijos de la Barbuda, Los, 46, 110, 142, 154
Hijos de Madrid, 6
Hill, John M., 82, 123, 124, 125, 126, 127, 210
Historia de la lengua y literatura castellana, 60
Historia de la literatura española, 4, 5, 108, 129, 188, 221, 232, 271
Historia de la literatura española desde los orígenes hasta el año 1900, 94
Historia de la literatura y del arte dramático en España, 252
Historia del teatro español, 83, 272
Historia general de las literaturas hispánicas, 84
History of Spanish Literature, 159, 266

Hohmann, L., 128
Homenaje a Archer M. Huntington, 47
Homenaje a Bonilla y San Martín, 153
Homenaje a Cervantes, 97
Homenaje a Menéndez y Pelayo en el año vigésimo de su profesorado. Estudios de erudición española, 147, 227
Hora de todos, La, 40
Horozco, Sebastián, 27
Hugo, Víctor, 238
Hurtado de Mendoza, Antonio, 133, 255
Hurtado y Jiménez de la Serna, Juan, 129

Ideas de los españoles del siglo XVII, 121
"*Iglesia sitiada* — a Calderonian Puzzle, La," 289
Ignez de Castro, 113, 116, 167
imagery, 63, 169, 179, 208, 239, 267
Inés de Castro, 115, 116
"Inés de Castro and Pedro of Portugal," 85
Inès de Castro, Contribution à l'étude du développement littéraire du thème dans les littératures romanes de l'histoire à la légende et de la légende à la littérature, 75
"Inés de Castro, 'cuello de garza'," 267
"Inés de Castro legend, 8, 15, 113, 115, 116, 148, 180, 184, 238, 257
"Inès de Castro ou literatura portuguesa desde Fernâo Lopes a Camões...," 257
Inesilla la de Pinto, 148
"Inez de Castro Theme in European Literature, The," 184
Infanzón de Illescas, El, 48
Inquiridion, El, 73
"Inquisición prohibe *Los tres portentos del cielo* de Vélez de Guevara, La," 259
Introducción al teatro religioso del Siglo de Oro (Evolución del Auto Sacramental: 1500-1648), 287

Introduction to Spanish Literature, An, 182
Isabel de Liar (romance), 257

Jacquot, Jean, 25, 52, 209
Jardín de Lope de Vega, El, 87, 276
Jocosería, La, 77
Jones, Royston Oscar, 130
José Prades, J. de, 131
Juan de Austria, 52
"Judging Authorship and Chronology in the *comedia*," 174
Juretschke, Hans, 132

Kennedy, Ruth Lee, 133
Kincaid, William A., 134
King, Willard F., 135, 136
Kirk, Charles F., 137, 138

Lacalle Fernández, Ángel, 139, 140, 151, 251, 260, 287
La Cerda, Mejía de. See Mexía de la Cerda
"Lágrimas poéticas," 153
La Motte, Houdar de, 85, 113, 115, 148, 238
Lasso de la Vega, Francisco de P., 83
Lasso de la Vega, Gabriel, 267
Laurel de Apolo, 87, 278
Lazarillo de Tormes, 68
Leavitt, Sturgis E., 12, 141
Legarda, P. Anselmo de, 142
Lego de Alcalá, El, 166
Leonard, Irving A., 143
Lesage, Alain René, 23, 32, 70, 99, 118, 144, 145, 159, 160, 182, 204, 245, 282, 288
Letanía moral, La, 73
Life and Works of Cristóbal Suárez de Figueroa, The, 79
"Life and Works of Luis de Belmonte Bermúdez (1587?-1650?)," 134
Life of Lope de Vega, The, 217
Limping Devil, The, 182
Liñán de Riaza, Pedro, 40, 255
Liñán y Verdugo, Antonio, 68
Lista y Aragón, Alberto, 132, 146
Literary History of Spain, A., 130, 292

Literatura española, resumen de historia crítica, La, 245
Literature of the Spanish People from Roman Times to the Present Day, The, 45
Loa para una égloga, 200
Lomba y Pedraja José R., 147
Lopes, Fernão, 8
López de Mendoza, Íñigo, marqués de Santillana, 161
"Luis Vélez de Guevara y su tiempo," 72
"Luis Vélez de Guevara y sus obras dramáticas," 78
"Luis Vélez de Guevara's *El gran Iorge Castrioto y Príncipe Escanderbey*, a Critical Edition, with Introduction and Notes," 18
Luna de la sierra, La, 4, 21, 24, 36, 63, 128, 195, 205, 219, 221, 242. 243, 271, 274, 292, 294
Lusíadas, Os, 15, 272

McCall, Johnston V., 148
MacCurdy, Raymond R., 149
McKendrick, Melveena, 150
Manual de historia de la literatura castellana, 169
Manual de literatura, principios generales de poética y retórica y resumen histórico de la literatura española, 99
Marcos de Obregón, 68
Marqués del Vasto, El, 97
Marqués, E. F., 151
Martín Robles, P. A., 64
Martínez, Enrique José, 152
"Más 'diabluras,'" 42
Más pesa el Rey que la sangre, 3, 9, 12, 65, 94, 128, 141, 165, 182, 252, 266, 271, 292
Mejor rey en rehenes, El, 126
Mélanges a la memoire de Jean Sarrailh, 23
Méndez Bejarano, Mario, 153
Menéndez Pidal, Ramón, 40, 43, 50, 76, 105, 154, 155, 156, 161, 177, 183, 202, 216, 225, 242
Menéndez y Pelayo, Marcelino, 43, 82, 94, 124, 147, 157, 158, 231
Menosprecio de corte, 68

Mérimée, Ernest, 159, 160, 161
Mesonero Romanos, Ramón de, 162, 163
Mexía de la Cerda, 15, 116, 148, 167, 238, 257
Michaëlis de Vasconcellos, Carolina, 44
Michels, Ralph J., 164
Mientras yo podo las viñas, 34, 154
Mier, Eduardo de, 252
Millé Giménez, Isabel, 165
Miller, Kenneth C., 166
Miscelânea de estudos em honra de D. Carolina Michaëlis de Vasconcellos, 44
Miscellanea di studi ispanici, 205, 237
Moir, Duncan, 292
Montalbán, Juan Pérez de. See Pérez de Montalbán, Juan.
Montesinos, José F., 167
Montherlant, Henri de, 25, 115, 119, 223, 230, 238
Montoliu, Manuel de, 168, 169
Morel-Fatio, Alfred, 170, 171
Moreto, Agustín, 2, 84, 132, 133, 243, 272, 294
Moriscos, Los, 77
Morley, S. Griswold, 159, 172, 173, 174, 175, 176, 177, 178
"'Mujer en hábito de hombre' in the *comedia*, La," 17
"Mula de Liñán; eine Bermerkung zu Guevaras *Diablo cojuelo*, La," 255
Muñoz Cortés, Manuel, 26, 81, 100, 179, 180
"Mythological and Other Classical Allusions in the Theater of Ruiz de Alarcón and Luis Vélez de Guevara," 281
"Mythological and Other Classical Allusions in the Theaters of Tirso, Alarcón and Vélez," 284

Narraciones extremeñas, 29
Nercasseau y Morán, Enrique, 181
New History of Spanish Literature, A, 65
Ninfa del cielo, La, 47, 161
"*Ninfa del cielo, La serrana de la Vera* and Related Plays, La," 47

Niña de Gómez Arias, La, 19, 27, 36, 212, 239, 240, 241, 263, 285
Niño diablo, El, 174, 178
No hay contra un padre razón, 163
Northup, George T., 105, 182, 183
"Noruega, símbolo de la oscuridad," 56
"Note critiche sull'opera di Vélez de Guevara," 205, 224
"Note on *El diablo cojuelo* and the French Sketch of Manners and Types, A," 204
"Notes on Collections of Types: A Form of *costumbrismo*," 117
"Notes on the *comedia*: A New Edition of a Vélez de Guevara Play," 19
"Noticias y documentos relativos a la historia y literatura españolas," 198
Novela de los tres hermanos, 128, 279
Novela del caballero invisible, 279
Novela picaresca española, La, 273
Novelistas posteriores a Cervantes con un bosquejo histórico sobre la novela española, 93
Novios de Hornachuelos, Los, 24, 48, 58, 82, 124, 127, 178
Nozick, Martin, 184
"Nueva comedia de Lope de Vega sobre Santa Teresa de Jesús, estudio bibliográfico, Una," 91
Nueva y manual historia de la literatura española, 63
"Nuevo dato para la biografía de Vélez de Guevara, Un," 106
"Nuevos datos para la vida de Luis Vélez de Guevara," 192

Objective Methods for Testing Authenticity and the Study of Ten Doubtful comedias Attributed to Lope de Vega, 74
Obligación de las mujeres, 46, 208
Obligaciones de honor, 47
Obras de Lopè de Vega, Vol. XII: *Crónicas y leyendas dramáticas en España*, 158
"Observaciones sugeridas por la lectura del drama de Coello, Rojas

y Vélez: *El Catalán Serrallonga y vandos de Barcelona,"* 102
"Observations on *La Estrella de Sevilla,*" 9
Ocho comedias desconocidas de don Guillén de Castro, del Licenciado Damián Salustio del Poyo, y de Luis Vélez de Guevara, 254
Ochoa, Eugenio de, 185, 241
Olivares, El conde de, 107
Oliver, J. J., 186
Ollero de Ocaña, El, 163, 249, 292
Olmsted, Richard H., 10, 125, 187
"Olvidado poema de Vélez de Guevara, Un," 89
"Origins of Sebastianism in Three Spanish Plays of the Golden Age, The," 194
"Orthoëphy of the Holographic *comedias* of Vélez de Guevara, The," 286

Palacín Iglesias, Gregorio B., 188
Palmero (romance del), 172
Palomo, María del Pilar, 189, 269
Panegírico por la poesía, 280
"Para la historia de *Los novios de Hornachuelos*," 82
Para todos, 98, 146, 196, 200, 207
"Partial Edition of *El lego de Alcalá*, A," 166
Pasajero, El, 79
"Patriarca Jacob, amante ejemplar del teatro del siglo de oro español, El," 103
Pavía, Mario N., 190
Paz y Meliá, Antonio, 124, 191, 192
Pellicer de Ossau, Salas y Tovar, José, 192, 193, 199
Penny, Carl O., 194
Peregrinación sabia, La, 234
Peregrino en su patria, El, 43, 167
Pérez de Guzmán y Gallo, Juan, 195
Pérez de Montalbán, Juan, 18, 52, 58, 98, 146, 196, 200, 207, 289
Pérez Galdós, Benito, 223
Pérez Pastor, Cristóbal, 197, 198
Pérez y González, Felipe, 42, 199, 200, 258
Peribáñez, 48, 219
Perinola, 207

Persiles y Segismunda, 97
Pfandl, Ludwig, 201, 202, 203
Place, Edwin B., 204
Pleito que tuvo el diablo con el Cura de Madrilejos, El, 266
poesías, 39, 80, 89, 107, 123, 139, 228, 231, 248, 249, 260, 291
Por campos del Romancero, estudios sobre la tradición oral moderna, 59
Preceptiva dramática de Lope de Vega y otros ensayos sobre el Fénix, La, 233
Précis d'histoire de la littérature espagnole, 160
Príncipe Escanderbey, El, 18, 58, 80, 134, 200
Príncipe esclavo y hazañas de Escanderbeg, El, 18, 200
Príncipe prodigioso y defensor de la Fe, El, 254
Príncipe transilvano, El, 67, 88
Príncipe viñador, El, 34, 154, 155
Privado perseguido, El, 292
"Procédé dans *El diablo cojuelo*, Le," 69
Prodigioso príncipe transilvano, El, 46, 74, 178
Profeti, Maria Grazia, 205, 206, 224, 225
Prosa novelística y academias literarias en el siglo XVII, 135

"Qualitative Analysis of the Versification of Selected *comedias* of Luis Vélez de Guevara, A," 33
"Querellas y rivalidades en las Academias del siglo XVII," 234
"Quevedo, Guevara, Lesage and the *Tatler*," 118
Quevedo y Villegas, Francisco Gómez de, 4, 41, 60, 68, 69, 70, 72, 84, 108, 118, 130, 179, 181, 201, 207, 236, 243, 261, 273.
Quiñones de Benavente, Luis, 77, 188
Quinque comedias famosas, 126
"Quinta de Florencia, fuente de Peribáñez, La," 48
"Quinta parte of *Comedias nuevas escogidas*, The," 213

Reas, Marjorie V., 208
Recoules, Henri, 209
Reed, Frank O., 127, 210
"*Régner après la mort* de Vélez de Guevara et *La reine morte* de Montherlant," 25
Reichenberger, Arnold G., 20, 36, 111, 175, 211, 212, 213, 214, 262, 290
Reinar después de morir, 2, 3, 4, 8, 13, 15, 16, 21, 25, 26, 31, 37, 63, 65, 75, 81, 85, 98, 100, 113, 115, 116, 119, 128, 131, 132, 141, 143, 146, 148, 149, 152, 153, 154, 159, 162, 180, 182, 184, 185, 188, 205, 214, 221, 223, 230, 238, 243, 246, 248, 252, 257, 267, 270, 271, 272, 274, 292, 294, 295
Reine morte, La, 25, 115, 119, 223, 230
Rennert, Hugo A., 58, 215, 216, 217, 218
Reparaciones históricas: Estudios peninsulares, 248
"Representación de obras clásicas en el teatro español," 195
"Representaciones teatrales en Cuba a fines del siglo XVIII," 16
Resende, García de, 15, 238, 267
Revuelta, Luisa, 219
"Rey D. Pedro en el teatro, El," 147
Rey don Sebastián, El, 46, 194, 253, 254
Rey en su imaginación, El, 13, 56, 71, 97, 104, 176, 186, 202, 268, 271, 286, 292, 293
Reyes, Alfonso, 220
Río, Ángel del, 221
Rodríguez Cepeda, Enrique, 222, 223, 224, 225, 226, 242
Rodríguez Marín, Francisco, 57, 227, 228, 229, 237, 260, 261
Rodríguez Padrón, Jorge, 230
Rojas, Agustín de, 231
Rojas Zorrilla, Francisco de, 2, 102, 137, 243, 266, 272
Román, Manuel Antonio (Canónigo), 181
Romance de El conde preso, 59
Romance de Grifos Lombardo, 59
"Romance del *Palmero*, El," 172
"Romance of Luis Vélez de Guevara, A," 123
Romancero general, 116
Romancero hispánico (Hispano-portugués, americano y sefardí) teoría e historia, 155
romances, 3, 4, 5, 21, 26, 29, 34, 59, 63, 75, 86, 116, 148, 154, 155, 156, 161, 172, 173, 176, 177, 180, 205, 222, 240, 241, 257, 274
Romances of Roguery, 64
Romera de Santiago, La, 59, 97, 146, 155, 173, 252
Romera-Navarro, Miguel, 232, 233, 234
Rosa de Alexandría, La, 110
Roscoe, Thomas, 235
Rosell, Cayetano, 276, 277, 278
Rosen, Harold E., 236
Rosselli, Ferdinando, 205, 237
Rossi, Giuseppe Carlo, 131, 238
Rozzell, Ramón, 19, 27, 239, 240, 241, 285
Ruiz, Juan (Archpriest of Hita), 161
Ruiz de Alarcón y Mendoza, Juan, 2, 84, 132, 220, 243, 272 281, 284
Rull, Enrique, 226, 242
"Rumbo y tropel de Vélez de Guevara, El," 21

Saber por no saber y vida de San Julián de Alcalá de Henares, El, 166
Sämtliche Werke, Vol. XV: *Spanische Studien*, 110
Sainz de Robles, Federico Carlos, 243, 244
Saladino, El, 137
Salas Barbadillo, Alonso, 234
Salcedo Ruiz, Ángel, 245
Salucio del Poyo, Damián, 137, 254
Samonà, Carmelo, 246
Sánchez, José, 247
Sánchez Mogul, Antonio, 248
Sánchez Pérez, José A., 249
Santa Liga, La, 191
Santillana, marqués de. See López de Mendoza, Íñigo, marqués de Santillana.

Santos, Francisco, 250
Sarna de los banquetes, La, 77
Saz, Agustín del, 251
Schack, Adolf Friedrich von, 124, 252
Schaeffer, Adolph, 49, 253, 254
Schäpers, Roland, 255
Schevill Rudolph, 11, 22, 36, 62, 111, 126, 164, 203, 256, 264, 281
Schwartz, Kessel, 65
Sená, Jorge de, 257
Señor don Juan de Austria, El, 52
Serrana de la Vera, La, 4, 7, 21, 28, 29, 36, 43, 47, 50, 53, 63, 76, 105, 150, 152, 154, 156, 158, 161, 177, 183, 205, 216, 221, 222, 225, 242, 243, 271, 272, 274, 286, 292
Serrano y Sanz, Manuel, 40, 258
Sete annos, 103
"Shipment of *comedias* to the Indies, A," 143
Si el caballo vos han muerto, subid, Rey, en mi caballo, 155, 252
"*Siglo de Oro* Plays in Madrid, 1820-1850," 2
Silla de San Pedro, La, 143
Simón Díaz, José, 259, 260
Sims, E. R., 261
Sloman, Albert E., 262, 263
"Sobre un tomo perdido de Lope de Vega," 44
Solís, Antonio de, 170
"Some Aspects of the Grotesque in the Drama of the *Siglo de Oro,*" 141
"Soneto inédito de Luis Vélez, Un," 107
"Song and Legend of Gómez Arias, The," 241
Sordos, Los, 77
Spain and the Western Tradition, Vol. II: *The Castilian Mind in Literature from El Cid to Calderón,* 109
Spanish Drama of the Golden Age: Twelve Plays, 149
Spanish Novelists: A Series of Tales from the Earliest Period to the Close of the Seventeenth Century, The, 235

Spanish Stage in the Time of Lope de Vega, The, 218
Spectator, The, 204
Spencer, Forrest E., 11, 22, 36, 111, 126, 164, 203, 264, 273
Studi di letteratura spagnola, 246
Studien zu Luis Vélez de Guevara, 128
style, 10, 18, 22, 33, 60, 68, 69, 70, 137, 146, 179, 205, 208
"Style de Vélez de Guevara, Le," 70
Suárez de Figueroa, Cristóbal, 79
Sueños, Los, 41, 68, 118, 181, 261, 273
Suppico, Pedro José, 247, 265

También la afrenta es veneno, 16
Tatler, The, 118, 204
Teatro de Montherlant, dramaturgia y tauromaquia, El, 119, 230
"Teatro de Vélez de Guevara," 163
Teatro español en su Siglo de Oro, El, 270
Teatro español, historia y antología desde sus orígenes hasta el siglo XIX, El, 243
Teatro español, las épocas en el desarrollo del drama, El, 66
Téllez, Gabriel, 2, 4, 47, 84, 132, 146, 149, 155, 161, 173, 183, 272, 281, 284
"Tema de Inés de Castro en el siglo xx, El," 37
"Tentative Edition, with Introduction and Notes, of Luis Vélez de Guevara's *El príncipe viñador,* A," 34
"Tentative Edition, with Introduction and Notes, of Luis Vélez de Guevara's *La corte del demonio,* A," 1
Tesoro del teatro español, 185
"Textos dispersos de clásicos españoles. XII, Vélez de Guevara," 260
Théâtre espagnol, Le, 98
Théâtre tragique, Le, 25
"Three Thematically Similar Plays Attributed to Luis Vélez de Guevara," 208
Ticknor, George, 134, 266
Timoneda, Juan de, 92

Tirso de Molina, pseud. See Téllez, Gabriel.
Torres Naharro, Bartolomé de, 101
Tragedia del rey don Sebastián, La, 194
"Tragedy in the Spanish Theater of the Golden Age," 152
Tres hermanos, Los, 94, 128, 279
Tres portentos del cielo, Los, 259
"Tricentenario — Haz y envés de de Luis Vélez de Guevara, Un," 90
Triwedi, Mitchell D., 267
Truhán del cielo y loco santo, El, 166
Turkiainen, V., 268

Umbral, Francisco, 269
"Uniqueness of the *comedia*, The," 214
"Uso de las combinaciones métricas en las comedias de Tirso de Molina," 173

Valbuena Prat, Ángel, 100, 270, 271, 272, 273, 274
Valdivielso, José de, 161
Valera, Juan de, 147, 227
Valiente Céspedes, El, 3, 254
Vaquero de Moraña, El, 34
Vega Carpio, Lope de, 2, 3, 4, 13, 21, 29, 33, 34, 43, 44, 47, 54, 58, 66, 72, 74, 78, 82, 87, 91, 101, 104, 124, 132, 146, 150, 152, 156, 157, 158, 163, 166, 174, 178, 183, 191, 194, 200, 217, 218, 219, 221, 232, 234, 235, 239, 246, 253, 254, 275, 276, 277, 278
Vélez de Guevara, Juan, 6, 192, 199, 222
"Vélez de Guevara, Luis," 295

Vera y Mendoza, Fernando de, 280
versification, 33, 34, 46, 47, 49, 134, 178, 180, 222
Veynar, Eva B., 281
Viaje del Parnaso, El, 13, 62, 293
Viaje entretenido, El, 231
Vic, Jean, 282
Vida de Lope de Vega, 58
Vida de los pícaros, La, 255
Vida es sueño, La, 138, 206, 256
Vida, obra, y pensamiento de Alberto Lista, 132
Vida y muerte de Santa Teresa de Jesús, 91
Viel-Castel, Louis de, 283
Villamediana, Conde de, 226
Villegas, Francisco de, 194
Virtudes vencen señales, 138, 206, 225, 256
"*Virtudes vencen señales* and *La vida es sueño*," 256
"*Vizcaíno* en la literatura castellana, Lo," 142

Wade, Gerald E., 284, 285, 286
Wardropper, Bruce W., 287
Willers, Hermann, 288
Wilson, Edward M., 289, 290, 291, 292
Wurzbach, Wolfgang, 293

Yndurain, Francisco, 294

Zabaleta, Juan de, 68, 262
Zahurdas de Plutón, 69
Zamora, Alonso, 295
Zur Charakteristik des spanischen Dramas im Anfang des XVII. Jahrhunderts (Luis Vélez de Guevara und Mira de Mescua), 3, 114

NORTH CAROLINA STUDIES IN THE ROMANCE LANGUAGES AND LITERATURES

I.S.B.N. Prefix 0-88438

Recent Titles

A CRITICAL EDITION WITH INTRODUCTION AND NOTES OF GIL VICENTE'S "FLORESTA DE ENGAÑOS", by Constantine Christopher Stathatos. 1972. (No. 125). -925-1.

LI ROMANS DE WITASSE LE MOINE. *Roman du treizième siècle.* Édité d'après le manuscrit, fonds français 1553, de la Bibliothèque Nationale, Paris, par Denis Joseph Conlon. 1972. (No. 126). -926-X.

EL CRONISTA PEDRO DE ESCAVIAS. UNA VIDA DEL SIGLO XV, by Juan Bautista Avalle-Arce. 1972. (No. 127). -927-8.

AN EDITION OF THE FIRST ITALIAN TRANSLATION OF THE CELESTINA, by Kathleen Kish. 1973. (No. 128). -928-6.

MOLIERE MOCKED: THREE CONTEMPORARY HOSTILE COMEDIES, by Frederick W. Vogler. 1973. (No. 129). -929-4.

INDEX ANALYTIQUE DE "CHATEAUBRIAND ET SON GROUPE LITTERAIRE SOUS L'EMPIRE" DE SAINTE-BEUVE, by Lorin A. Uffenbeck. 1973. (No. 130). -930-8.

THE ORIGINS OF THE BAROQUE CONCEPT OF PEREGRINATIO, by Juergen S. Hahn. 1973. (No. 131). -931-6.

THE "AUTO SACRAMENTAL" AND THE PARABLE IN THE SIXTEENTH AND SEVENTEENTH CENTURIES, by Donald T. Dietz. 1973. (No. 132). -932-4.

FRANCISCO DE OSUNA AND THE SPIRIT OF THE LETTER, by Laura Calvert. 1973. (No. 133). -933-2.

ITINERARIO DI AMORE: DIALETTICA DI AMORE E MORTE NELLA VITA NUOVA, by Margherita de Bonfils Templer. 1973. (No. 134). -934-0.

L'IMAGINATION POETIQUE CHEZ DU BARTAS, ELEMENTS DE SENSIBILITE BAROQUE DANS LA "CREATION DU MONDE," by Bruno Braunrot. 1973. (No. 135). -935-9.

ARTUS DÉSIRÉ, PRIEST AND PAMPHLETEER OF THE SIXTEENTH CENTURY, by Frank Giese 1973. (No. 136). -936-7.

JARDIN DE NOBLES DONZELLAS BY FRAY MARTÍN DE CÓRDOBA, by Harriet Goldberg. 1974. (No. 137). -937-5.

MOLIERE: TRADITIONS IN CRITICISM, by Laurence Romero. 1974 (Essays, No. 1). -001-7.

STUDIES IN TIRSO, I, by Ruth Lee Kennedy. 1974. (Essays, No. 3). -003-3.

LAS MEMORIAS DE GONZALO FERNÁNDEZ DE OVIEDO, Vols. I and II, by Juan Bautista Avalle-Arce. 1974. (Texts, Textual Studies, and Translations, Nos. 1 and 2). -401-2; 402-0.

ESTUDIOS DE LITERATURA HISPANOAMERICANA EN HONOR A JOSÉ J. ARROM, edited by Andrew P. Debicki and Enrique Pupo-Walker. 1975. (Symposia, No. 2). 952-9.

When ordering please cite the *ISBN Prefix* plus the last four digits for each title.

Send orders to:

    University of North Carolina Press
    Chapel Hill
    North Carolina 27514
    U. S. A.

The Department of Romance Studies Digital Arts and Collaboration Lab at the University of North Carolina at Chapel Hill is proud to support the digitization of the North Carolina Studies in the Romance Languages and Literatures series.

www.ingramcontent.com/pod-product-compliance
Lightning Source LLC
Chambersburg PA
CBHW022022220426
43663CB00007B/1182